Kirklees
COUNCIL

Library and Information Centres

Red doles Lane

Huddersfield, West Yorkshire

HD2 1YF

This book should be returned on or before the latest date stamped below. Fines are charged if the item is late.

You may renew this loan for a further period by phone, personal visit or at www.kirklees.gov.uk/libraries, provided that the book is not required by another reader.

NO MORE THAN THREE RENEWALS ARE PERMITTED

A Mother's Reckoning

Living in the aftermath of the Columbine tragedy

Sue Klebold

Introduction by Andrew Solomon

1 3 5 7 9 10 8 6 4 2

WH Allen, an imprint of Ebury Publishing,
20 Vauxhall Bridge Road,
London SW1V 2SA

WH Allen is part of the Penguin Random House group of companies whose
addresses can be found at global.penguinrandomhouse.com

Penguin
Random House
UK

First published in the United Kingdom by WH Allen in 2016
First published in the United States by Crown Publishers in 2016

www.eburypublishing.co.uk

A CIP catalogue record for this book is available from the British Library

Hardback ISBN 9780753556795
Trade Paperback ISBN 9780753556801

Printed and bound in Great Britain by Clays Ltd, St Ives PLC

Penguin Random House is committed to a sustainable future for
our business, our readers and our planet. This book is made from
Forest Stewardship Council® certified paper.

MIX
Paper from
responsible sources
FSC® C018179
www.fsc.org

To all who feel alone, hopeless, and desperate—
even in the arms of those who love them

Klebold family photo, Christmas 1991
(from l to r: me, Byron, Dylan, and Tom).
Photography by Pekari

CONTENTS

Introduction

And must I, indeed, Pain, live with you
All through my life?—sharing my fire, my bed,
Sharing—oh, worst of all things!—the same head?—
And, when I feed myself, feeding you, too?
—*Edna St. Vincent Millay*

We have consistently blamed parents for the apparent defects of their children. The eighteenth- century theory of imaginationism held that children had deformities because of their mothers' unexpressed lascivious longings. In the twentieth century, homosexuality was said to be caused by overbearing mothers and passive fathers; schizophrenia reflected the parents' unconscious wish that their child did not exist; and autism was the result of "refrigerator mothers," whose coldness doomed their children to a fortress of silence. We've now realized that such complex and overdetermined conditions are not the result of parental attitude or behavior. We nonetheless continue to assume that if you could only get inside the households in which killers were raised, you'd see the parents' errors writ large. The perception of children as tractable has been a hallmark of social justice; it has led us to seek rehabilitation for juveniles rather than simply punishment. According to this logic, a bad adult may be irrecoverably bad, but a bad kid is only a reflection of negative influences, the product of pliable nurture rather than immutable nature. There can be truth in that pleasant optimism, but to go from there to presuming parental culpability is a gross injustice.

We cling to the notion that crime is the parents' fault for two primary reasons. First, it is clear that severe abuse and neglect can trigger aberrant behavior in vulnerable people. Poor parenting can push such children toward substance abuse, gang membership, domestic violence, and thievery. Attachment disorders are frequent in victims of childhood cruelty; so is a repetition compulsion that drives them to recapitulate the aggression they have known. Some parents damage their children, but that does not mean that all troubled children have incompetent parents. In particular, extreme, irrational crimes are not usually triggered by anything the parents have done; they come out of an illogic too profound to be instigated by trauma.

Second, and far more powerfully, we want to believe that parents create criminals because in supposing that, we reassure ourselves that in our own house, where we are not doing such wrong things, we do not risk this calamity. I am aware of this delusion because it was mine. When I met Tom and Sue Klebold for the first time on February 19, 2005, I imagined that I would soon identify their flaws. I was working on a book, *Far from the Tree*, about parents and their challenging offspring, and I thought these parents would be emblematic of erroneous parenting. I never imagined they had egged their child on to heinous acts, but I did think that their story would illuminate innumerable, clear mistakes. I didn't want to like the Klebolds, because the cost of liking them would be an acknowledgment that what happened wasn't their fault, and if it wasn't their fault, none of us is safe. Alas, I liked them very much indeed. So I came away thinking that the psychopathy behind the Columbine massacre could emerge in anyone's household. It would be impossible to predict or recognize; like a tsunami, it would make a mockery of all our preparations.

In Sue Klebold's telling, she was an ordinary suburban mother before Columbine. I didn't know her then, but in the wake of that tragedy, she found the strength to extract wisdom from her devastation. To sustain your love in these circumstances is an act of courage. Her generosity in friendship, her lively gift for affection, and her capacity for attention, all of which I've been privileged to know, render the tragedy more bewildering. I started off thinking that the Klebolds should have disavowed their child, but I ended up understanding that it took far more steel to deplore what he had done yet be unflagging in their love. Sue's passion for her son is evident in every one of these grief-stricken pages, and her book is a testament to complexity. She argues that good people do bad things, that all of us are morally confused, and that doing something terrible does not erase other acts and motives. The ultimate message of this book is terrifying: you may not know your own children, and, worse yet, your children may be unknowable to you. The stranger you fear may be your own son or daughter.

"We read our children fairy tales and teach them that there are good guys and bad guys," Sue said to me when I was writing *Far from the Tree.* "I would never do that now. I would say that every one of us has the capacity to be good and the capacity to make poor choices. If you love someone, you have to love both the good and the bad in them." At the time of Columbine, Sue worked in the same building as a parole office and had felt alienated and frightened getting on the elevator with ex-convicts. After the tragedy, she saw them differently. "I felt that they were just like my son. That they were just people who, for some reason, had made an awful choice and were thrown into a terrible, despairing situation. When I hear about terrorists in the news, I think, 'That's somebody's kid.' Columbine made me feel more connected to mankind than anything else possibly could have." Bereavement can give its dupes great compassion.

Two kinds of crime upset us more than any others: crimes in which children are the victims, and crimes in which children are the perpetrators. In the first case, we mourn the innocent; in the second, our misapprehension that children are innocent. School shootings are the most appalling crimes of all, because they involve both problems, and among school shootings Columbine remains something of a gold standard, the ultimate exemplar to which all others are indebted. The extreme self-importance tinged with sadism, the randomness of the attack, and the scale of the advance planning have made Eric Harris and Dylan Klebold heroes to a large community of causeless young rebels, while they are hailed by most people as psychologically damaged and by some religious communities as icons of Satanism. The boys' motives and purposes have been analyzed time and again by people who want to protect their children from such assaults. The most dauntless parents also wonder how to be certain that their children are incapable of committing such crimes. Better the enemy you know than the enemy you don't know, says the adage, and Columbine was above all an ambush of unknowability, of horror hidden in plain sight.

It has been impossible to see the killers clearly. We live in a society of blame, and some of the victims' families were relentless in their demand for impossible "answers" that were being kept "hidden." The best evidence that the parents didn't know is the surety that if they had, they'd have done something. Jefferson County magistrate John DeVita said of the two boys, "What's mind-boggling is the amount of deception. The ease of their deception. The coolness of their deception." Most parents think they know their children better than they do; children who don't want to be known can keep their inner lives very private. The victims' families' lawsuits were predicated on the dubious principles that human nature is knowable, that interior logic can be monitored, and that tragedies follow predictable patterns. They have sought some missing information that would change what happened. Jean-Paul Sartre once wrote, "Evil is not an appearance," adding that "knowing its causes does not dispel it." Sartre seems not to have been read very much in the Denver suburbs.

Eric Harris appears to have been a homicidal psychopath, and Dylan Klebold, a suicidal depressive, and their disparate madnesses were each other's necessary condition. Dylan's depressiveness would not have turned into murderousness without Harris's leadership, but something in Eric might have lost motivation without the thrill of dragging Dylan down with him. Eric's malice is shocking, Dylan's acquiescence, equally so. Dylan wrote, "Thinking of suicide gives me hope that i'll be in my place wherever i go after this life—that ill finally not be at war w. myself, the world, the universe—my mind, body, everywhere, everything is at PEACE— me—my soul (existence)." He described his own, "eternal suffering in infinite directions through infinite realities." The most common word in his journals is *love*. Eric wrote, "how dare you think that I and you are part of the same species when we are soooooooooo different. you arent human, you are a robot ... and if you pissed me off in the past, you will die if I see you." His journal describes how in some imagined collegiate future he would have tricked girls to come to his room and raped them. Then, "I want to tear a throat out with my own teeth like a pop can. I want to grab some weak little freshman and just tear them apart like a fucking wolf, strangle them, squish their head, rip off their jaw, break their arms in half, show them who is god." Eric was a failed Hitler; Dylan was a failed Holden Caulfield.

Sue Klebold emphasizes the suicidal element in her son's death. Karl Menninger, who has written extensively on suicide, said that it requires the coincidence of "the wish to kill, the wish to be killed, and the wish to die." The wish to kill is not always directed outward, but it is an essential piece of the puzzle. Eric Harris wanted to kill and Dylan Klebold wanted to die, and both thought their experience contained seeds of the divine; both wrote of how the massacre would make them into gods. Their combination of grandiosity and ineptitude contains echoes of ordinary adolescence. In the commons at Columbine High School, toward the end of the spree, a witness hiding in the cafeteria heard one of the killers say, "Today the world's going to come to an end. Today's the day we die." This is an infantile conflation of the self with the other. G. K. Chesterton wrote, "The man who kills a man kills a man / The man who kills himself kills all men. / As far as he is concerned, he wipes out the world."

Advocates for the mentally ill point out that most crime is not committed by people with mental illnesses, and that most people with mental illnesses do not commit crimes. What does it mean to consider Columbine as the product of minds that were not mentally ill? There are many crimes that people resist either because they know they'd get in trouble or because they have learned moral standards. Most people have seen things they'd like to steal. Most people have felt an occasional flash of murderous rage toward someone with whom they are intimate. But the reasons for not killing kids you barely know at school and holding the place hostage is not that you fear punishment or grapple with received morality; it's that the whole idea never crosses healthy minds. Though he was depressed,

Dylan did not have schizophrenia, PTSD, bipolar illness, or any other condition that fits the neat parameters of psychiatric diagnosis. The existence of disordered thinking does not mitigate the malevolence of Dylan's acts. Part of the nobility of this book is that it doesn't try to render what he did into sense. Sue Klebold's refusal to blame the bullies, the school, or her son's biochemistry reflects her ultimate determination that one must simply accept what can never be explained away. She does not try to elucidate the permanently confused borderline between evil and disease.

Immediately after the massacre, a carpenter from Chicago came to Littleton and erected fifteen crosses—one for each victim, including Dylan and Eric. Many people piled flowers at Eric's and Dylan's crosses just as they did at the others. Brian Rohrbough, father of one of the victims, removed Harris's and Klebold's markers. "You don't cheapen what Christ did for us by honoring murderers with crosses," he said. "There's nowhere in the Bible that says to forgive an unrepentant murderer. You don't repent, you don't forgive them—that's what the Bible says." There is obviously scope for revising this interpretation of Christian doctrine, but Rohrbough's assertion hinges on the mistaken notion that mourning the deaths of the killers is tantamount to forgiveness, and that forgiveness conceals the horror of what was done. Sue Klebold does not seek or even imagine forgiveness for her son. She explains that she didn't know what was happening, but she doesn't exonerate herself; she presents her not knowing as a betrayal of her son and the world. The death of someone who has committed a great crime may be for the best, but any dead child is some parent's vanquished hope. This mournful book is Sue's act of vicarious repentance. Hatred does not obliterate love. Indeed, the two are in constant fellowship.

Sue told me at our first meeting about the moment on April 20, 1999, when she learned what was happening at Columbine High School. "While every other mother in Littleton was praying that her child was safe, I had to pray that mine would die before he hurt anyone else," she said. "I thought if this was really happening and he survived, he would go into the criminal justice system and be executed, and I couldn't bear to lose him twice. I gave the hardest prayer I ever made, that he would kill himself, because then at least I would know that he wanted to die, and I wouldn't be left with all the questions I'd have if he got caught by a police bullet. Maybe I was right, but I've spent so many hours regretting that prayer: I wished for my son to kill himself, and he did."

At the end of that weekend, I asked Tom and Sue what they would want to ask Dylan if he were in the room with us, Tom said, "I'd ask him what the hell he was thinking and what the hell he thought he was doing!" Sue looked down at the floor for a minute before saying quietly, "I would ask him to forgive me, for being his mother and never knowing what was going on inside his head, for not being able to help him, for not being the person that he could confide in." When I reminded her of this conversation five years later, she said, "When it first happened, I used to wish that I had never had children, that I had never married. If Tom and I hadn't crossed paths at Ohio State, Dylan wouldn't have existed and this terrible thing wouldn't have happened. But over time, I've come to feel that, for myself, I am glad I had kids and glad I had the kids I did, because the love for them—even at the price of this pain—has been the single greatest joy of my life. When I say that, I am speaking of my own pain, and not of the pain of other people. But I accept my own pain; life is full of suffering, and this is mine. I know it would have been better for the world if Dylan had never been born. But I believe it would not have been better for me."

We tend to lose someone all at once, but Sue's loss came in repeated waves: the loss of the boy himself; the loss of her image of him; the loss of her defenses against recognizing his darkest self; the loss of her identity as something other than the mother of a killer; and the loss of the fundamental belief that life is subject to logic, that if you do things right you can forestall certain grim outcomes. Comparative grief is not a fruitful measurement, and it would be wrong to say that Sue Klebold's was the most shattering of all the losses in Littleton. But she is stuck with the impossibility of disentangling the pain of finding she had never known her son from the pain of knowing what devastation he caused others. She fights the sadness of a dead child, the sadness of the other dead children, and the sadness of having failed to bring up a happy child who makes the world better.

It's a heady experience to have young children and be able to fix the little problems they bring to you; it's a terrible loss when they start to have problems beyond your ability to resolve. That universal disappointment is presented here on a vastly inflated scale. Sue Klebold describes her natural impulse to please people, and makes it clear that writing has required a disavowal of that predilection. Her book is a tribute to Dylan without being an excuse, and a moving call to action for mental health advocacy and research. Moral, determined, and dignified, Sue Klebold has arrived at an impenetrable aloneness. No one else has had this experience. To some degree, it has made Sue unknowable, just as Dylan was. In writing of her experience, she has chosen a kind of public unknowability.

Ovid delivered a famous injunction to "welcome this pain, for you will learn from it." But there is little choice about such pain; you do not have the option of not welcoming it. You can express displeasure at its arrival, but you cannot ask it to leave the house. Sue Klebold has never complained of being a victim, but her narrative echoes that of Job, who says, "Shall we receive good from God and shall we not receive evil?" And then, "For the thing which I greatly feared is come upon me, and that which I was afraid of is come unto me. / I was not in safety, neither had I rest, neither was I quiet; yet trouble came." And finally, "Though I speak, my grief is not assuaged." Sue Klebold's book narrates her Job-like descent into an incomprehensible hell, her divorce from safety. Perhaps most impressively, her book acknowledges that speech cannot assuage such grief. She doesn't even try. This book is not a cathartic document intended to make her feel better. It is only a narrative of acceptance and of fight, of harnessing her torment in hopes of sparing others pain like hers, like her son's, and like his victims'.

—Andrew Solomon

Preface

On April 20, 1999, Eric Harris and Dylan Klebold armed themselves with guns and explosives and walked into Columbine High School. They killed twelve students and a teacher, and wounded twenty-four others, before taking their own lives. It was the worst school shooting in history.

Dylan Klebold was my son.

I would give my life to reverse what happened that day. In fact, I would gladly give my own in exchange for just one of the lives that was lost. Yet I know that such a trade is impossible. Nothing I will ever be able to do or say can possibly atone for the massacre.

Sixteen years have passed since that terrible day, and I have dedicated them to understanding what is still incomprehensible to me—how a promising boy's life could have escalated into such a disaster, and on my watch. I have interrogated experts as well as our family, Dylan's friends, and, most of all, myself. What did I miss, and how could I have missed it? I have scoured my daily journals. I have analyzed our family life with the ferocity of a forensic scientist, turning over mundane events and exchanges in search of the clues I missed. What should I have seen? What could I have done differently?

My quest for answers began as a purely personal mission, a primal need to know as strong as the shame and horror and grief that overwhelmed me. But I have come to see that the fragments I hold offer clues to a puzzle many are desperate to solve. The hope that what I have learned may help has led me to the difficult but necessary step of going public with my story.

There is a world between where I stand now and the view I had before Columbine, when our family life looked like that of a typical suburban American family. In more than a decade of searching through the wreckage, my eyes have opened—not only to those things once hidden to me about Dylan and the events leading up to that day, but also to the realization that these insights have implications that extend far beyond Columbine.

I'll never know whether I could have prevented my son's terrible role in the carnage that unfolded that day, but I have come to see things I wish I had done differently. These are small things, threads in the larger tapestry of a normal family's life. Because if anyone had peeked inside our lives before Columbine, I believe that what they would have seen, even with the tightest zoom lens, was thoroughly ordinary, no different from the lives unfolding in countless homes across the country.

Tom and I were loving, attentive, and engaged parents, and Dylan was an enthusiastic, affectionate child. This wasn't a kid we worried and prayed over, hoping he would eventually find his way and lead a productive life. We called him "The Sunshine Boy"— not just because of his halo of blond hair, but because everything seemed to come easily to him. I was grateful to be Dylan's mother, and loved him with my whole heart and soul.

The ordinariness of our lives before Columbine will perhaps be the hardest thing for people to understand about my story. For me, it is also the most important. Our home life was not difficult or fraught. Our youngest child was not a handful, let alone someone we (or others who knew him) would have imagined to be a risk to himself or to anyone else. I wish many things had been different, but, most of all, I wish I had known it was possible for everything to seem fine with my son when it was not.

When it comes to brain health issues, many of our children are as vulnerable today as children a hundred years ago were to infectious diseases. Far too often, as in our case, their susceptibility goes undetected. Whether a child flames out in a horrifying scenario, or whether their potential for happiness and productivity merely fizzles, this situation can be as confounding as it is heartbreaking. If we do not wake up to these vulnerabilities, the terrible toll will continue to rise. And that toll will be counted not just in tragedies such as Columbine or Virginia Tech or Newtown or Charleston, but in countless quieter, slow-burning tragedies playing out every day in the family lives of our coworkers, friends, and loved ones.

There is perhaps no harder truth for a parent to bear, but it is one that no parent on earth knows better than I do, and it is this: love is not enough. My love for Dylan, though infinite, did not keep Dylan safe, nor did it save the thirteen people killed at Columbine High School, or the many others injured and traumatized. I missed subtle signs of psychological deterioration that, had I noticed, might have made a difference for Dylan and his victims—all the difference in the world.

By telling my story as faithfully as possible, even when it is unflattering to me, I hope to shine a light that will help other parents see past the faces their children present, so that they can get them help if it is needed.

Many of my own friends and colleagues have changed their parenting styles as a result of knowing our story. In some instances, their interventions have had dramatic results, as when a former colleague noticed that her thirteen-year-old daughter seemed slightly withdrawn. With Dylan in mind, she pressed (and pressed, and pressed). Eventually, her daughter broke down and confessed that a stranger had raped her while she was sneaking out to see a friend. The girl was deeply depressed and ashamed and afraid, and she was seriously considering taking her own life.

My colleague was able to help her child because she noticed subtle changes, and kept asking. I take heart in knowing that my colleague effected a happier ending for her daughter's story because she knew ours, and I believe only good can come from widening the circle of people who know it.

It is not easy for me to come forward, but if the understanding and insights I have gained in the terrible crucible of Columbine can help, then I have a moral imperative to share them. Speaking out is frightening, but it is also the right thing to do. The list of things I would have done differently if I had known more is long. Those are my failures. But what I have learned implies the need for a broader call to action, a comprehensive overview of what should be in place to stop not only tragedies like the one committed by my son but the hidden suffering of any child.

Notes to the Reader

The italicized passages beginning many of the chapters are excerpts from my diaries.

In the days after Columbine, I filled notebook after notebook with words in an effort to process my confusion and guilt and grief. Like most diaries, mine are unpublishable, but they are invaluable source material for this book. People refer to the fog of war, and I am sure something similar applies to my situation. If I hadn't kept a running record of the days, weeks, and years, the fog would have swallowed too much of the story for me to provide a reliable account. My journals serve as helpful reminders not only of events and facts, but also of the phases of my own evolution.

I am in a very different place than I was in the days following Columbine; it's not hyperbole to say I'm no longer the same person. The excerpts from my diaries provide a window into the immediate thoughts and feelings I was having as the events occurred, while the chapters incorporate the perspective that has come with the passage of time and a tremendous amount of research and self-reflection.

. . .

Some of the names and identifying details in this book have been changed to protect people's privacy.

. . .

In the process of writing this book, I interviewed many experts in fields ranging from law enforcement to threat assessment to journalistic ethics to sociology, psychology, psychiatry, and neurobiology. This book would not have been possible without their generosity and dedication to the spirit of inquiry.

A Mother's Reckoning

PART I

The Last People on Earth

With Dylan on his fifth birthday.
The Klebold Family

CHAPTER 1

"There's Been a Shooting at Columbine High School"

APRIL 20, 1999, 12:05 P.M.

I was in my office in downtown Denver, getting ready to leave for a meeting about college scholarships for students with disabilities, when I noticed the red message light on my desk phone flashing.

I checked, on the off chance my meeting had been canceled, but the message was from my husband, Tom, his voice tight, ragged, urgent.

"Susan—this is an emergency! Call me back immediately!"

He didn't say anything more. He didn't have to: I knew just from the sound of his voice that something had happened to one of our boys.

It felt as if it took hours for my shaking fingers to dial our home phone number. Panic crashed over me like a wave; my heart pounded in my ears. Our youngest son, Dylan, was at school; his older brother, Byron, was at work. Had there been an accident?

Tom picked up and immediately yelled: "Listen to the television!" But I couldn't make out any distinct words. It terrified me that whatever had happened was big enough to be on TV. My fear, seconds earlier, of a car wreck suddenly seemed tame. Were we at war? Was the country under attack?

"What's happening?" I screamed into the receiver. There was only static and indecipherable television noise on the other end. Tom came back on the line, finally, but my ordinarily steadfast husband sounded like a madman. The scrambled words pouring out of him in staccato bursts made no sense: "gunman . . . shooter . . . school."

I struggled to understand what Tom was telling me: Nate,

Dylan's best friend, had called Tom's home office minutes before to ask, "Is Dylan home?" A call like that in the middle of the school day would have been alarming enough, but the reason for Nate's call was every parent's worst nightmare come to life: gunmen were shooting at people at Columbine High School, where Dylan was a senior.

There was more: Nate had said the shooters had been wearing black trench coats, like the one we'd bought for Dylan.

"I don't want to alarm you," he'd said to Tom. "But I know all the kids who wear black coats, and the only ones I can't find are Dylan and Eric. They weren't in bowling this morning, either."

Tom's voice was hoarse with fear as he told me he'd hung up with Nate and ripped the house apart looking for Dylan's trench coat, irrationally convinced that if he could find it, Dylan was fine. But the coat was gone, and Tom was frantic.

"I'm coming home," I said, panic numbing my spine. We hung up without saying good-bye.

Helplessly fighting for composure, I asked a coworker to cancel my meeting. Leaving the office, I found my hands shaking so uncontrollably that I had to steady my right hand with my left in order to press the button for my floor in the elevator. My fellow passengers were cheerfully chatting with one another on the way out to lunch. I explained my strange behavior by saying, "There's been a shooting at Columbine High School. I have to go home and make sure my son's okay." A colleague offered to drive me home. Unable to speak further, I shook my head.

As I got into the car, my mind raced. It didn't occur to me to turn on the radio; I was barely keeping the car safely on the road as it was. My one constant thought, as I drove the twenty-six miles to our home: *Dylan is in danger.*

Paroxysms of fear clutched at my chest as I sifted again and again through the same jagged fragments of information. The coat could be anywhere, I told myself: in Dylan's locker or in his car. Surely a teenager's missing coat didn't mean anything. Yet my sturdy, dependable husband had sounded close to hysterical; I'd never heard him like that before.

The drive felt like an eternity, like I was traveling in slow motion, although my mind spun at lightning speed and my heart pounded in my ears. I kept trying to put the pieces of the puzzle together so it would come out okay, but there was little comfort to be found in the meager facts I had, and I knew I'd never recover if anything happened to Dylan.

As I drove, I talked out loud to myself and burst into uncontrollable sobs. Analytic by nature, I tried to talk myself down: I didn't have enough information yet. Columbine High School was enormous, with more than two thousand students. Just because Nate hadn't been able to find Dylan in the chaos didn't necessarily mean our son was hurt or dead. I had to stop allowing Tom's panic to infect me. Even as terror continued to roll over me in waves, I told myself we were probably freaking out unnecessarily, as any parent of an unaccounted-for child would in the same situation. Maybe no one was hurt. I was going to walk into our kitchen to find Dylan raiding our fridge, ready to tease me for overreacting.

I nonetheless couldn't stop my mind from careening from one terrible scenario to another. Tom had said there were gunmen in the school. Palms sweaty on the wheel, I shook my head as if Tom were there to see. Gunmen! Maybe no one knew where Dylan was because he had been shot. Maybe he was lying injured or dead in the school building—trapped, unable to get word to us. Maybe he was being held hostage. The thought was so awful I could barely breathe.

But there was, too, a nagging tug at my stomach. I'd frozen in fear when I heard Tom mention Eric Harris. The one time Dylan had been in serious trouble, he'd been with Eric. I shook my head again. Dylan had always been a playful, loving child, and he'd grown into an even-tempered, sensible adolescent. He'd learned his lesson, I reassured myself. He wouldn't allow himself to get drawn into something stupid a second time.

Along with the dozens of other frightening scenarios whirling through my fevered brain, I wondered if the horror unfolding at the school might not be an innocently planned senior prank, spun terribly out of hand.

One thing was for sure: Dylan couldn't possibly have a gun. Tom and I were so adamantly anti-gun, we were considering moving away from Colorado because the laws were changing, making it easier to carry concealed firearms. No matter how hideously ill-conceived the stunt, there was no way Dylan would ever have gotten involved with a real gun, even as a joke.

And so it went, for twenty-six long miles. One minute I was awash with images of Dylan hurt, wounded, crying out for help, and then I'd be flooded with happier snapshots: Dylan as a boy, blowing out his birthday candles; squealing with happy pleasure as he rode the plastic slide with his brother into the wading pool in the backyard. They say your life flashes before you when you die, but on that car ride home, it was my son's life flashing before me, like a movie reel—each precious frame both breaking my heart and filling me with desperate hope.

That hellish ride home was the first step in what would become a lifetime's work of coming to terms with the impossible.

. . .

When I arrived home, my panic kicked into an even higher gear. Tom told me what he knew in spotty bursts: shooters at the school, Dylan and Eric still unaccounted for. Whatever was happening was serious. He'd called our older son, Byron, who'd said he would leave work and come to us immediately.

Tom and I raced around the house like demented wind-up toys, flooded with adrenaline, unable to stop or to complete a task. Our wide-eyed pets crouched in the corners, alarmed.

Tom was single-minded in his focus on the missing coat, but I was personally confounded by Nate saying Dylan had missed bowling. He'd left the house that morning with more than enough time to get there; he'd said good-bye as he left. Thinking about it, I found myself haunted by the peculiar nature of that farewell.

That morning, the morning of April 20, my alarm had gone off before first light. As I dressed for work, I watched the clock. Knowing how much Dylan hated to get up early, Tom and I had tried to talk him out of signing up for a 6:15 a.m. bowling class. But Dylan prevailed. It would be fun, he said: he loved bowling, and some of his friends were taking the class. Throughout the semester, he'd done a good job of getting himself to the alley on time—not a perfect record, but nearly. Still, I needed to keep an eye on the time. No matter how dutifully he set his alarm, on bowling mornings Dylan usually needed an extra call-out from me at the bottom of the stairs to get him out of bed.

But on the morning of April 20, I was still getting dressed when I heard Dylan bounding heavily down the stairs, past our closed bedroom door on the main floor. It surprised me that he was up and dressed so early without prompting. He was moving quickly and seemed to be in a hurry to leave, though he had plenty of time to sleep a little more.

We always coordinated our plans for the day, so I opened the bedroom door and leaned out. "Dyl?" I called. The rest of the house was too dark for me to see anything, but I heard the front door open. Out of the blackness, his voice sharp and decisive, I heard my son yell, "Bye," and then the front door shut firmly behind him. He was gone before I could even turn on the hallway light.

Unsettled by the exchange, I turned back to the bed and woke Tom. There had been an edge to Dylan's voice in that single word I'd never heard before—a sneer, almost, as if he'd been caught in the middle of a fight with someone.

It wasn't the first sign we'd had that week to indicate Dylan was under some stress. Two days before, on Sunday, Tom had asked me: "Have you noticed Dylan's voice lately? The pitch of it is tight and higher than usual." Tom gestured toward his vocal cords with his thumb and middle finger. "His voice goes up like that when he's tense. I think something may be bothering him." Tom's instincts about the boys had always been excellent, and we agreed to sit down with Dylan to see if something was on his mind. It certainly made sense that Dylan would be feeling some anxiety as his high school graduation loomed. Three weeks before, we'd gone to visit his first-choice college, the University of Arizona. Though Dylan was highly independent, leaving the state for school would be a big adjustment for a kid who'd never been away from home.

But I was unsettled by the tight quality I'd heard in Dylan's voice when he said good-bye, and it bugged me that he hadn't stopped to share his plans for the day. We hadn't yet had the chance to sit down and talk with him, as Dylan had spent most of the weekend with various friends. "I think you were right on Sunday," I told my sleepy husband. "Something *is* bothering Dylan."

From bed, Tom reassured me. "I'll talk to him as soon as he gets home." Because Tom worked from home, the two of them usually shared the sports section and had a snack together when Dylan got back from school. I relaxed and continued to get ready for work as usual, relieved to know that by the time I arrived home, Tom would know if something was bothering Dylan.

In the wake of Nate's phone call, though, as I stood in our kitchen trying to piece together the fragments of information we had, I felt chilled by the memory of the nasty, hard flatness in Dylan's voice as he'd said good-bye that morning, and the fact that he'd left early but hadn't made it to class. I'd figured he was meeting someone early for coffee—maybe even to talk through whatever was bugging him. But if he hadn't made it to bowling, then where on earth had he been?

The bottom didn't fall out from my world until the telephone rang, and Tom ran into the kitchen to answer it. It was a lawyer. My fears so far had been dominated by the possibility that Dylan was in danger—that either he'd been physically hurt or done something stupid, something that would get him into trouble. Now I understood that Tom's fears also included something for which Dylan could need a lawyer.

Dylan had gotten into trouble with Eric in his junior year. The episode had given us the shock of our lives: our well-mannered, organized kid, the kid we'd never had to worry about, had broken into a parked van and stolen some electronic equipment. As a result, Dylan had been put on probation. He'd completed a Diversion program, which allowed him to avoid any criminal charges. In fact, he'd graduated early from the course—an unusual occurrence, we were told—and with glowing praise from the counselor.

Everyone had told us not to make too much of the incident: Dylan was a good kid, and even the best teenage boys have been known to make colossally stupid mistakes. But we'd also been warned that a single misstep, even shaving cream on a banister, would mean a felony charge and jail time. And so, at the first indication that Dylan might be in trouble, Tom had contacted a highly recommended defense attorney. While part of me was incredulous that Tom imagined Dylan could be involved in whatever was happening at the school, another part of me felt grateful. In spite of Tom's worry, he'd had the foresight to be proactive.

I was still miles away from the idea that people might actually be hurt, or that they'd been hurt by my son's hand. I was simply worried that Dylan, in the service of some dumb practical joke, might have jeopardized his future by carelessly throwing away the second chance he'd been given with the successful completion of his Diversion program.

The call, of course, brought much, much worse news. The lawyer Tom had contacted, Gary Lozow, had reached out to the sheriff's office. He was calling back to tell Tom the unthinkable was now confirmed. Although reports were wildly contradictory, there was no doubt something terrible involving gunmen was happening at Columbine High School. The district attorney's office had confirmed to Gary Lozow that they suspected Dylan was one of the gunmen. The police were on their way to our home.

When Tom hung up the phone, we stared at each other in stunned horror and disbelief. What I was hearing couldn't possibly be true. And yet it was. And yet it couldn't possibly be. Even the most nightmarish worst-case scenarios I'd played out in my mind during the car ride home paled with the reality now emerging. I'd been worried Dylan was in danger or had done something childish to get himself into trouble; now it appeared that people had been hurt because of whatever he was doing. This was real; it was happening. Still, I could not get my brain to grasp what I was hearing.

Then Tom told me he was going to try to get into the school.

I yelled, "No! Are you crazy? You could get killed!"

He looked at me steadily, and then he said, "So?"

All of the noisy confusion swirling around us came to a dead stop as we stared at each other. After a moment, I bit back my protests and turned away. Tom was right. Even if he died, at least we'd be sure he'd done everything he could to stop whatever was happening.

Shortly after one o'clock, I called my sister, my fingers shaking as I dialed. My parents were both dead, but my older sister and younger brother lived near each other in another state. My entire life, my sister has been the one I reach out to when things are going well, and the one I reach out to when they aren't. She has always taken care of me.

The minute I heard her voice, whatever composure I'd been maintaining collapsed, and I burst into tears. "Something horrible is happening at the school. I don't know if Dylan is hurting people or if he's hurt. They're saying he's involved." There was nothing Diane could say to stem my tears, but she did promise to call our brother and the rest of the family. "We're here for you," she said fiercely as we said good-bye so I could keep the line free. I had no idea then how much I would need her over the years to come.

By the time our older son, Byron, arrived, my frenzied attempts to do something—anything—had ground to a halt, and I was sitting at the kitchen counter, sobbing into a dish towel. As soon as Byron put his arms around me, every ounce of strength left my body and I collapsed, so he was holding me up more than he was hugging me.

"How could he do this? How could he do this?" I kept asking. I had no idea what "this" was. Byron shook his head in silent disbelief, his arms still around me. There was nothing to say. Part of me thought, *I'm his mother. I should pull myself together, be a role model here, be strong for Byron.* But it was impossible for me to do anything other than weep helplessly, a rag doll in my son's arms.

The police began to arrive, and they escorted us out of the house to wait in the driveway. It was a beautiful day, sunny and warm, the kind of day that makes you feel like spring might finally be here to stay. Under other circumstances, I'd be rejoicing we'd survived another long Colorado winter. Instead, the beauty of the weather felt like a slap in the face. "What are they looking for? What do they want?" I kept asking. "Can we help?" Eventually, an officer told us they were searching our house and our tenant's apartment for explosives.

It was the first time we'd heard anything about explosives. We could find out nothing more. We were not allowed into our house without a police escort. Tom would not be permitted to go to the school, or anywhere else. Later, we learned that no one had been allowed in the school. The first responders hadn't entered the building until long after Dylan and Eric were dead, surrounded by the bodies of their victims.

As we stood there, waiting in the sunny driveway, I noticed that three or four of the officers were wearing SWAT team uniforms and what appeared to be bulletproof vests. The sight of them was more puzzling than alarming. Why were they at our house instead of at the school? They crouched and entered our home through the front door, their guns drawn and held at arm's length with both hands as if in a movie. Did they think we were harboring Dylan? Or that Tom and I would somehow be a danger to them?

It was completely surreal, and I thought very clearly: *We are the last people on earth anyone would expect to be in this situation.*

We spent hours pacing the driveway like frightened animals. Byron was still smoking then, and I watched him light cigarette after cigarette, too overwhelmed to protest. The police would not engage with us, though we begged for information. What had happened? How did they know Dylan was a suspect? How many gunmen were there? Where was Dylan? Was he okay? Nobody would tell us a thing.

Time warped, as it does in emergencies. Media and police helicopters began circling noisily overhead. Our tenant, Alison, who lived in the studio outbuilding on our property, brought us bottles of water and granola bars we couldn't bear to eat. If we needed to use the bathroom, we did so with two armed policemen guarding the other side of the door. I wasn't sure if they were protecting us or if we were suspects. Both options horrified me: I'd never done anything illegal in my life, and it had never, ever occurred to me to be afraid of my son.

As the afternoon stretched on, we continued to pace the drive-way. Conversation was impossible. The Rocky Mountain foothills surrounding our home had always soothed me; Tom and I often said we didn't feel any need to travel because we already lived in the most beautiful place on earth. But that afternoon, the tall stone cliffs seemed cold and forbidding—prison walls around our home.

I looked up to see a figure coming up the driveway. It was Judy Brown, the mother of one of Dylan's childhood friends, Brooks. Alerted by the Littleton rumor mill that Dylan was involved in the events at the school, she had come to our house.

I was startled to see her. Our boys had been good friends in first and second grades and then reunited in high school, but they hadn't been close, and I'd only seen Judy a few times in the years since elementary school. We'd chatted warmly a few weeks before, at a school event, but we'd never done anything together except when our boys were involved, and I wasn't sure I could manage any social niceties. I was too disoriented to question why she was there, but it did seem odd for her to have materialized during this most private of times. She and Alison sat on either side of me on our brick side-walk, urging me to drink the water they'd brought. Tom and Byron paced up and down the front walk with brooding expressions as we all struggled with our own splintered thoughts.

My mind was a chaotic swirl. There was no way to square the information we had with what I knew about my life, and about my son. They couldn't be talking about Dylan, our "Sunshine Boy," such a good kid, he always made me feel like a good mother. If it was true that Dylan had intentionally hurt people, then where in his life had this come from?

Eventually, the detective in charge told us he wanted to inter-view each of us separately. Tom and I were happy and eager to co-operate, especially if there was anything we could do to shed light on whatever was happening.

My interview took place in the front seat of the detective's car. It's unthinkable now, but during that interview, I really believed

I could straighten the whole mess out if I could only explain why everything they were thinking about Dylan was wrong. I did not realize I had entered a new phase in my life. I still thought the order of the world as I'd known it could be restored.

I pressed my trembling hands together to still them. Solemn and intimidating, the detective got right to the point: Did we keep any weapons in our home? Had Dylan been interested in weapons or in explosives? I had little of relevance to share with him. Tom and I had never owned any guns. BB guns were standard fare for young boys where we lived, but we'd bucked the trend for as long as we could—and then made our kids create and sign handwritten safety contracts before giving in. They'd used the BBs for target practice for a while, but by the time Dylan was a young teenager, the air rifles had found their way to a shelf in the garage with the model airplanes and G.I. Joe action figures and the other forgotten relics of the boys' childhoods.

I remembered aloud that Dylan had asked the year before if I would consider buying him a gun for Christmas. The request was made in passing and came out of the blue. Surprised, I had asked why he wanted a gun, and he'd told me it would be fun to go to a shooting range sometime for target practice. Dylan knew how avidly anti-gun I was, so the request had taken me aback—even though we'd moved to a rural area, where hunting and hanging out at the shooting range were popular pastimes. As alien as it might have been to me personally, guns were an accepted part of the culture where we lived, and many of our neighbors and friends in Colorado were recreational firearm enthusiasts. So while I would never allow a gun under our roof, Dylan's request for one didn't set off any special alarm bells.

I'd suggested we search for his old BB gun instead. Dylan rolled his eyes, a teasing smile on his face: Moms. "It's not the same thing," he said, and I shook my head decisively. "I can't imagine why you'd want a gun, and you know how your dad and I feel about them. You're going to be eighteen shortly, and if you really want one, you can get one for yourself then. But you know I would never, ever buy you a gun."

Dylan nodded fondly at me, and smiled. "Yeah, I knew you'd say that. I just thought I'd ask." There was no intensity to the request, and no animosity when I dismissed it. He never mentioned a gun to me again, and I filed it in the same category as the other outlandish Christmas requests he'd made over the years. He hadn't seriously thought we were going to get him a muscle car or gliding lessons, either.

The detective had another question: Was Dylan interested in explosives? I thought he was asking about firecrackers, and I answered truthfully: Dylan did like those. He'd accepted fireworks as payment when he'd worked at a fireworks display stand, one of his first summer jobs. (It's legal to sell them in Colorado.) So he had a lot of them, which he kept safely stored in a big rubber bin in the garage. He set the firecrackers off on the Fourth of July, and enjoyed them; the rest of the year, they sat in the bin in the garage, forgotten. Dylan was a collector of a lot of things. I hadn't heard anything yet about propane tanks or pipe bombs, so I had no idea what the detective was really asking me.

I felt small and frightened in the front seat of the detective's car, but I was dedicated to answering his questions fully and truthfully. When he asked if I had ever seen any gun catalogs or magazines around the house, his question jarred something loose in my memory. A few catalogs with guns on the cover *had* arrived in the stacks of unwanted junk mail we received on a daily basis. I hadn't paid any more attention to them than I had to the catalogs advertising personalized baby clothes or orthopedic devices for the elderly, and had thrown them away without looking at them. Dylan had pulled one of those catalogs out of the trash. He'd been looking for a pair of heavy-duty work boots to fit his large feet, and he found a pair of boots he liked in the catalog. When we learned they didn't carry his size, I threw the catalog away a second time. He'd eventually found a pair of boots at an army surplus store.

I felt like the detective was looking at me with knowing eyes. *Gotcha.* Suddenly defensive and self-conscious, I heard myself begin to babble, trying to get this police officer to understand how many catalogs came every day, and why I hadn't checked the addressee.

I thought he'd understand if only I could make myself heard. I had always relied on my aptitude for addressing problems logically, and on my ability to communicate effectively. I did not yet understand—and would not for some time—that my version of reality was the one out of sync.

The detective asked about recent events, and I told him everything I could remember. A few weeks earlier, we'd visited the University of Arizona. Dylan had been accepted, and we wanted him to be able to plant his feet on the ground of his number-one pick to make sure the fit felt right. Just three days before, Dylan, handsome in a tuxedo, had posed with his prom date, smiling awkwardly while we snapped a picture. How could that boy be the one they were accusing?

But there was no answer forthcoming, nor any hope. The interview was over. As I climbed out of the detective's car, I felt as if I were about to explode into a thousand pieces, bits of me spinning out into the stratosphere.

We still weren't permitted into the house. Tom and Byron were still pacing the driveway. A police officer told us the investigators were waiting for the bomb squad, a piece of information that only added to our terror and confusion. Were they looking for a bomb? Had our home been booby-trapped by someone Dylan knew? But nobody would answer any of our questions, and we couldn't tell if this was because they didn't yet know exactly what had happened, or because we were suspects.

Because we had been standing for so long in our driveway, cut off from any media or news updates, we probably knew less than anyone else in Littleton—or the rest of the world, for that matter—about what was going on. Cell phones were not yet as ubiquitous as they are now; although Tom had one for work, its signal was blocked by the sandstone cliffs surrounding our house. The police had commandeered our home phone. Frightened and bewildered, all we could do was pray for our son.

We waited outside in the sun, perched on concrete steps or leaning against parked cars. Judy approached me. Dropping her voice confidentially, she told me about a violent website Eric had made.

Still out of my mind with worry about Dylan, I didn't understand why she was telling me about it, until I did: she'd known Eric was disturbed and dangerous for a long time.

"Why didn't you tell me?" I asked, genuinely baffled. She'd told the police, she said.

The house phone rang constantly. The detective called me to the phone to speak to my elderly aunt. She'd heard about a shooting in Littleton. (Dylan's name had not yet been mentioned on air.) She was in frail health, and I worried about telling her the truth, but realized that protecting her would soon be impossible.

I said as gently as possible, "Please prepare yourself for the worst. The police are here. They think Dylan is involved." As she protested, I repeated what I had already said. What had been inconceivable hours before had already begun to solidify into a new and horrible reality. Just as nebulous shapes resolve into letters and numbers with every progressive click of the machine at the eye doctor's, so was the magnitude of the horror starting to come into focus for me. Everything was still an incomprehensible blur, but I already knew two things: this would not be the case for much longer, and the confusion was resolving into a truth I did not believe I could bear.

I promised my aunt I would be in touch, and hung up to keep the line open for communication from the school.

As the shadows lengthened, time slowed. Tom and I muddled through our uncertainty in hushed whispers. We had no choice but to accept Dylan's involvement, but neither of us could believe he had participated in a shooting under his own free will. He must have become mixed up with a criminal, somehow, or a group of them, who forced him to participate. We even considered that someone had threatened to harm us, and he had gone along in order to protect us. Maybe he had gone into the school thinking it was a harmless joke, some kind of theater, only to learn at the last minute he was using live ammunition?

I simply could not, would not, believe Dylan participated voluntarily in hurting people. If he had, the kind, funny, goofy kid that we loved so much must have been tricked, threatened, coerced, or even drugged into doing it.

Later we would learn that Dylan's friends spun similar explanations for the events unfurling around them. Not one of them considered he might willingly be involved. None of us would learn the true level of his involvement—or the depths of his rage, alienation, and despair—until many months later. Even then, many of us would struggle to reconcile the person we knew and loved with what he'd done that day.

We stayed out there in the driveway, suspended in limbo, the passing hours marked only by our helpless confusion as we careened from hope to dread. The phone rang and rang and rang. Then the glass storm door of our house once again swung open, and this time I could hear the television Tom had left on in our bedroom, echoing inside the empty rooms. A local news anchor was reporting from outside Columbine High School. I heard him say the latest reports had twenty-five people dead.

Like mothers all over Littleton, I had been praying for my son's safety. But when I heard the newscaster pronounce twenty-five people dead, my prayers changed. If Dylan was involved in hurting or killing other people, he had to be stopped. As a mother, this was the most difficult prayer I had ever spoken in the silence of my thoughts, but in that instant I knew the greatest mercy I could pray for was not my son's safety, but for his death.

CHAPTER 2

Slivers of Glass

As the afternoon turned to twilight and then to darkness, I let go of my last hope that Dylan would zoom up the drive in the dented old black BMW he'd fixed up with his dad, laughing and wondering about dinner.

Late in the day, I cornered a member of the SWAT team and asked him a question, point-blank:

"Is my son dead?"

"Yes," he told me. As soon as he said it, I realized I had already known it to be true.

"How did he die?" I asked him. It seemed important to know. Had Dylan been killed by the police or by one of the shooters? Had he taken his own life? I hoped he had. At least if Dylan died by suicide, I'd know he had wanted to die. Later, I would come to regret that wish almost as bitterly as I've ever regretted anything.

The SWAT team member shook his head. "I don't know," he said. And then he turned away, leaving me alone.

• • •

It will perhaps seem callous that my focus was so squarely on Dylan—on the question of his safety, and later on the fact of his death. But my obligation is to offer the truth to the degree to which my memory will allow, even when that truth reflects badly on me. And the truth is that my thoughts were with my son.

Over the course of the afternoon, I had come to understand Dylan was suspected of shooting people, but this fact registered with me only in an abstract way at first. I was convinced Dylan could not have been responsible for taking anyone's life. I was beginning to accept he had been physically present during the shootings, but Dylan had never hurt anyone or anything in his life, and I knew in my heart he could not have killed anyone. I was wrong, of course—about that and many things. At the time, though, I was sure.

So, in those first hours and even days, I wasn't thinking about the victims or about the anguish of their loved ones and friends. Just as our bodies experience shock when we experience extreme trauma—we've all heard stories of soldiers in combat who run for miles unaware of a severed limb—a similar phenomenon occurs with severe psychological trauma. A mechanism to preserve our sanity kicks in and lets in only what we can bear, a little at a time. It is a defense mechanism, breathtaking in its power both to shield and to distort.

Whatever mercy there was in not knowing was short-lived. My anguish over the lives lost or destroyed by my son's hand, and for the pain and suffering this caused their families and friends, is with me every single day. It will never go away, as long as I live. I will never see a mother in the cereal aisle with her little girl without wondering if that beautiful child will reach adulthood. I will never see a cluster of teenagers laughing and bumping each other at Starbucks without wondering if one of them will be robbed of life before he's had the chance to live it in full. I will never see a family enjoying a picnic or a baseball game or walking into church without thinking of the relatives of those my son murdered.

In writing this book, I hope to honor the memories of the people my son killed. The best way I know to do that is to be truthful, to the best of my ability. And so, this is the truth: my tears for the victims did eventually come, and they still do. But they did not come that day.

· · ·

We were still standing in the gravel driveway when the bomb squad arrived. Shortly after, it began to drizzle, and I sought shelter on our doorstep with Tom, Byron, our tenant Alison, and Judy Brown. We clustered tightly together under the narrow ledge over our front door.

It grew dark and cold suddenly, and the change in weather heightened our sense of vulnerability and our fear of what was to come.

Reflexively, I thought to pray, and then—for the first time in my life—I stopped myself from reaching for that comfort.

While my mother's parents were Christian, my father had been brought up in a Jewish home, so my siblings and I were raised in both traditions. There are significant differences between the two religions, but both shared a conception of God as a loving, understanding Father. Since childhood, I had taken refuge in that understanding of Him. However, there was no solace for me there in the early evening of April 20, 1999. Instead, I felt a real sense of fear. I was afraid to make eye contact with God.

Every night since the birth of my children, I had asked God to protect and guide them. I truly believed those prayers watched over my sons. As the boys grew, I'd amended my evening prayer to include the safety of others. When Byron was first entering adolescence, I heard a dreadful story on the news: a teenager had stolen a stop sign from an intersection, a lark resulting in a fatal accident. The idea that one of my children would unwittingly cause harm became my worst nightmare. I never worried they'd hurt someone deliberately; I'd never had any cause to worry about such a thing, from either of them. But, especially as I gripped the dashboard while they were first learning to navigate the narrow, winding canyon roads between our house and town, I hoped no expression of pure teenaged stupidity or carelessness would ever result in injury to someone else. Now those prayers had resolved themselves into a reality so horrific, I lacked the moral imagination to fully grasp it.

I hadn't lost my faith. I was afraid to attract God's attention, to further draw down His wrath.

I had always imagined God's plan for me was aligned with my own plan. I believed with all of my heart that if I was a caring and loving and generous person—if I worked hard and gave what I could to charity, if I did my best to be a good daughter and friend and wife and mother—then I would be rewarded with a good life. Exiled to our front steps, the light from the hallway casting harsh shadows on our faces, I felt suddenly ashamed, as my lifelong understanding of God was starkly revealed as a naive fiction, a bedtime story, a pathetic delusion. It was the loneliest I have ever felt.

Soon, there was no time to think or to feel. The police would not let us back into our house; we would have to find another place to stay. Tom, Alison, and I would each be allowed to go inside for five minutes to collect a few personal belongings. We would have to go in one at a time, and under the close watch of two guards.

Before the burst of activity to follow, I had a short, vivid vision that I was standing with a multitude of spirits, all of whom suffered. They were all ages, sizes, and races; I couldn't tell who was male and who was female. Their heads were bowed and covered with tattered white robes. My old life had come to an end, and a new one had begun: a life in which joy, once so abundant, would be simply a memory. Sorrow, I understood with a painful clarity, would transport me through the rest of this life. The vision ended when needles of rain began to fall on my face, like slivers of glass.

The two police officers escorting me into the house stayed on me like basketball guards, watching my hands closely and keeping their own hands near to mine as I packed. This confused and frightened me, and I felt embarrassed as I rifled through drawers to find underthings and hygiene products. Years afterward, I spoke to one of the officers who'd been at our home. When I described how nervous I'd been, he explained the close attention had been for my own protection: they'd been watching to make sure I didn't try to kill myself. I was strangely touched by that, later.

I narrated what I was doing as I packed, a breathless monologue to focus my scattered concentration. The need to be systematic and organized returned me to myself. "Something to sleep in. A nightgown. The weather is set to change. Warm coat. You'll need boots if it snows." Our cat Rocky was ill, and I fumbled about for his medicines, conscious of how ridiculous it seemed against the backdrop of the tragedy. Worried our two little cockatiels would not survive the cold night in our car, I grabbed our thickest beach towels to wrap around their cage.

I dug through a downstairs closet for the old nylon duffel bags we used for luggage, but couldn't find two of the bags. Months later,

I would learn Dylan used them to carry explosives into the school cafeteria.

With the two officers flanking me, I stood at my closet door. The realization I would have to select clothing to wear to Dylan's funeral hit me like a punch in the gut; I was still hoping to be rescued from the truth. After a few deep breaths, I hung a brown tweed skirt, a white blouse, and a dark wool blazer on a single hanger.

• • •

Tom and I packed the car in a frenzy.

We had to go, but where? How could we bring this to someone else's door? The road around our property was thick with media trucks and disaster tourists peering out of their cars. Once we passed the police barricade surrounding our house, we'd be at their mercy. To whose home could we bring a swarm of reporters and curiosity seekers—an inconvenient invasion of privacy at best, and the threat of outright danger at worst? We would arrive, not knowing when we would leave, and with a menagerie of sick and messy animals in tow. We needed help, but from whom?

Judy offered to host us at her house. Grateful to have an option, we agreed, and she left to get ready for us.

Byron wanted to pick up a change of clothes at his own apartment, but the idea terrified me. Could he think clearly enough to drive safely? Reporters and photographers surrounded our property, their cameras and sound equipment aimed toward our house from every vantage point. Would a similar reception greet Byron at his apartment? In truth, I simply didn't want to let him out of my sight. I relented only after Byron reminded me his lease was in his roommate's name: he'd likely be able to pick up a few things without attracting attention. He assured me he'd meet up with us later.

As we finished loading the car, some of our neighbors showed up carrying a roast beef wrapped in towels, a gift from yet another neighbor—probably her own family's dinner. I'd been crying all day, but that act of spontaneous generosity set off a fresh jag. In just a few hours, we'd shed our old identities as valued members of a vibrant community to take on a new one: we were the parents of a perpetrator now, the agent of that community's destruction. It felt significant, as I clutched the warm glass dish in my arms, that people would still be kind to us.

It was time to go. Some of our neighbors masterminded our escape: one opened the gate at the foot of the drive while another took his own car down to the bottom of the drive and skidded into the middle of the road, blocking anyone who might follow us. The rest of us raced after him in three separate cars—Byron in one, Alison in the next, with Tom and me in the last. As we careened out of the gate at top speed and flew down the dark, twisting road, I was thrumming with fear—of an accident, of exposure, of what would come next.

When Tom and I finally slowed down, we found ourselves alone for the first time since noon, driving aimlessly through the suburbs before our 8:30 meeting with our new attorney. I don't know how or when Tom contacted him in the chaos, but they'd arranged a meeting in the parking lot of a convenience store near our house. This plan was so cloak-and-dagger that under any other circumstances I would have laughed. Once again, I thought: *We are the last people in the world.* There was no solace to be found in an old identity, though. Whatever was happening, it was happening to us—and it was happening because of whatever Dylan had done.

We still had little actual information about what had gone on in the school. We knew for sure only that Dylan had been seen inside with Eric during a shooting incident that left many killed and wounded, and investigators believed he'd been involved. I knew my son had died that day, but I did not know yet exactly what he had done.

As we slowly wound our way through the darkened suburb, Tom and I realized we were both having second thoughts about our plan for the night. We were worried Judy's close connection to the community would mean we might be too exposed if we stayed with her. I was also afraid we'd put her family at risk. We needed a place to collapse and grieve. Mostly, we needed somewhere safe—a place to hide.

As parents and business partners and spouses, Tom and I were good at coordinating complicated logistics with each other, and we relied on those skills as we tried to figure out how to handle what the next few hours would bring, let alone the next few days. We had not yet begun the emotional work of grieving for Dylan, or of struggling to understand what led him to wreak such terrible destruction—a journey we would not weather together as smoothly.

That night, our sole focus was on the most basic of human needs: shelter. Hotels and motels were out of the question as the media flocked to Denver. We couldn't give our distinctive last name at the front desk, or register with a credit card. We couldn't leave town. Even if the police would allow such a thing, what would happen to Dylan?

A possibility entered my mind. Too absorbed in our own crisis, we'd barely considered what our friends and family members must have been going through as they watched the tragedy evolve, but Tom's half sister Ruth and her husband, Don, lived in a quiet suburban neighborhood about twenty-five minutes away from the epicenter of the tragedy, and they did not share our last name. If they were willing to have us, their home would be a good place to be.

We didn't see Don and Ruth often, although they had always been there for us. When we'd first moved to the Denver area, they'd been invaluable in helping me to get settled. After Dylan was born, Ruth was one of my only visitors at the hospital, as I hardly knew anyone else in town.

They were good people. When my children were small, we'd endured a long season of illness, passing chicken pox and a bad flu around the family for several weeks. On my birthday, I was too ill even to answer the doorbell when it rang; I dragged myself downstairs in time to see Ruth's car pulling away down the drive—and at my feet, an entire home-cooked dinner, complete with a chocolate birthday cake and candles.

I was appalled we hadn't thought of them sooner, and could only attribute the oversight to my impaired level of thinking. I pressed the number into Tom's cell phone while he cruised the silent streets. The houses we passed looked inviting and cozy with their lit windows, and I could imagine kids getting help with their homework after the soup kettle had been cleared from the table, and all the other ordinary weekday activities that should have been taking place inside. That night, though, I knew that every family in the area would be tuned in to breaking coverage of the horror at Columbine High School. In some of those houses, as in our own, nothing would ever be normal again.

When Ruth answered the phone, I was relieved to hear the welcome in her voice, and I nearly wept with gratitude when she said we could stay with them. I called Judy to thank her for her offer, and Tom called Byron at his apartment to let him know the new plan. Years later, Byron told me he'd mistaken his father's voice for his brother's. For one joyful moment, he thought Dylan was calling to tell him he was fine, and that the entire day had been a huge misunderstanding. It was not the first time, or the last, that one of us would engage in the kind of magical thinking that allowed us to hope we could erase the events of the day.

Before we could take shelter at Don and Ruth's, we had to meet with our lawyer. At 8:30 p.m., we pulled into the convenience store parking lot and waited only a moment in the light rain before a car drew into the space next to ours. Gary Lozow looked over his shoulder to make sure nobody was watching, then approached the driver's side of our car. I reached over Tom and put my hand out the window to introduce myself, grasping Gary's wet hand in my own.

We opened the back door so he could come in from the rain. Gary folded himself carefully into the available space in the backseat, wedging his feet between a litter box and a cat-carrying case. One of the shoulders of his camel-colored overcoat pressed against the steamy car window, the other against a towel-covered birdcage. He asked us to drive into a nearby neighborhood so we could talk. A short distance later, Tom parked the car, turned off the ignition, and we both twisted in our seats to look into the face of the man who would help us through the difficult times ahead.

Gary's manner comforted me. He not only had a great deal of professional experience, but there was an underlying compassion

in the way he spoke to us. He conveyed his concern for us as a bereaved family and acknowledged our need to cope with a devastating loss. Then he asked a series of probing questions about Dylan,
about our family, and about our role as parents. As we had done
earlier in the day with the detective, we told him everything we
knew to be true about our son.

He was trying to establish whether we knew of Dylan's plans.
After listening to our answers, he announced he did not have "one
scintilla of doubt" we had not. I felt a flood of relief. Though it didn't
make the slightest difference in the world, I was desperate to know
someone believed us. The earth might be roiling and shifting under
my feet, but the fact that we'd no inkling of whatever Dylan had
been up to was the only truth I could still be sure of.

But our lawyer's face was serious as he told us: "Your son is responsible for this, but he's dead. You're the closest that people can
get to Dylan, so they're going to come after you. After the last victim is buried, there will be a firestorm of hatred leveled against your
family. It will be a very difficult time. You will be blamed, and you
will be sued, and in the weeks to come, you must think seriously
about your safety."

Firestorm of hatred. I would have cause to think of the phrase
many times over the years: it would turn out to be an eerily prescient, pitch-perfect description of what was to come.

Gary suggested steps to ensure our privacy and protection, and
he told us he'd be in touch with the officials about retrieving Dylan's
body. I appreciated how clearly he outlined his next steps, and that
he told us exactly when he would speak to us again. Then we drove
him back to his car. The rest of our drive was silent, as Tom and I
struggled to process what Gary had said.

Don and Ruth were looking out for us, and they opened the garage door as we approached so our car wouldn't be spotted on the
street. I'll never forget that slit of light slowly opening to a bright
rectangle in the blackness, or how deeply surreal and science-
fictional it felt to glide into their garage, as if we were docking a
spaceship. At the time, I was conscious of a profound sense of unreality. I was wrong. This *was* our new reality.

Tom turned off the ignition, and we sat together a moment in silence. I took a deep breath before opening the passenger-side door. I was upset to be inconveniencing Tom's family so greatly, and afraid we were bringing the threat of exposure to their lives, but the predominant emotion I was feeling was shame. It was hard to get out of the car.

Both of Tom's parents were dead by the time he was twelve. He had been raised by his half brother, but Ruth was older and out of the house by then. (Tom and I are nearer in age to Ruth and Don's children than we are to Ruth and Don.) Although there was great affection between us—I thought of them like an aunt and uncle—I still felt a bit formal, too, always trying to put my best foot forward.

Don is the son of a farmer, generous to a fault—the kind of salt-of-the-earth, hardworking Midwestern guy you hope to end up with as a neighbor. Ruth is known for her loving generosity. They're both gentle and soft-spoken and kind and have four beautiful daughters, all of them successful in their own right. And yet, there I was, slinking into their home under cover of darkness, the mother of a criminal.

Don and Ruth's greeting was warm but quiet as they helped us unload the car. I was profoundly thankful when Byron arrived minutes after we did. We set up camp in the basement apartment. I was relieved to see two alert faces with bright-orange cheeks peering out at their new surroundings when I removed the towels from the birdcage. Because of Ruth's allergies, we put our two cats, Rocky and Lucy, in the utility room, and they slunk behind the dryer in the unfamiliar space. I wished I could do the same.

When we joined Don and Ruth upstairs, I discovered that being inside a normal home was even more nightmarish than the frantic limbo we'd endured outside of our own. Those long hours in the driveway, we'd been suspended in time, without any access to news. But Don and Ruth, like everyone else in the country (and, we would discover later, around the world) were glued to the nonstop television coverage of the shootings.

We went from having no information to having too much. The chaos inside my mind was hard enough to bear, but the sudden flood of televised speculation and information was infinitely worse. We could see the horrifying aftermath of what our son had done, the incongruity of a triage center set up on a suburban front lawn. We could hear the shock and horror in the voices of the kids who had escaped the school, see the grim looks on the faces of the first responders. There was no escaping the enormity of it all.

The eyewitness descriptions were so horrific I could feel them bouncing right off my brain. It must have been then, too, that I heard early descriptions of the victims for the first time, although I do not remember that part. I would later learn it is common for people in the immediate throes of desperate grief to experience this type of denial, and in the years since, I have talked with many people who are puzzled and ashamed by it—as I was—but the brain takes in only what it can bear.

Outside our home, insulated from news, we'd still been able to keep the tragedy at arm's length. All at once, it was suffocatingly close: the difference between seeing a fire at a distance and standing knee-deep in live coals while the inferno rages around you. When I began to moan, "My God. This can't be true. I can't watch this," Ruth quickly told Don to turn off the TV. The silence was better, even if the echoes of the horrors we'd seen and heard still bounced off the walls around us.

Near midnight, it became clear our hosts needed to go to bed. All day long, I had wanted privacy so I could collapse in grief, and silence so I could focus on the incomprehensible situation and the loss of my son. With that moment upon me, though, I felt terrified of being alone with the unspeakable truth.

Ruth put fresh sheets on the guest beds in the basement and then left us. Byron was to sleep on a hideaway bed in the downstairs office, right outside the spare room where Tom and I were staying. I left the door open all night, so I could see the lump Byron's feet made under the blanket; it was vital for me to know he was there. I must have checked for that lump a hundred times.

As the house grew quiet, Tom and I lay sleepless beside one another, touching each other's hands and shoulders to offer what precious little comfort there was to be had. We had lost our son: Dylan was dead. We did not know where, or in what condition, his body was. We did not know if he had taken his own life, or if he had been killed by the police, or by his friend. Despite the horrifying reports we had heard on the news, we still did not know exactly what he had done.

That first night, the idea that Dylan could have been centrally involved in this monstrous event was beyond my ability to grasp, and I refused it. Instead, I conjured a million alternative explanations. I could not fathom how Dylan could have obtained a gun, or why he would have wanted one. I obsessed instead on a million other possible scenarios: Was he duped into participating, thinking the ammunition was fake? Had it been a prank gone terribly wrong? Had he been forced to participate, under some kind of duress? I told myself that even if our son had been a part of what had happened, he hadn't necessarily shot anyone. Both Tom and I believed with all of our hearts that Dylan could not have killed anyone, and we clung, not just for hours and days, but for months, to that belief.

In the long hours of that night, and in the following days, my mind would only occasionally light upon the idea that there were people Dylan might have hurt, but then that intolerable thought would skitter away just as fast. It shames me, even now, to admit this. At the time, I simply felt crazy. By many standards, I was.

After Tom fell into a fitful sleep, I pressed a pillow against my face to silence my sobbing. For the first time I truly understood how "heartbroken" had come to describe a sensation of terrible, terrible grief. The pain was actual, physical, as if my heart had been smashed to jagged fragments in my chest. "Heartbroken" was no longer a metaphor, but a description.

I did not sleep, and my thoughts as I lay there were as circular and disjointed as they'd been all day. I'd told the detective Dylan had attended prom the weekend before with a big group of his friends, and I returned to my memories of that night and the next day. I'd gotten up from bed to check in with him when he got home early the morning after prom. He'd had a great night, and thanked me for buying his ticket. He'd danced! Not for the first time in his life, I had reflected on how our youngest son always seemed to do things right. *I've done a good job with this kid*, I'd thought to myself as I returned to my room that night. A mere seventy-two hours later, and I was lying rigid in an unfamiliar bed, that feeling of warm satisfaction supplanted by utter confusion, growing horror, and sorrow. Integrating the two realities seemed impossible.

The day before his prom, Dylan had sat shoulder to shoulder with his father, looking at the floor plans of various dorm rooms, working out the comparative square footage of each configuration. At six foot four (and as someone who'd never shared a bedroom with anyone before), Dylan had wanted to secure as much real estate as possible. I'd laughed, then, to see the two of them there, scribbling sums on scrap paper. It was so quantitative—and so like Dylan!—to choose his college dorm room by using math.

Those memories were so recent as to be still warm, and reflecting back on them threw me into even greater confusion. Was any of that the behavior of a person preparing to go on a killing spree?

This only started to make sense when I began to learn more about people who are planning to die by suicide. They often make concrete plans for the future: surviving family members are frequently baffled by recently purchased cars and booked cruises. Talking with people who have survived their own suicide attempts has helped researchers to shed light on the mystery. In some cases, these future plans are a way to throw concerned friends and family members off a trail of suicidal behavior. If you were concerned a person close to you was planning self-harm, wouldn't your concerns be assuaged if they booked a cruise?

In other cases, such plans are simply sign and symptom of the genuinely "broken" logic driving the suicidal brain. They may signal the ambivalence the person feels—a desire to live that is, at times, as strong as the desire to die. A person with intent to self-harm can also believe simultaneously in both realities: that they will take a Caribbean vacation, and that they will have died by suicide before they have the chance to go.

I knew none of this then, and so the idea of Dylan eagerly making plans for his future at college while planning a shooting rampage that would end in his own death seemed absurd—and thus more evidence that he could not have meant to participate.

In the months and years to follow, I would be forced many times to confront everything I did not know about my son. This Pandora's box will never empty; I will spend the rest of my life reconciling the reality of the child I knew with what he did. That night was the last time I was able to hold Dylan in my mind exactly as I had held him in life: a beloved son, brother, and friend.

And so it was that, when the blue-gray light of dawn finally appeared through the basement windows, I was still asking the question—first to Dylan, and then to God—the question that would bedevil and perplex me, and ultimately animate the rest of my life: "How could you? How could you do this?"

CHAPTER 3

Someone Else's Life

Yesterday, my life entered the most abhorrent nightmare anyone could possibly imagine. I can't even write.

—Journal entry, April 21, 1999

The next morning, it felt as if I'd been dropped without warning into someone else's life.

Just the month before, an old friend had come to town. Catching up over dinner, I'd told her my life had never been more satisfying. I had recently turned fifty. I had a loving husband, and a marriage that had withstood twenty-eight years of ups and downs. Byron was fully supporting himself, and sharing an apartment with a friend. Dylan had recovered from an episode of trouble in his junior year and had done a great job of getting back on track; he was heading into the homestretch before graduation, hanging out with his friends and planning for college. I even had a little free time to draw and paint. The single biggest worry in my life, I told her, was the declining health of our beloved elderly cat, Rocky.

On April 20, 1999, I woke up an ordinary wife and mother, happy to be shepherding my family through the daily business of work, chores, and school. Fast-forward twenty-four hours, and I was the mother of a hate-crazed gunman responsible for the worst school shooting in history. And Dylan, my golden boy, was not only dead, but a mass murderer.

The disconnect was so profound that I could not wrap my head around it. Over the course of that first night in Don and Ruth's basement guest room, I had come to accept that Dylan was dead, but Tom and I were still in complete denial that he could have taken the lives of others.

More than anything else, this is what stands out about those early days in the aftermath of Columbine: the way we were able to cling, in strange and stubborn ways, to an unreality shielding us from a truth we could not yet bear. But those contortions could not protect us for very long from the wrath of a community we had come to love, or from the emerging truth about our son.

. . .

Don and Ruth were infallibly generous and kind, but they were utterly helpless in the face of our bewilderment and grief, as anyone would have been.

I could barely speak. When I did open my mouth to make a comment, more often than not, I'd trail off mid-thought. The idea of eating was inconceivable: a fork looked like an alien instrument in my hand, and the mere smell of Ruth's delicious cooking made my stomach churn.

I was exhausted, lower in energy than I'd ever been in my life, moving through the hours as if buried in wet cement. I dimly remember a worried Ruth covering me with an afghan as I lay motionless on her couch. Sleep provided only a temporary reprieve: the second I became conscious, I'd be crushed all over again by the enormity of what Dylan had done, and by the senselessness of it. It's a cliché, I suppose, to say I was behaving like a zombie, but that is the closest description I have for the way I felt in those early days.

Under normal circumstances—if any circumstances involving the death of a child can ever be called normal—we would have called family members and friends to share the awful news. They would have gathered to grieve with us, and to offer support. We would have been kept busy readying the house for visitors, and friends would have come bearing stories, poems, and photographs to honor Dylan. These coping mechanisms in the face of grief are time-honored and shared across many cultures because they are effective; they give families comfort at a time when very little can.

For us, nothing could have been further from normal than our lives during the days following Dylan's death.

Almost everyone who'd ever known us knew of our son's connection to the Columbine tragedy within hours of it happening, but they couldn't get in touch with us because we had fled for our lives. Horrified family members and friends who called our home that afternoon either received no answer or found themselves talking to the law enforcement officials still searching our house.

Clearly, we couldn't have any of our out-of-state family members or close friends come to Littleton to be with us. Even if we had anywhere for them to stay, we couldn't guarantee their safety. In hiding at Don and Ruth's house, we were insulated from how frightening the situation in the community was. We wouldn't really know how much danger we'd been in until I read about one of Tom's long-lost cousins in the paper: he was going public to say he'd never met Dylan, and begging people to stop sending him death threats. In the forty-eight-hour period following the shootings, a cluster of family members received more than two thousand phone calls from media and members of the community. Not all were threatening, of course—even in the immediate aftermath, people reached out in support—but it was still unmanageable. A local reporter tried to push his way into my eighty-five-year-old aunt's home in Ohio. (She was proud she'd stood up to him by asking him to leave, though she insisted he take a fresh-baked cookie with him.)

I couldn't in good conscience invite the people I loved to a community whose grief was mingled with rage toward our family. In choosing seclusion, we had chosen safety. We had also cut ourselves off from the comfort of others who had loved Dylan.

According to the police report released months later, we were officially notified of Dylan's death on the day after the massacre. I don't remember it. Neither does Tom. I do remember learning our son's body had been moved to the coroner's for autopsy, news that gave a solid, tangible weight to the fact of Dylan's death it had not yet had for us. I found the idea of him lying, all alone, on a frigid steel table intolerable. I'd been by his side for every visit to the pediatrician, had held his hand for every vaccination; I'd never missed one of his dental appointments. I longed to go to the coroner's office to be with him, just so he would not have to be alone.

At the same time, Tom and I held out hope for the autopsy, praying the results would come back positive for drugs. At least drug abuse might give us a way to explain how Dylan could have been involved with this monstrous event.

It felt like death surrounded and threatened to suffocate us. Tom began saying he didn't think he could go on without Dylan, his buddy. That morbid sentiment was one of the only things that could rouse me out of my near-catatonic state: How would I cope if Tom took his own life, too? After what had happened with Dylan, there was no way I could trust myself to take an accurate read on the emotional state of the other members of my family. For all I knew, Tom and Byron were actively planning their own deaths. The thought made me frantic.

I was having suicidal thoughts, myself. It was the most natural thing in the world to explore a way to silence the grief and guilt and shame I felt. But knowing those feelings were a normal response didn't make them any less scary.

It was also normal for me to worry excessively about Byron, even if it was unhealthy. As soon as he left my sight, I felt anxious and abandoned. I could not let go of the fear that something horrendous was going to happen to him—or that, out of the depths of his despair over what Dylan had done, he was going to do something terrible to himself. This dynamic between us would intensify over the months to come.

Byron had lived a life touched little by loss: he'd only been to a single funeral in his life, for a Little League coach who'd suffered a sudden heart attack. Tom and I had both survived parents and other relatives, and we knew Byron was unprepared for what the next few days would bring. On the other hand, what preparation could there be? Byron's first real experience of loss would be a catastrophe of such magnitude and incomprehensibility that all of us would spend the rest of our lives struggling to understand it.

. . .

I could not watch television or read the newspaper at Don and Ruth's house, but I would peek through the cracks once in a while, as you would from a bomb shelter to confirm the utter devastation outside. And so I could not entirely avoid what every headline and front page and news crawl in the world was screaming: "TERROR IN LITTLETON. The two boys believed to have been the shooters, Eric Harris and Dylan Klebold, were students at Columbine High School. . . ."

I became fixated on the picture that aired over and over: the most terrible school picture Dylan ever had taken, so unflattering that when he brought it home, I urged him to have it reshot. It made him look like the kind of kid teachers as well as students would find a reason to pick on—the guy you'd move your tray to avoid in the lunchroom. It didn't look like *him*. Even in my near-madness in those early days after the tragedy, I knew how ridiculous it was for me to be upset that the media were using an unbecoming photograph of Dylan, instead of showing him as the nice-looking young man he had been. My son was an alleged murderer—and there I was, dithering over an ugly photo. It was a spectacular example of the tricks the mind plays when we're juggling unbearable emotions. Absurd as it was, I wanted Dylan to be shown the way I remembered him.

Every channel ran graphic accounts of the carnage, and of the horrifying things Dylan and Eric had said and done. There were detailed descriptions of the weapons the boys had carried, and of the clothing they wore. There were diagrams of their movements through the school. In the absence of information, there was endless speculation as to the motives behind the attack.

Theories abounded, many of them conflicting, and each one of them more perplexing than the one before. The papers reported that Dylan and Eric had been goths. They'd been members of a death cult. They'd been sworn members of an antisocial clique at the school called the Trench Coat Mafia. They'd been spoiled, over-indulged brats who were never taught the difference between right and wrong. They'd been gay. They had been bullied. They'd been bullies themselves. The attack had been cold-blooded, and planned for a long time. Alternatively, it had been impromptu: the boys had simply snapped.

Much has been written in the years since about the media coverage of the event—in particular about how quickly early misinformation about the boys solidified into received truth.

For me, listening to the flood of speculation felt like looking into a kaleidoscope. I was as hungry for enlightenment as anyone else; I had no idea anymore what to believe. As every new piece of information tumbled into place, each one uglier than the last, a different picture of my son came into focus. Invariably, that picture was of someone I did not recognize. When one of the component pieces was discounted, or determined to be false, the arrangement would shift again—and with it, the ground under my feet. To the rest of the world, these kaleidoscopic shifts probably made it seem like investigators and the press were closing in on a plausible explanation for why and how the tragedy had occurred. But each explanation took me further away from the boy I knew.

Early on, I flinched from the news coverage about Columbine because it was wildly inaccurate, or reporting things about my son I could not bear to hear. I now flinch because, as an antiviolence activist and brain health advocate, I understand how frighteningly irresponsible much of it was. We now know that press coverage with excessive details—fetishizing what the killers wore, for instance, or providing precise accounts of their movements during the crime—inspire copycats, and give them a blueprint upon which to model their own plans.

At the time, though, the contradictory reports and the inaccuracies served to fuel my desperate hope it was all a terrible misunderstanding. If they'd gotten this fact wrong, or that one, then perhaps all of it was false. As I would come to learn too well over the weeks, months, and years to follow, the mind plays tricks to hold itself together when under tremendous strain. Ordinarily logical to a fault, I spent those early days clinging to any shred of hope I could salvage or manufacture, no matter how irrational or far-fetched.

The first and most widely spread inaccuracy was the characterization of the boys as "outcasts." This startled me, although it shouldn't have: as I was to learn, it is a commonly held (and even more commonly reported) misconception about mass shooters.

It was true Dylan had always been reserved and self-conscious; he never liked to be the center of attention, or to stand out from the crowd in any way. It was also true he had grown more reserved as he entered adolescence, although he was never the ostracized, friendless, antisocial stereotype offered up by the media. Throughout his life, Dylan was quick to make and keep good, close friends, both girls and boys. During his high school years, our phone rang to the point of distraction with invitations to go bowling or to the movies, or to play fantasy baseball. If the media could be wrong about Dylan's social status, my broken mind reasoned, there was still the possibility it was all wrong—that the reporters and police had their facts mixed up and Dylan was a victim, not the agent, of violence.

It was also reported that Eric had been Dylan's only friend, which wasn't remotely true. We'd frankly discouraged the relationship after the two of them had gotten in trouble together the previous year, and Tom and I had been pleased to notice Dylan keeping his distance. At the time of his death, I'd definitely have named Nate as Dylan's closest friend.

Similarly, when the media identified Dylan and Eric as swastika-wearing haters, I felt strangely buoyed; there was simply no way this part of the reporting could be right. I had been raised in a Jewish home, and our own family had hosted an informal Passover seder two short weeks before. As the youngest, Dylan had read the Four Questions at the celebration. I had spent my career as a teacher and an advocate for people with disabilities, and Tom and I were both lifelong proponents of tolerance and inclusion. Neither of us would ever have tolerated any hate speech or anti-Semitic imagery in our home or on Dylan's clothing.

Again and in the same vein, I focused obsessively on the contradictory and changing numbers—how many hurt, how many dead. If the authorities still weren't sure about fatalities, what else might they be wrong about? Much as I was riveted to those tallies, I did not yet—could not—translate the numbers into what they really meant: children and a teacher who had been violently and permanently torn from their families and robbed of their lives, of their futures. I wanted the number of fatalities and injuries to be small, as if that would make Dylan's actions seem less awful. I hope I do no dishonor to those who died and were injured or traumatized that day, or to their families, by being truthful about this. It would be weeks before the veil lifted and I would cry for Dylan's victims. We all grieve first for the ones we love, and Dylan was my son. And I still didn't believe he could really have killed anyone.

I might have been eager to avoid the full truth about the degree of Dylan's involvement, but the complete denial insulating me in those early days was not sustainable. The magnitude and severity of the attack crashed over me with every headline and every call from our lawyer, newly overwhelming me each time. In addition to the fifteen who had died, twenty-four individuals were being treated for injuries at local hospitals. The status of the severely injured children was updated constantly. If they survived, they would likely sustain permanent disabilities as a result of their injuries. I had spent the latter half of my career working with students with disabilities, so I knew very well what that meant.

My mind reeled. How could there be no way to press a reset button, to live the last weeks of Dylan's life over again, to change the outcome of that life, to stop what had happened? I ached for the other parents grieving their own children and praying by hospital beds, and had to constantly remind myself no magical thinking would rewind the clock. Not only was there nothing I could do to stop it: now that it had happened, there was absolutely nothing I could do to make it better.

All I wanted to do was to hold my son—and then to have one more chance to stop him before he committed his final, terrible act. The loop in my brain ran constantly, always starting and ending in the same place: "How could he have done this? How could he have done this?" We were left to face the catastrophe Dylan had left behind, without the only person who could possibly shed light on what had happened, and why.

. . .

Although Don and Ruth could not have been more hospitable, they were beginning to look almost as exhausted as Tom, Byron, and I did. It's natural to want a break from even the most charming and welcome houseguests, and we were hardly that, although we did try to stay out of their way as much as possible, and to minimize the burden of our confusion and grief. I knew Don wanted to watch news coverage of the tragedy; I also knew I could not bear to hear it, and so I spent more and more time in the basement. Years later, Byron admitted he'd hidden behind a shrub outside of their house so he could have a place to cry without being seen.

When we had parted with our new attorney the night before in the parking lot of the convenience store, we had scheduled an appointment for the next day: he wanted us to come to his office to meet his staff. Our neighbors and close friends Peggy and George urged us to come to their home after the appointment with our lawyer. I said we would, after I got my hair cut.

Left to my own devices, I wear a man's flannel shirt and jeans, and can count on one hand the number of manicures I've had. Early in my working life, though, I'd realized that if I had a good haircut, regularly maintained, I could look tidy and professional without having to fuss—indeed, on most mornings, without even having to resort to a comb. So I scheduled a standing monthly cut-and-color appointment. I regarded it as a necessary grooming chore, like showering or brushing my teeth. That month, my standing hair appointment fell on the day after Columbine.

I decided to keep it. I wasn't thinking about how it would look to the outside world; I wasn't thinking about anything. A haircut was the last thing in the world I wanted, but then, so was choking down the bowl of Cheerios Ruth had insisted I eat earlier in the day. Keeping the appointment, I reasoned, would get me out of Don and Ruth's house for a while, allowing them a modicum of privacy and recovery time away from us. Also, it required nothing of me except sitting in a chair. I wasn't up to much, but this I thought I could handle.

More important, it would make me presentable. I grew up with the understanding that personal presentation is a way to show respect. I might be most comfortable in jeans and an old T-shirt, but I dress up to go to the theater out of admiration for the performers. I wouldn't dream of wearing sweatpants to temple, or to church. Over the next few days, we would have to have a funeral for Dylan, and I did not want to look like a scarecrow when I said good-bye to my son.

Tom drove us to Gary Lozow's office, where we met his staff. So it was that we sat with a table full of attorneys even before we had made funeral arrangements for our son. Looking back on it now, I realize we probably could have refused to discuss legal matters until after the funeral, but we were stunned into helplessness. This juxtaposition of legal and personal affairs was to become a pattern in our lives after Columbine, and one we would negotiate over the years to come. The need to tend to legal concerns shadowed our grief—always. Fortunately, we had found an ethical and compassionate lawyer, who genuinely had our interests at heart.

At the meeting, Gary summarized the legal aspects of our situation: no lawsuits had yet been filed, but they were imminent. I sat there, numb, while the lawyers talked over my head. Still in shock, I could barely understand what was being said, and I simply couldn't rouse myself to care. They were acting as if my future was at stake, but as far as I was concerned, I had no future. My life was over.

Leaving the meeting, I asked Gary about my hair appointment. Unconsciously, I had already begun to ask for his input on the most minor decisions, realizing I had no idea what the right thing to do was, and no barometer for how I should behave. I was still in zombie mode. He told me gently, "I think you should do whatever you would normally do. That's what will help." So I called my hairdresser and asked her if she could move my appointment to the evening, so I could see her after all her other clients were gone. She agreed.

Later in the evening, Tom dropped me off at the salon, and went to our friends' house to wait. My hairdresser was cordial but visibly uncomfortable. We didn't know each other well. It was my first attempt at trying to look and act normal for someone outside my inner circle of family and friends, and I saw immediately it was hopeless. I had thought getting a haircut would require little of me, but even that minimal social interaction was leagues beyond what I could manage. I wished I could put the poor woman at ease, but I understood she wouldn't ever be able to see me as a normal human being after what Dylan had done.

The darkness outside the large storefront windows left me feeling terribly exposed; I could barely make eye contact with the bedraggled, haunted creature staring back at me from the mirror. My hairdresser chatted nervously as I cowered under the glaring fluorescent shop lights. In the course of conversation, she mentioned that one of the victims' mothers had been to the salon for her own hair appointment, earlier in the day.

That stunned me. I might have been sitting in the same chair where that other mother had sat—perhaps under the same stained plastic cape. The thought of the two of us performing this perfunctory grooming task in order to get ready for our children's funerals touched me and horrified me in equal measure. For a split second, I felt as I had in our driveway, like I was part of a community of people who were grieving.

But then it became intolerable, the sorrow my own son had caused another mother. I wanted to feel close to her, and I did, but I was the last person on earth she would allow to offer her words of comfort, and the sense of isolation and grief and guilt following so quickly on the heels of that sense of connection devastated me.

I practically dissolved in gratitude when my friend Peggy and her daughter Jenny arrived—a surprise. They'd left Tom with Peggy's husband, George, so the men could talk. It was humiliating to be seen in such a pathetic position, my wet hair plastered to my face while I slumped over, almost too weak to sit up in the chair. My friends could see how hard I was working to keep myself together, and the two of them held my hands and kept up my end of the conversation with the hairdresser while I struggled imperfectly to hold back my tears.

I finally got out of the chair with my hair still wet, as I always did. As I went to pay, I remembered my cash supply was limited: the Browns had lent us some money to walk around with so we wouldn't have to reveal our identity through checks or credit cards, but I was loath to spend any of it before I knew when we'd next be able to get to the bank. So I asked if my hairdresser would allow me to mail her a check instead of paying cash as I usually did.

The subsequent silence startled me; I sensed mistrust in her hesitation. Then she summoned her courage and explained it was the salon's policy to request payment at the time of service. A flush of shame crawled up my throat as I fumbled with the bills and paid her. I was not the person she knew before the tragedy; I was the mother of a criminal now. Dylan's actions had changed who I was to others, as well as to myself.

Still preoccupied by my dwindling money supply, I was caught off guard when my hairdresser asked if it was okay to tell people she'd seen me. I flashed on that other mother sitting in the salon chair, and the fleeting moment of connection I'd felt with her over the simple grooming ritual we'd shared. Foolishly, I told the hairdresser it was okay to talk about my visit. Perhaps she would be able to create a bridge between me and the community ripped apart by my son.

Those were still early days, and it frankly did not occur to me that she would talk to the press. She gave an interview that night. It was a generous gesture, an attempt to help us: she described my shock and grief, my insistence that we hadn't known anything about what had been planned. But the story took off, and suddenly I was Marie Antoinette, getting in some self-indulgent "me time" while parents grieved over children lying dead in the school. The story got national attention, and I got hate mail from as far away as Texas.

This narrative fed into a story the media had already been cultivating: that Dylan was a spoiled brat raised by negligent, self-serving parents. News reports focused on Dylan's BMW—never mind that Tom had picked it up for $400, vandalized and virtually undrivable, so he and Dylan could fix it up together. Aerial shots of our house made it look like a massive compound but didn't mention it had been a handyman's special with a mouse problem we'd gotten for a song because of its neglected condition.

These misperceptions and others bothered me. Tom was more immediately tuned in to his grief for Dylan, his beloved son and close companion. The two of them had spent hours at a time shooting the breeze about baseball scores, fixing up cars, building speakers, playing chess. Tom was heartbroken Dylan hadn't said good-bye. It was one thing that our son could commit this appalling act, but he had done so with no explanation at all. A note, as insufficient as it would have been, would have been something.

My own focus was on the response of the community around us. Like many women, I was raised to think first about others, and to care about their good opinion of me. I had taken pleasure and pride in being an active and respected part of my community, in being thought of as a good mom. The censure beginning to emerge was excruciating.

The gentlest portrayal of us as parents in the media was that we were checked out, useless: bumbling and blindly oblivious. In other accounts, we had knowingly shielded a hateful racist, turning a blind eye to the arsenal he was assembling under our roof, thereby exposing an entire community to danger.

I completely understood why people were blaming us. I'd certainly be furious beyond measure with the parents of *that child*, had it been the other way around. I'd hate them. Of course I'd blame them. But I also knew that neither of those caricatures of us was true—and that the truth was far more disturbing.

• • •

On April 22, two days after the shootings, we learned from our attorney that Dylan's death had been ruled a suicide. The coroner was ready to release his body.

With that announcement, a new and appalling problem reared its head: What would we do with his body? We assumed we would automatically be turned away from any funeral home in Littleton. Even if they didn't refuse us, it was sickening to imagine we might further upset or dishonor the victims' families, or interfere with their own ceremonies. I had no idea what to do.

Years earlier, I had served on a committee advising the mortuary science program at a local college on creating opportunities in that field for students with disabilities, and had worked closely with the head of the program. We had not spoken in years, but desperate and unsure where else to turn, I reached out to her for guidance.

When we connected on the phone, Martha's tone was warm and filled with concern: I'd already been in her thoughts, she told me, and she'd been wondering if there was anything she could do to help, but she'd had no way of getting in touch. As soon as we got off the phone, she immediately contacted one of the most respected funeral directors in Denver. Martha and John would show an extraordinary measure of generosity and compassion toward us over those next few days.

Initially, Tom and I didn't want a funeral of any kind for Dylan. It simply felt too disrespectful to his victims. I will be forever grateful to Martha and John, though, for convincing us to reconsider. They promised we would be able to keep the ceremony private both from the media and from enraged community members. Together, we planned a simple service, attended only by a few friends and family members. Byron would be there, of course, as would Ruth and Don, and the parents of Dylan's two best friends, Nate and Zack. The pastor of the church we'd belonged to when Dylan and Byron were small agreed to officiate for us.

Tom and I understood cremation was our only option. The likelihood that a gravesite would be vandalized was too great, and we might not be able to stay in the area; if we buried Dylan and then moved, we'd be forced to leave him behind. I explained I needed to see my son one last time, and Martha and John told me the technicians would do everything they could to cover the bullet wounds in his head so we could see him as we'd known him.

I hardly remember making the arrangements. I do remember being amazed to hear myself speaking calmly about practical matters when the only sound I could hear in my own head was a continuous, endless screech of agony and disbelief. This was my son, the person I had nurtured, protected, and loved with all my heart. The thought that I would never hear his voice or touch his face again took my breath away. It took every ounce of strength I could summon to make preparations for our final separation. My parenting of

Dylan was over. The love and work that had gone into the creation of this human being had ended—and in the most disastrous way.

. . .

Amid the nightmarish covert planning sessions for Dylan's funeral, it became clear that our old cat Rocky's health was worsening rapidly, and I became obsessed with getting him medical attention.

Ruth later admitted that my hysteria over the ailing cat seemed evidence to her I had totally snapped under the pressure. We'd been in their home for three days, and I'd been so weak I had to prop my head up with my arm at the table to prevent myself from collapsing under the weight of my exhaustion and grief. I could barely shower or feed myself, let alone care for my family—but I would not stop fretting about Rocky.

Driving myself to the vet was out of the question: even I was self-aware enough to realize I was in no shape to get behind the wheel of a car. With resignation, and simply because they had no idea what else to do, Ruth and Don packed Rocky into their car and drove us to the veterinary clinic in our neighborhood.

I am unapologetically tenderhearted where animals are concerned, but I can see now there was obviously more going on that day with Rocky than merely responsible pet ownership. There was so much suffering in Littleton for which I felt responsible, and nothing I could do about it. Caring for this one suffering animal was something I *could* do, a situation still salvageable.

Terrified of being recognized, I entered the clinic through a side door. When it came time to hand Rocky over to the vet, I found I couldn't do it. Rocky was Dylan's cat. He'd chosen him from a neighbor's litter of kittens when he was in third grade. The big white cat had stretched out with us for all those family nights on the couch as we watched the *Pink Panther* movies together in the den. Letting go of Rocky felt like letting go of Dylan. I struggled to communicate to the doctors without sobbing and asked them to do what they could for him, and to keep him until I was able to come back. Finally, I allowed a vet to take the frightened cat from my arms.

As I made my way across the parking lot, heading for the sanctuary of Don and Ruth's car, I heard someone running after me, calling my name. I turned to see one of the clinic's staff members heading toward me, and for a moment I wasn't sure whether to walk toward her or run away. Gary had warned us repeatedly we would need to be careful for our safety: there were many people in Colorado and around the world who held us responsible for the shootings, and who would be happy to see us dead. The day before, a large delivery of hot food had arrived for us at his office—a gesture of sympathy and goodwill from a stranger, like the boxes of mail we were beginning to receive there. Gary wouldn't allow us to eat a bite of the food for fear it was poisoned. Even years afterward, I would find myself on heightened alert whenever I had to give my full name to schedule a delivery, or to a teller at the bank. But that moment in the vet clinic's parking lot was the first time I had ever recoiled in fear from an interaction with anyone in the place where we lived.

As it happened, I had nothing to worry about. The petite woman threw her arms around me. She told me she'd raised boys, and knew how unbelievably stupid they could be. It was a sentiment many, many mothers would share with me over the years. Though I towered over her, I let her hold me while I sobbed, soaking both of us with my tears. Later I realized I didn't even know her name.

That woman was not the only person to show us generosity. Even before we left Don and Ruth's, our longtime friends and neighbors closed ranks around us. The newspaper ran a photograph of our friends hanging a poster on the gate at the foot of our driveway:

Sue & Tom
We Love You
We're Here for You
CALL US

The sight of those familiar, dear faces felt like a Radio Free Europe message transmitted across enemy lines. The memory of so many kindnesses, both large and small, humbles me to this day. Even as our friends and family showed their love and compassion for us, though, I felt sure they must also be wondering, *What on earth did you people do to create such anger in a child? How could you not see what was happening?*

I was asking those questions myself.

CHAPTER 4

A Resting Place

On Saturday, the twenty-fourth of April, we cremated our son. Martha had offered to pick us up and drive us to the funeral home. Her experience with the bereaved was a gift, and she talked easily with us as she drove, but the paralyzing dread I felt intensified with every mile. Still, my social training prevailed and I tried to keep up my end of the conversation, even as I trembled violently and unsuccessfully fought back tears.

Both Martha and John were genuinely concerned about our security and privacy. They assured us there would be no posted sign or guest book available outside the room where Dylan lay, which had a single entrance and no windows. But even with the precautions, a member of the press had called the funeral home minutes before we arrived, so we entered the room furtively, casting glances over our shoulders like frightened prey.

No words are adequate to describe the pain of seeing Dylan's body in that casket. The expression on Dylan's face was unfamiliar, which Byron later confessed made it easier for him. That unfamiliar expression was perhaps the only thing that allowed us to get through that first, horrific, unreal moment. I smoothed Dylan's hair and kissed his forehead, searching his face for clues and finding none. Tom and I had brought a number of Dylan's childhood stuffed animals, and we placed them in the coffin so they rested against his cheeks and neck. Byron and Tom and I held one another's hands, and together we held Dylan's. We were finally by his side, a family again.

It was a chilly spring day, and I was overcome by a compulsive, almost biological need to make Dylan warm. I could not stop rubbing his ice-cold arms, exposed by the short-sleeved hospital gown he was wearing. I had to hold myself back from climbing into the casket so I could cover him with the warmth of my body.

Martha had recommended we each take some time alone with Dylan. Byron went first. As I waited in the main sitting room of the funeral home, I braced myself to be alone for the last time with what remained of my son, and I began to panic. A surge of animal protectiveness came over me. How could I allow Dylan to be destroyed, to be burned in a fire? I jumped out of my chair and started to pace, my mind racing. The other options—above- and below-ground burial—brought me no comfort. I tried to think how we could steal his body out of the mortuary and sneak him to safety. *I can't do this*, I thought over and over, in an endless loop. There was a fireplace in the funeral home's sitting room. It looked cheerful and inviting on that cold, snowy day, and I was drawn to it. Eventually, I was able to recover some calm by looking into the flames. Most of my panic turned to resignation, and then my grief resurfaced. *How sad*, I thought as I stared at the fire, *that this is the way I must warm my son.*

Since that day, I have experienced a number of recurring dreams about Dylan: dreams where I have a second chance to keep him safe, and fail; dreams where I lift his shirt to expose hidden wounds; dreams where I am simultaneously protecting him and protecting others from him. But there was a particular dream I only had once.

In it, I see Dylan's bloody bones scattered across a forest floor. I collect them, one by one in my arms, afraid to put them down lest they be stolen or lost, but there is no safe place for them, so I am left helplessly clutching the sticky, blood-soaked bones to my chest.

There is a famous Buddhist tale about a woman called Kisa Gotami. The story begins when her baby dies. Unable to accept his passing, she demands medicine from the doctor, who knows full well that nothing will cure the child. He sends her to the Buddha, who tells her to go out and find four or five white mustard seeds from a household where no one has suffered. Kisa Gotami goes door to door, explaining she needs medicine for her baby. Many people offer to give her mustard seeds, but every time she asks the householder if they have lost someone close to them, the answer is always yes. Eventually, she goes back to the Buddha.

"Have you brought me the mustard seeds?" he asks.

"No," she tells him. "But now I understand there is no one who has not lost someone they love, and I have laid my child to rest."

It would take me years to find a resting place in my mind for Dylan—and even longer to uncover some of the answers that would permit me to find one for myself.

CHAPTER 5

Premonition

Dylan, wherever you are, I love and miss you. I'm struggling in the chaos you left behind. If there is any way to absolve you of these actions, please point the way. Help us find answers that will give us peace and help us live with this life we have been thrust into. Help us.
—Journal entry, April 1999

On the evening of Dylan's funeral on Saturday, we stripped the beds, packed up our pets, and left Ruth and Don's basement apartment in order to return to our own home. Byron followed, in his own car.

We approached our house with trepidation. The media swarm had not abated. Journalists had surrounded the houses of our friends, bombarding them with business cards and messages. One blocked a friend's driveway when she refused to speak to him, and then followed her as she ran errands until she threatened to call the police. More than once, a friend called to tell us in a whisper that a famous news anchor was sitting *right there* in their den.

I understood the world was united by a single question, which was to know why the shootings had taken place. I understood they expected us to provide an explanation, though we had none to give. All we wanted was to be left alone to mourn the loss of our son, as well as those he had killed and injured. Thankfully, our driveway was deserted as we approached that night; after a fruitless four-day vigil, the journalists had given up and gone.

Our homecoming brought no relief. I'd expected us to feel better, just by virtue of being home again and closer to Dylan's things.

Instead, as soon as the front door closed behind us, I felt more vulnerable than I had at Don and Ruth's. Our large picture windows looked out over the spectacular Colorado scenery surrounding the house. We'd never covered them; privacy wasn't an issue out where we were, and we hadn't wanted to obscure the views. Now, all I could think was how unprotected those windows made me feel. Once the house was lit from the inside, anyone outside could see right in.

The lamp Tom had left burning in a front window while we were gone served as our only source of illumination as we moved through the deserted house. Tom found a flashlight, but, confusingly, our entire supply of batteries was gone from the kitchen drawer, so we resorted to the half-burned taper candles I'd saved in case of a power failure. Out of habit, I still kept the wooden matches on a top shelf, away from small children who had outgrown me years earlier, but the matches, like the batteries, were gone. The police had confiscated anything in the house that might provide evidence of bomb-making.

Rummaging around in the darkness, I found a set of old sheets, a few flannel blankets, and newspapers destined for the recycling bin. I groped around in drawers for thumbtacks and masking tape. We tackled the kitchen first, standing on chairs and using the light of the open refrigerator to hang a set of makeshift curtains. With candles lit from the gas stove, the three of us moved from room to room, using whatever scraps we could find to block sightlines into our house. Only when we were sealed in this patchwork cocoon did we finally turn on another light at the very back of the house.

After helping us to get settled, Byron went back to his own apartment. It was hard to let him go. I was sure his physical similarity to his brother and our distinctive last name would mean he'd never again have a normal life, and his grief and confusion frightened me far more than my own. I'd lost one son, and was terrified by the new possibility that I might lose another to despair.

I wonder, too, if I wasn't clinging to Byron because the simple fact of his presence restored me to myself. Despite everything, when I was with Byron, I was still someone's mother.

Now alone, Tom and I wandered through the darkened rooms. Driving home, I'd imagined I was going to ground, like a hunted animal, but I felt more like one so badly injured that it crawls into a burrow to die alone. Our house no longer felt like a home. Covering the windows had changed the acoustics in the rooms, and the absence of sound in our suddenly childless home felt like an absence of oxygen. I kept thinking I heard the refrigerator door open, one of the many fantasies I would have over the years that Dylan was still with us, in body and soul.

From the ground floor we could see upstairs to the mezzanine, where furniture, books, and papers spilled out of Dylan's room into the hallway. His mattress, stripped of sheets, leaned against the second-floor banister. The bed itself was in pieces next to it. As much as we had wanted to be close to his belongings while we were at Don and Ruth's, neither of us had the strength to go near his room that night.

It hurt too much to remain conscious, so Tom and I went to bed. We kept the light on, because our bedroom overlooked the road and we were afraid the press or a vigilante would notice if we shut it off. When its glare made it impossible for us to sleep, we finally agreed we were being foolish.

．．．

It's hard to imagine we slept at all that first night home, but the mind eventually shows mercy and shuts down. As it would be for years, waking was the cruelest moment of the day—the split second where it was possible to believe it had all been a nightmare, the worst dream a person could ever have.

That first morning in our own bed, Tom's hand crept across the coverlet, and we lay there together in silence, staring at the ceiling and gripping each other's hands. Finally, one of us swung our feet to the floor, and together we ventured out of the bedroom. I flinched as I walked through the house in the daylight and confronted photographs of the boys—hiking and fishing with their dad, in their baseball uniforms, whitewater rafting with another family, standing on the rocks near our house. From table surfaces and book-shelves, Dylan's impish, joyful face beamed out at me.

The main room of our beloved house, the place we'd lived in for more than ten years, home to countless classic movie nights and homework skirmishes and family dinners, was unrecognizable. We could not have survived without the privacy, but the blocked windows made the wide-open space look dark and sinister. The clean sunlight that usually flooded the house bounced off the newspaper and filled the air with the dirty smell of wet dog. I could hear birds at the feeder outside, but I couldn't see them.

The short journey from the bedroom to the kitchen exhausted me, and I gripped the counter to hold myself up. Standing there, I thought suddenly of an unsettling moment I'd had years ago in the hospital, right after Dylan's birth.

He'd been born in the early morning of September 11, 1981. As with his older brother, Tom and I had named our second son for a poet, the Welsh playwright Dylan Thomas. The sheets in the hospital birthing room had yellow flowers on them, and Dylan's arrival was so quiet and uneventful I could hear the whispers of nurses in the hallway while I was in labor. He cried out once before settling into my eager arms and squinting into the light.

Like every new mother, I was delighted to meet this brand-new creature I already had such an intimate relationship with. The next morning, we finally got a minute alone, and I was thrilled to kiss his smooth cheeks and wonder at his tiny, perfect fingers and toes. But as I held him, I experienced a deep and unsettling sense of foreboding, strong enough to make me shiver. It was as if a bird of prey had passed overhead, casting us into shadow. Looking down at the perfect bundle in my arms, I was overcome by a strong premonition: this child would bring me a terrible sorrow.

I am not superstitious by nature, and this was a feeling I had never experienced before, and haven't since. I was so startled by it, I could hardly move. Was this a mother's intuition? Was my seemingly healthy baby sick? But everything checked out fine, and the hospital sent me home with my new little boy.

Two weeks later, Dylan vomited profusely after a feeding, and then after the next. Badly frightened, I took him to the emergency room. The doctors kept him two nights for observation, but found nothing. At the follow-up visit I insisted upon later that week, three-week-old Dylan was pale, dehydrated, and below his birth weight. By then, the condition had developed enough to show up on an X-ray, and Dylan was diagnosed with pyloric stenosis, a narrowing at the base of the stomach. The doctor sent us back to the hospital. The situation was so serious, Dylan might have died without immediate surgery.

After he pulled through that harrowing ordeal and turned into his sweet, plump, rosy-cheeked baby self, I felt all the obvious relief and more besides, sure that this serious illness—disaster averted—was my premonition realized.

That childhood illness was also the last time, until his junior year of high school, that I ever had real cause to worry about Dylan.

CHAPTER 6

Boyhood

With Dylan as a toddler, playing in the snow.
The Klebold Family

*The terror and total disbelief are overwhelming. The sorrow of losing
my son, the shame of what he has done, the fear of the world's hatred.
There is no respite from the agony.*

—Journal entry, April 1999

I've kept a diary most of my life. In late elementary school and
junior high, I poured my hopes and dreams onto the pages of
little books I kept locked and hidden—not that anyone on earth
cared what blouse I'd worn, or where I'd taken my dog for a
walk. I filled one page to the bottom, every day. If my sister grew

impatient and turned off our bedroom light, I'd finish the page in the dark.

In high school and college, I focused more on writing letters to my sister and my mother and my grandparents, although I did make time to write (bad) poetry. After I married and had children, I journaled whenever I wanted to remember landmark events or cope with difficult emotions. I took pleasure in recording the developmental milestones of both my children, and captured the dates when they noticed their own hands for the first time, or rolled over, or took their first steps. As the boys grew, and managing their busy lives took more of my time, the entries grew shorter and more quotidian: "Byron to dentist, must floss. Dylan's team won: 6–3!"

In the first days after Columbine, I turned again to writing as an outlet, in a journal Dylan had given me for Christmas. Tom and I always told the boys not to bother buying us expensive gifts, and so I had been touched, in 1997, to find a leather-bound writing journal in my stocking. I made such a fuss over how great it was that Dylan got me another diary for Christmas in 1998, this one with a reproduction of Edvard Munch's *The Scream* on the cover. The image seemed ominously symbolic afterward, of course, but at the time I was simply touched by the thoughtful gift—both art- and writing-themed, and therefore perfect for me.

After Columbine, the relief I got from writing felt almost physical, if temporary. My diaries became the place for me to corral the myriad, often-contradictory feelings I had about my son and what he had done. In the earliest days, writing allowed me to process my tremendous grief for the sorrow and suffering Dylan had caused. Before I could reach out personally to the families of the victims, the journals were a place for me to apologize to them with all my heart, and to grieve privately for the losses they had sustained.

The diaries were also a place for me to "set the record straight." In the immediate aftershock of the tragedy, we weren't mourning simply Dylan, but also his very identity—and ours. It was impossible to correct the floods of misinformation in the media, but I wanted to tell our side of the story, if only in private. The pages of my notebook became a place for me to silently respond to the people who called us animals and monsters, to correct misapprehensions about my son and our family. Some of those pages reflect my feelings of defensiveness and even anger toward those who judged us without knowing us. I was not proud of those feelings, and was glad to keep them hidden, but they were necessary for me at the time, and I see the details I obsessed over as unwitting testaments to the shock and grief I was feeling.

Writing in my diary also allowed me the space to reflect on my own loss when I did not feel safe enough to speak about it openly. Our lawyer had told me I could not attend a support group without putting the other members at risk of being deposed, but I needed a safe space to remember and eulogize my son. To the rest of the world, Dylan was a monster; but I had lost my child.

And so, especially in those very early days, a great deal of what I filled my diaries with was memories. Later, I would revisit these as a form of forensic accounting, an attempt to see where things had gone so horribly wrong. Much of grieving is the process of encapsulating the individual in your memory, and for years my grief would be tangled up with wondering what had been in Dylan's mind at the end of his life. Trying to unravel the mystery would come later. In those first days, I wrote simply out of love.

I downloaded every memory I could dredge up of Dylan—as a child, a young boy, a teenager. I revisited his triumphs and disappointments, as well as a host of small, ordinary moments from our life together. Petrified I'd forget, I recorded the well-worn family stories and inside jokes we'd cherished together, words and phrases that could reduce any one of the four of us to helpless laughter while remaining incomprehensible to an outsider. Writing made me feel close to him.

I know telling these stories here exposes me to further criticism. The thought fills me with fear, although there's no criticism of my parenting I have not already heard over the last sixteen years. I've heard that Tom and I were too lenient with Dylan, and that we were too restrictive. I've been told that our family's position on gun control caused Columbine; perhaps if Dylan had been habituated to guns, they would not have had the same mystique for him. People have asked me if we abused Dylan, if we permitted someone else to abuse him, if we ever hugged him, if we ever told him that he was loved.

Of course I look back skeptically on the decisions we made. Of course I have regrets, in particular about the clues I missed that Dylan was in danger of hurting himself and others. It is precisely because I missed them that I want to tell these stories, because whatever parenting decisions Tom and I might have made, they were done thoughtfully and in good conscience, and to the best of our abilities. I tell these stories not to burnish my son's reputation, or our own as parents. But I do think it's important, especially for parents and teachers, to understand what Dylan was *like*.

In the fifteen years I've worked in suicide and violence prevention, I've heard hundreds of stories of lives that ended in tragedy. Sometimes, parents tell me they knew their kid was in trouble. They describe a baby they couldn't settle; disturbingly antisocial behaviors in elementary school; an angry, violent teenager they grew to fear. In many cases, these parents tried repeatedly, and often without success, to get their kids help. I will talk more about cases like these later in this book; we must make it easier for parents and other gatekeepers to get help for a child who is obviously having a hard time before that child becomes a danger to himself and others. But I mention those struggling families here because I want to make an important differentiation. That child, whose difficulties surface early and strain his or her whole family for years? *That was not my son.*

There were hints that Dylan was troubled, and I take responsibility for missing them, but there was no deafening klaxon, no blinking neon danger sign. You wouldn't nervously herd your child away from Dylan if you saw him sitting on a park bench. In fact, after a few minutes of chatting with him, you'd be more likely to invite him home for Sunday dinner. As far as I'm concerned, it is precisely this truth that makes us so vulnerable.

In the aftermath of Columbine, the world's judgment was understandably swift: Dylan was a monster. But that conclusion was also misleading, because it tied up too neatly a far more confounding reality. Like all mythologies, this belief that Dylan was a monster served a deeper purpose: people needed to believe they would recognize evil in their midst. Monsters are unmistakable; you would know a monster if you saw one, wouldn't you? If Dylan was a fiend whose heedless parents had permitted their disturbed, raging teen to amass a weapons cache right under their noses, then the tragedy—horrible as it was—had no relevance to ordinary moms and dads in their own living rooms, their own children tucked snugly into soft beds upstairs. The events might be heartbreaking, but they were also remote. If Dylan was a monster, then the events at Columbine—however tragic—were anomalous, the equivalent of a lightning strike on a clear, sunny day.

The problem? It wasn't true. As monstrous as Dylan's actions were, the truth about him is much harder to square. He wasn't the pinwheel-eyed portrait of evil we know from cartoons. The disquieting reality is that behind this heinous atrocity was an easygoing, shy, likable young man who came from a "good home." Tom and I were hands-on parents who limited the intake of television and sugary cereals. We monitored what movies our boys could see, and put them to bed with stories and prayers and hugs. With the exception of some troubling behavior the year before the tragedy (hardly out of the ordinary for a teenage boy, we were told), Dylan was the classic good kid. He was easy to raise, a pleasure to be with, a child who had always made us proud.

If the portrayal of Dylan as a monster left the impression that the tragedy at Columbine had no relevance to average people or their families, then whatever measure of comfort it offered was false. I hope the truth will awaken people to a greater sense of vulnerability—more frightening, perhaps, but crucial—that cannot be so easily circumscribed.

. . .

I'd wanted to be a mother since I was a child myself. Tom had lost both of his parents when he was a child, and despite the loving care he received from the family members who raised him, he felt the loss of his mother and father acutely. This strengthened his own resolve to be an active, involved, and present parent. My own 1950s childhood looked like the traditional postwar life depicted in the television shows of the day. Although the world had changed significantly (and I worked four days a week, instead of staying home full-time, as my mother had with her three kids), that close-knit, suburban family model was the one Tom and I followed in raising our own children.

We were confident parents, especially by the time we had our second child. Anxious by nature, I never stopped fussing over choking hazards and good manners. But I'd been babysitting since childhood, and I'd spent the majority of my career teaching both children and adults. My graduate degree had required me to take courses in child development and psychology. Naively, I believed the combination of knowledge and intuition honed by experience was sufficient to stand my own children in good stead. At the very least, I reasoned, we'd know where to turn if we encountered problems.

Our confidence as parents was supported by what we saw in our children. As a small child, Byron, our first, was a joyful whirling dervish. He reminded me of Lucille Ball's character in *I Love Lucy*, always getting up to (or into) something. Byron was the kid who whizzed out of the restaurant bathroom, straight into the waitress with the loaded tray. He was the kid who hooked a plate of potato salad so it crashed into his own face, pie-fight style, while demonstrating an armpit fart—and then did it again with a bowl of oatmeal the next morning during a breakfast reenactment. It was pure boyish tomfoolery without an ounce of malice in it. Even Tom was usually laughing too hard at Byron's antics to get mad.

After Byron's energy, Dylan's willingness to sit on the floor and play quietly was a revelation. Both boys were active and playful, but Dylan sought out sedentary tasks that required patience and logic, and after his always-on-the-go brother had outgrown snuggling, Dylan would still slow down for a book or a puzzle or a cuddle with me. Our younger son was observant, curious, and thoughtful, with a gentle personality. Curious about what was going on around him, patient, even-tempered, and quick to giggle, Dylan could make the most routine errand fun. He was up for anything—a social, affable child, who loved to *do* stuff.

And he was smart. Dylan's giftedness emerged early. Shortly after he learned to hold objects by himself as a baby, Dylan went through a brief spell of crying at night. We tried everything we could think of to comfort him, and then took him to the pediatrician to see if the problem might be a physical one. The doctor checked him over carefully, and then advised us to put Dylan to bed with safe toys and soft books so he could entertain himself if he woke up. That night, we heard Dylan wake and make quiet sounds as he played with the toys and looked at the books. When he was finished, he went back to sleep. He'd just been bored.

As a teacher, I marveled at his precociousness. Maybe it shouldn't have mattered so much to me, but he learned so quickly! In third grade he fell in love with origami, an interest that lasted until his adolescence. (A short while after he made his first paper crane, we hosted two Japanese exchange students in our home. Dylan was disappointed to discover the girls didn't know much more about paper-folding than I did.) Over the years we collected a lot of origami books, and Dylan mastered the most complicated designs, ones with seventy or eighty folds. He moved fast, and his pudgy fingers couldn't always get the creases razor-sharp, but these were nonetheless little works of art. I still see his handiwork in the homes of our friends, and when his fifth-grade teacher paid us a condolence call after the tragedy, she brought one of her most treasured possessions to show us: an origami tree, decked with tiny origami ornaments—a Christmas gift it had taken Dylan hours to make.

As a toddler, he was fascinated by snap-together construction toys; as he grew older, he spent countless hours building with Legos. Precise and methodical, he loved to follow the printed instructions exactly, meticulously building ships, castles, and space stations, only to dismantle and build them again. Dylan had a bunk bed in his bedroom, and Tom placed a large sheet of plywood over the lower bed so Dylan would have an out-of-the-way spot to work on larger and more complicated structures over a period of days. Byron preferred freestyle construction, and his imagination was the source of some wildly creative projects. Dylan was the opposite. Occasionally concerned he was too focused on perfection, Tom and I would talk to him about how it was okay to substitute an alternate piece if he couldn't find the exact right one.

Similarly, we saw his competitive nature emerge when the four of us played board games together, like Monopoly and Risk. Losing was humiliating for Dylan, and his humiliation sometimes turned to anger. Of course, it's as important to know how to lose as it is to win, so we continued to play games as a family until Dylan learned to control his temper. He also played Little League baseball, where he learned the importance of sportsmanship. As we hoped, Dylan's need to win leveled out as he matured. Looking back, however, I wonder if we were inadvertently encouraging Dylan to suppress his feelings, under the guise of learning appropriate play.

Since I'd been a real scaredy-cat as a child, I was impressed by how free of ordinary childhood fears Dylan was. He wasn't afraid to go to the doctor or the dentist, as I had been at his age. He got his first haircut with a big smile on his face. He wasn't afraid of the water, or to be left alone in the dark, or of thunder and lightning. Later, when we started going to amusement parks, Dylan could be counted on to pick the scariest rides. Sometimes he had to ride them alone while we waved from below because no one else had the courage to join him.

Tom and I called Dylan "our little trouper" because of his ability to withstand frustration. He wouldn't quit until he'd conquered a problem, and he rarely abandoned an idea without seeing it through. He didn't like to ask for help. Then again, he rarely needed it. Because he was so tall and academically gifted, he entered school a year early. For most of his life, he was the youngest kid in his class, and almost always the biggest.

He wasn't always great at sharing his toys, to the point of hiding his favorites when a particularly grabby playdate was coming over. As a toddler, an exhausted Dylan would occasionally throw himself down in a tantrum at the checkout when my grocery shopping was taking too long, and the way he flaunted how much better he knew his multiplication tables than his older brother was not the most charming thing in the world. But he was nothing if not normal, and we loved him. Tom and I both believed he was destined to do great things.

In the years since, I have thought a great deal about Dylan's need to convince himself and others that he was completely in control. It was part of his nature from early childhood. While we were proud of this trait when he was young, I wonder now if that pride was misplaced. Because when Dylan really did need help toward the end of his life, he did not know how to ask.

In the wake of Columbine, many people have come forward to share their own stories of hidden pain with me. I find it striking how many of those stories come from so-called perfect kids: the science-fair winner, the track star, the young musician offered a full scholarship to the conservatory of her choice. Sometimes there were glaring signs in the lives of these children that all was not well: declining grades, promiscuity or drug use, trouble with the law. In many cases, though, these kids were able to fly under their parents' radar precisely because they were the shiny pennies, hiding the terrible pain they were in from their parents as capably as they did everything else.

Whenever I wonder why I am writing this book, exposing myself once again to the judgment and vitriol of the world, those parents are the ones I think about. Dylan may not have been a valedictorian or a star athlete, but we were confident he would handle the inevitable challenges of life gracefully. Would I have parented differently if I had known those stories of kids suffering under the surface while presenting a happy, well-adjusted face to the world? Hindsight is 20/20, but I think if I had known, I would not have been so easily convinced by how effortlessly Dylan seemed to move through his life.

Tom and I always joked that Dylan was on autopilot. At five or six, Dylan asked me to teach him how to give himself a bath. I showed him how to put soap on the washcloth, which parts of his body needed extra attention, and how to rinse himself off thoroughly. Three years older, Byron was still having too much fun in the tub to wash his ears without prompting. I only needed to show Dylan the steps once—and he hung his towel up afterward without me saying a word about it.

In addition to being an easy child, Dylan was a *happy* one. He was more introverted than his brother but still quick to make friends. When we lived on a street with a lot of kids, Dylan moved comfortably along with a pack of boys his age as they rode around the neighborhood. (We always knew where they were by the herd of bikes lying on the lawn outside whichever house they'd stopped at for a snack.)

As our sons got older, Tom and I were particularly impressed by how seamlessly Dylan fit in with Byron and his friends. One of my favorite pictures, on my desk as I write this, is of Dylan clinging to Byron's arm like a little monkey, both of them sporting huge grins.

There's a story from Dylan's childhood I think about a lot. When he was about ten, he had to have a misplaced, deeply embedded tooth removed. Unfortunately, we had friends coming into town to visit the next day. I probably should have insisted Dylan and I stay home while he recuperated, but there was no way he was going to miss sightseeing with our friends, even with his cheeks swollen up like a chipmunk's.

I winced whenever I looked at his pale, swollen face, but he didn't miss a beat—riding go-karts, eating ice cream, and taking the train up Pikes Peak, a mountain with an elevation of more than 14,000 feet and some of the most spectacular scenery in the world. When I anxiously made eye contact with him through the rearview mirror on our way from one place to the next, he smiled softly at me to dispel my worries. Despite my concern, Dylan was having the time of his life.

And when the other mom on the trip and I were too afraid to take the first step out onto the Royal Gorge Bridge, it was Dylan who skipped back to us, alternately teasing and cajoling and encouraging us across the highest bridge in the United States. I can still feel his hand in mine.

· · ·

Tom and I had moved several times before we finally found the house we wanted to raise our family in. With its large picture windows and high ceilings, the house had been quite the show home. It had been badly neglected, though, and by the time we bought it, it had fallen into serious disrepair. The pool didn't hold water, and weeds grew six feet tall through the cracks on the tennis court. The house had a leaky roof and several broken windows, creating easy access routes for the hundreds of ground squirrels, voles, and mice that had taken up residence in and around the house.

The property was too much for us, given our income, but it was surrounded by breathtaking scenery. The extraordinary light in the foothills made the rocks behind our house glow a fiery orange in the mornings and a sweet, deep lavender at dusk. Set among the massive pink sandstone cliffs were twisted, gnarly scrub oaks, bristling prickly pears, and spiky yucca—hardy desert survivors, every one.

The boys and I would sit and watch the wildlife from our picture windows like other families watched television. Scrub jays, flickers, magpies, and chickadees patronized our bird feeders, and deer families and foxes and raccoons shared whatever seeds spilled to the ground. We hosted a family of bobcats in our backyard for a while. One night after dinner, Tom looked up from doing the dishes to see a black bear staring right back at him through the kitchen window, not eighteen inches away. One morning, he saw another bear blissfully lying on his back in the middle of our swimming pool, soaking in a depression in the pool cover that had trapped just enough water for his bath.

One of our neighbors told me the land used to be a wintering ground for a local Native American tribe, and the property had a spiritual feel to it. I had wanted my boys to grow up safely surrounded by the beauty of nature, to roam free in a place that would reward their imaginations. When we found the house in the foothills, as decrepit and neglected as it was, I believed we'd found that place.

We moved in early December of 1989, when Dylan was in third grade. A friendly neighbor gave us an old minibike from his garage, and Tom found a second one, used, in the newspaper classifieds. He and the boys rebuilt the bikes to get them running, and before long, Dylan and Byron had worn trails throughout our property. They had tremendous freedom to roam; on the other hand, the new house was so remote that their activities in town had to be scheduled so Tom or I could provide transportation. The boys couldn't simply get on their bikes to visit friends, or ride to the corner for an ice cream. Our relative isolation in the country meant the two boys spent a great deal of time together.

As he grew, Dylan took a lot of pride in his independence. To my amusement, he asked me to show him how to do his own laundry when he was ten. That independence, combined with the determination we'd seen when he was young, made him a force to be reckoned with. I remember taking him and Byron to the roller rink. I wasn't an accomplished skater by any stretch of the imagination, but I could stay on my feet, and I offered to help Dylan, who was struggling to stay on his. He insisted he could do it alone, and so I dutifully planted myself against the railing as he stumbled away from me. He took a few halting steps on his skates without gliding, and then fell, hard, to the floor. I rushed to help, but he waved me off impatiently. "I can skate. You wait here and watch. Don't move! I don't need help."

And so I watched as he crawled on his hands and knees to the railing and pulled himself up. Then he took another few awkward steps before falling again. I held myself back and watched as the tiny figure inched around the huge rink: a few hesitant steps, the inevitable fall, and then the laborious crawl back to the railing. I have absolutely no idea how long it took him to go all the way around. It felt like an hour.

Finally, he lurched up to where I stood. Sweat poured from his face, and tendrils of blond hair stuck to his forehead. I winced to think about the bruises covering his legs under his dusty jeans. Holding the wall to steady himself, his legs shaking with the effort to keep himself upright after all that work, he stood tall and proud in front of me.

"See? I told you I could skate!"

Incidents like this convinced Tom and me that Dylan would be able to accomplish anything he set out to do, if only by sheer force of will. This was the foundation of our belief in him. He had a lot of confidence in himself, and we did too.

Dylan spent fourth, fifth, and sixth grades in a gifted class-room. It was almost a private-school setting: small classes, lots of chess and math games and individual attention. By the end of sixth grade, challenged academically and spending his days with kids who shared his interests, Dylan seemed to be on top of the world. He left a record of the confidence he felt in a drawing: a boy in a plaid shirt, standing on top of a range of yellow, green, and purple mountains, waving to the viewer with a huge smile on his face. The principal of his elementary school chose the picture for the school's permanent collection, framed it with a gold nameplate, and hung it in the hallway.

After Columbine, afraid someone would destroy or steal it, we asked his favorite teacher to return it to us.

. . .

One of the traits that marked Dylan throughout his life was an ex-aggerated reluctance to risk embarrassment, something that inten-sified as he entered adolescence. Both Tom and I are self-deprecating by nature, the first ones to poke fun at ourselves. But Dylan did not laugh easily at his own foibles. He could be unforgiving of himself when he failed at anything, and he hated to look foolish.

One summer afternoon, when Dylan was about eight, we went on a picnic with Judy Brown and her two boys. The kids were catch-ing crayfish in the creek, and Dylan lost his balance on the slippery rocks and fell into the shallow water with a splash. He emerged unhurt but furious: livid about the pratfall, and even angrier that everyone else had laughed. We tried to help him to see the humor in it—Byron would likely have hammed it up further by taking an elaborate bow—but Dylan went to the car and refused to speak to anyone until he felt able to face the world again. The reaction seemed outsized, but it only cemented what we already knew: Dylan felt embarrassment more acutely than other kids did.

When he was about ten and a cousin was visiting from out of state, she and the boys and I went horseback riding together. Midway through our ride, Dylan's horse stopped in the middle of the trail to pee. Childishly, the rest of us laughed. Dylan's face grew red and hot with embarrassment, his humiliation growing with every passing second. Still, while Dylan might have been more self-conscious than Byron had been, his insecurities still fell well within normal parameters for a preteen.

By junior high, the gifted program Dylan was in had come to an end. Like many kids that age, he was excruciatingly conscious of anything that might make him stand out from the crowd. In junior high, he told me, it wasn't cool to be smart.

Despite this, he continued to do well academically. By the time he was in eighth grade, his junior-high math teacher recommended he enroll in an algebra class at Columbine High School. Dylan refused to go. All three of us met with his teacher to weigh the pros and cons. It's intimidating enough to start high school as a ninth grader, let alone to go there a year early, and the logistics of getting him back and forth safely were complicated. Together we concluded it would be best to let Dylan stay at the junior high for math.

It was a relief to us that Dylan was doing well, because Byron's entry into adolescence had been challenging. He needed a great deal of parental poking and prodding to get through his daily routines. We'd established clear expectations for the boys when they were young. They were never permitted to speak to us, or to any adult, in a disrespectful way. We asked them to care for their rooms and belongings, and to help us with projects around the house. I expected them to do what they could to stay safe: wear sunscreen, drive responsibly, and say no to drugs. On top of that, they were required to keep up with their schoolwork, and so when Tom and I saw Byron's high school academic performance (never stellar) decline, we searched his room and discovered he was smoking marijuana.

Marijuana is legal in Colorado now, so our reaction might seemed old-fashioned and outsized, but drugs had never been a part of either of our lives, and we were frankly afraid of them. We'd been pretty closely monitoring Byron's movements before, but after we found the pot, we got right up on top of him. We searched his room as a matter of routine. We insisted he end friendships we believed weren't in his best interests. We sent him to see a counselor.

I'm sure we annoyed him beyond measure, but Byron had the same good-natured, loving spirit as always. He was funny and open, and I'd spend hours in his room talking to him, making sure he was okay. There wasn't a lot of conflict in the house, but Byron was definitely receiving the lion's share of our parental attention, which may have meant we did not recognize the intensity of Dylan's emerging needs.

During those trying years, Dylan kept doing what he was supposed to be doing. He seemed to enjoy the role of the cooperative, responsible child, the kid who did the right thing, and Tom and I needed him to fulfill that role more than ever when we were preoccupied with Byron's welfare. Dylan's commitment to self-reliance obscured how much he needed help at the end of his life. It unquestionably contributed to our inability to see him as troubled.

In the summer after eighth grade, Dylan began to develop the lean, angular look he'd have for the rest of his life. We wanted to reward his transition into high school, so we offered to send him to a summer camp in the mountains. The camp was rustic, and the kids shouldered the majority of what needed to be done to keep the place running. Dylan never hesitated to complain at home when he felt he'd been assigned more than his fair share of chores, but he had no complaints about camp. He loved being outdoors, and the counselors told us he got along well with the other kids.

· · ·

Both of our sons played baseball from the time they were small; the sport was the common thread woven through their childhoods and adolescence. They watched games on television, fought over the sports pages, and took turns going to baseball games with their father. Tom loved the game, and the three of them would spend summer nights playing catch in the backyard, or throwing balls through a plywood sheet Tom had customized for pitching practice. Dylan's walls were covered with posters of his baseball heroes: Lou Gehrig, Roger Clemens, Randy Johnson. One of our favorite movies was *The Natural*, which starred Robert Redford as a baseball prodigy. The boys watched it so often that they knew parts by heart.

Baseball was not only a wholesome pastime for the boys; it was a shared love between Tom's family and my own. One of my grandfathers had been asked to join a professional team as a young man (he declined: he didn't want to leave his widowed mother), and both Tom's father and his brother played amateur ball well into their adult years. I loved that our boys played this classic American sport, just as their grandfathers and great-grandfathers had before them. Both Dylan and Tom were devastated when Dylan, entering Columbine High School as a ninth grader, didn't make the Columbine High School baseball team.

Byron's smooth right-handed pitch kept him in the game until he grew tired of it. Dylan also pitched, but he was a lefty and fired the ball like a cannon, trying to strike the batter out. Throwing hard was his trademark, and he often sacrificed accuracy for speed. In time, his pitching style took its toll on his arm. The summer before Dylan went into eighth grade, Tom hired a coach to help both boys with their form. During one of their sessions, Dylan seemed to be struggling. Suddenly, he stopped throwing altogether, his eyes downcast. Tom hurried over, worried he or the coach had pushed Dylan too hard. He saw Dylan's eyes were filled with tears.

"My arm hurts too much to pitch," Dylan told his dad.

Tom was shocked. Dylan had never mentioned any pain before, though we later learned it had been going on for months, worsening with each throw. It was typical of Dylan not to mention it: he'd been determined to overcome the problem by force of will. Tom took him to the doctor immediately. Dylan had a painful inflammation around the tendons of the elbow, and the doctor recommended he take a break from baseball. He stayed away until the following summer, when he began to practice for the Columbine High School baseball team tryouts.

Tom had also begun to experience serious joint pain. (Right around the time Dylan was entering high school, Tom was diagnosed with rheumatoid arthritis, and would undergo surgeries on his knees and shoulders in the next few years.) His ability to help Dylan practice was limited as he could no longer throw a ball, so he hired the pitching coach to come back. As it turned out, Dylan's arm was still sore. The day of the tryouts, the two of them made quite a pair—Dylan favoring his elbow, and Tom's knees hurting so badly he could barely walk out to the field.

Given his injury, we greeted the news that Dylan hadn't made the team with mixed emotions. Although disappointed he wouldn't be participating in a sport in high school, neither Tom nor I wanted to push him into an activity that might cause him lasting physical damage. As a family, we tried to minimize the loss and move on. For his part, Dylan claimed he hadn't liked some of the kids on the team anyway.

His passion for the sport didn't come to an end. He still followed professional baseball religiously, and went occasionally to games with his dad; in time, he'd join a fantasy baseball league. Not making the team was a much greater loss than we knew, though, as the focus of his attention shifted from baseball to computers.

Dylan and Byron weren't eligible for bus service to Columbine High School, so Tom or I had to drop them off and pick them up. When Dylan began ninth grade, we worked out a plan that honored his growing sense of independence: after school, he would take the city bus a couple of miles to the college where I worked, and stay with me until it was time to go home. I loved having Dylan at my office with me while I worked. I kept a file drawer full of snacks for him, which often went unopened because the women in my department spoiled him with homemade treats. If his homework was done, he'd head to the student lounge to watch television, or to the cafeteria for a milkshake. Occasionally he'd stretch his long legs out under a table in my office to take a nap.

When he was a sophomore, he volunteered at the day care on

campus. The director was a colleague of mine, and I'd occasionally stop by to watch him work. True to form, Dylan would be out there on the playground, making sure the little kids were lining up neatly to get a turn on the swing.

Every mother worries about the social aspects of high school, but I was less worried than most. Dylan was tall and geeky, and never part of that top rung of the social hierarchy reserved for athletes, but his social life flourished in high school. He had three close friends with whom he spent most of his free time. On any given weekend, one of them was at our house, or Dylan was at one of theirs. The four of them—Dylan, Zack, Nate, and Eric—had other friends too, but these were the kids we considered Dylan's inner circle.

Dylan met Nate, the boy I always considered his closest friend, in junior high school. Nate was an only child, raised by his mother and stepfather. Like Dylan, Nate was gangly: tall and thin, with long dark lashes and black hair. Unlike Dylan, though, he was effusive and happy to talk a mile a minute about everything under the sun. In the early years of their friendship, the two of them spent most of their free time outdoors, playing catch and other games. Nate handily outplayed Dylan in basketball, but Dylan beat him soundly when they played pool back at our house. When Nate spent the night, the boys would stay up late playing pool or video games, or trying out recipes from late-night cooking shows. (Dylan was famous, even among the voracious adolescents he hung out with, for his appetite. He was adventurous, too. When his friends came out with us for dinner, they'd usually stick with the fried standards, while Dylan experimented with calamari or barbecued duck.)

Nate spent a lot of time at our house. He was the first one on his feet to help if I came in carrying groceries or laundry, and quick to compliment my cooking. I'm happiest when I have a full house, and never complained when a group of teenagers descended upon my kitchen like locusts, although our house was sufficiently remote that it didn't happen very often.

Dylan met his friend Zack freshman year. Zack's dad was a university professor turned administrator, and his mom ran the children's youth group at the church we'd attended when the boys were younger. Zack was friendly and outgoing, with a stocky build, a round face, and short brown hair. His house was ground zero for all kinds of zany activity—someone always seemed to be barbecuing or going boating or throwing a pool party—and Dylan spent a lot of time there. I was especially pleased by Dylan's friendship with Zack, because of how gregarious and outgoing Zack was. He didn't mind being the center of attention, which drew Dylan out a little.

Both Zack and Dylan were interested in technology. One summer, they hit rummage sales in Zack's neighborhood for old telephone equipment, determined to build a portable telephone system. (This was before cell phones.) The boys were proud of the contraption they came up with—an old telephone bolted to a sprung suitcase—and they got it working well enough to cause some static on the phone system in our house.

It was Zack who got Dylan interested in doing sound tech for theater productions at the end of their sophomore year. After watching a production of *Bye Bye Birdie*, I visited Dyl in the sound booth and was impressed by his command of the many switches and levers on the complicated board. Dylan loved it. He spent hours at rehearsals, and experimented with manipulating sounds on his computer to make an original soundtrack for a production of *Frankenstein* directed by his friend Brooks. People occasionally approached him to run the sound system for their talent shows, church events, and less formal after-school productions.

Zack was the first of Dylan's friends to have a girlfriend. Dylan was jealous of his friend's good fortune, but nonetheless became friends with Zack's girlfriend, Devon. After Dylan's death, Devon made a book of photographs and stories about him for me. What struck me was how much she trusted in and confided in Dylan. When her feelings were hurt or when she had conflicts with others, it was Dylan she turned to for support: "I would call Dylan on the phone or talk to him on the computer. It was the best therapy I could hope for. Dylan was the best listener I had ever met."

Eric was the fourth member of the crew. Dylan and Eric had also met in junior high school. Eric's dad had been in the military, and he'd retired to the Denver area; the family was still quite new there when Eric and Dylan met. We met the Harrises when the boys started hanging out, and we liked them, although we didn't see them socially. At the end of eighth grade, Dylan and Eric were both recognized for their achievement in math. When they walked up to the stage to accept their awards, I whispered to Tom that they looked like two peas in a pod. (This was before Dylan's growth spurt.)

In junior high, Dylan and Eric watched tons of movies together, and loved to go bowling. One time, they built a contraption to launch potatoes from one side of a pocket park to another. As they grew older, they added to their interests an attraction to girls, computer games, and music, as well as baseball games and concerts. In high school, Eric remained small and relatively slight, while Dylan shot up in height. Eric was older, and got his license before Dylan.

Their friendship didn't seem any more intense than Dylan's relationships with other boys; if anything, I would have said that Dylan was closer to Nate. It did seem more private, somehow. I never felt as close to Eric as I did to Nate and Zack, although he was always respectful and perfectly polite when he was around Tom and me. I don't remember him asking me any questions, or volunteering ridiculous stories about Dylan, the way Zack and Nate did, but he was clearly smart, friendly, and funny.

Perhaps it's significant I don't have the same kinds of memories of connecting with Eric that I do with Dylan's other friends. I wonder how much of that has to do with spending time with Zack and Nate after Dylan's death, and the fact that I had the privilege of seeing them as they grew into adulthood. I still talk to Nate; he checks in with me at holiday time, and comes to visit when he's in town. I do know that we did not perceive there to be anything unusual or unsettling about Eric, or about his friendship with Dylan prior to the trouble they had near the end of junior year, or Tom and I would not have permitted it to continue.

Dylan didn't have a girlfriend in high school, but he and his other friends did hang out with girls; "herd dating" was common among their age group. He met his prom date, Robyn, in class; they studied calculus together. When Dylan first started spending time with Robyn, I peppered him with questions about her and her family, as I did about all of his friends. He laughed: "Believe me, Mom: you have nothing to worry about with Robyn. She's exactly the kind of person you'd want me to be with, an A student." When I asked what she was like, Dylan shrugged and told me, "She's just a nice person." I met her a few days later, and realized Dylan had been right: Robyn was lovely. I was impressed by how comfortable she seemed around Tom and me.

Before Dylan and his friends could drive, it was easy to interact with them and get to know their parents because the boys needed transportation in order to get together. Tom and I always stopped in to say hi to the other parents and to coordinate plans when we were dropping Dylan off. It made me feel good to know we could speak freely with one another about our children if we had concerns, though we almost never had cause.

When Dylan and his friends were old enough to work, his closest friends ended up working at Blackjack Pizza. Zack got a job there first; Dylan joined him a little while after, and Eric and Nate after that. Dylan bragged about his ability to make a great pizza quickly. When paychecks started rolling in, I helped him open checking and savings accounts at the bank, and after he died, I found neat folders containing his bank statements, payment stubs, and tax information. Tom or I would drop him off and pick him up from work if he couldn't get a ride from one of his friends. We both got a kick out of calling to find out what time he needed to be picked up; it was the only time we got to hear Dylan's professional customer service voice.

Dylan's high school grades ebbed and flowed with his level of enthusiasm for the subject and the teacher. It disappointed us that he was not fulfilling his academic potential as he had in elementary school. On the other hand, I was relieved to see him lighten up. When he was younger, Dylan's perfectionism had frustrated him, and sometimes frustrated us—although I could relate. So I didn't mind when his orderly room turned into the more typical teenage sty. He'd eventually find areas of interest he'd excel in, just as Tom and I had; my own grades had been mediocre until graduate school.

I have since learned that perfectionism is frequently a characteristic of kids with special abilities. Ironically, it can sometimes undermine their potential. A mistake or setback that most kids would shrug off can devastate a child with unrealistic and unattainable standards. It can lower their self-esteem, causing them to disengage from the intellectual challenges that once fired them up. In retrospect, I believe that Dylan's innate perfectionism, and our inability to help him manage his unrealistic expectations for himself, contributed to his feelings of alienation at the end of his life.

· · ·

Dylan planned to major in computer science at college. Like his dad, he loved to tinker, and they did a lot of that together: customizing speakers and fixing up cars. He and Tom also liked to play pranks on one another, like setting each other's computer to surprise the user with obnoxious sounds when the machine was turned on, such as a dog "singing" a Christmas carol.

In tenth grade, Dylan built his own computer. He and his friends liked playing video games and experimenting with visual and audio effects; eventually, he became a beta tester for Microsoft products. I often referred to him as a computer geek. I would have preferred it if he and his friends had spent more time outside, especially because we lived near some of the best hiking and skiing and snowboarding terrain in the world. But neither Tom nor I thought Dylan's time on the computer was inherently bad. His social life did not suffer, and he'd reluctantly pull himself away to go out for dinner or watch a movie with us if we asked him to. Neither of us saw the computer as a tool for destructive or malicious behavior. If we had, we would not have allowed him to use it.

That said, Tom and I did not look at what Dylan did on his computer. This seems shockingly naive now, but it was a different time—and anyway, I would not have known how to check his browser history or usage in those days; I had only just begun using the Internet myself. I did find excuses to go in and out of Dylan's room so I could take a peek at what he was up to. One time he was in a chat room, and he looked edgy when I peered over his shoulder. When I asked him to translate the jargon, it sounded like a typical (and dumb) teenage conversation. I knew sexual images were readily available on the Internet, and assumed they'd appeal to him, as they would to most teenage boys, although I never discovered him looking at any.

Even if I had been aware of dangerous content online, I would never have suspected Dylan to be interested in material that would lead him to hurt himself or anybody else.

．．．

Byron had no desire to go to college, at least not immediately. Tom and I didn't want to be in conflict with him over our rules (no drinking, drugs, or smoking cigarettes on our property, for starters), but we worried too that Byron would struggle in a less structured environment.

After endless conversations, Tom and I went with Byron to see his counselor. The counselor asked Byron outright if he was ready to hold down a job and an apartment by himself, and Byron assured him he was. For our part, we could only hope the demands of real life would help him mature. With the counselor's blessing, Byron and his best friend rented a cheap apartment across town, and the two of them set off from our house in a pickup truck loaded down with spare furniture, kitchen utensils, and a few boxes of food. Ever the optimist, I even included cleaning supplies.

Dylan couldn't wait to move into his brother's room, which was bigger and had more windows. Redecorating was a family affair. Tom and I replaced the sliding closet doors with mirrored ones, so the room looked twice as big as it had before. Dylan requested that one wall be painted a sleek black, which looked sharp with the modern black furniture Byron had left behind. Dylan put his computer against the dark wall and covered the rest of the room with posters.

Tom hung a shelf over the computer so that Dylan would have a place for his CDs, and attached a fluorescent light to the underside.

For me, Dylan moving into Byron's room marked the end of his childhood. Even though he was over six feet tall, I watched with sadness as he packed up boxes of toys from his own room and labeled them for storage. After his death, I opened boxes filled with his once-precious Lego sets. Most contained the original packaging and instructional diagrams, nearly torn along the folds from use. I was struck by how like Dylan that was, to meticulously organize even the things he was putting away for storage.

Around the time he moved into his brother's old room, Dylan got his learner's permit. As difficult as it was for us to watch him take this next step away from us, we were glad, too. His friends had always been generous with rides, but we lived a good fifteen or twenty minutes out of their way, and it had been annoying for him to be the only person in his group of friends too young to drive.

At first, Tom took Dylan to empty parking lots in the evening to get the feel of driving the car. Then they worked their way up to driving on city streets, freeways, and finally the twisting mountain roads. The first time we went to Byron's new apartment for dinner, we allowed Dylan to drive us halfway. (Byron proudly presented us with a double batch of Hamburger Helper. Anticipating a shortage of vegetables on the menu, I'd brought a salad.) By August, Dylan was taking driving lessons so he could get a lower auto insurance rate.

The process leading up to Byron's move had been painful, but once we saw him settled in his new apartment, we knew it was the right decision. "Now we can focus on Dylan," I told Tom, except there didn't seem to be all that much to focus on. Our younger son just seemed to stay on track. Most of the time, if he understood why a rule was in place, he'd follow it.

Maybe Dylan wasn't as demonstrative, cuddly, or communicative as he had been when he was younger. What teenage boy is? But until he hit a patch of trouble in his junior year, I saw nothing—*nothing*—in our life together as a family to foreshadow the tragedy to come.

CHAPTER 7

One Mother to Another

Today, I began the task of writing condolence letters to the victims'
families. It was so hard. The tragic loss of all those children. It's so
hard, but it's something I must do. From the heart of one mother to
another.

—Journal entry, May 1999

E ver since childhood, I have found comfort in being helpful.
My grandfather threw huge picnics at the farm he owned
for the people who worked at his company and for the charities he
supported, and I made myself useful by rounding up paper plates
and empties. At school, I preferred to help the lunch ladies clean
the cafeteria than to go out to the playground at recess. I'm still like
this. "Put me to work," I say at a wedding, and I keep saying it until
the host hands me something to pass or to pour.

But there was absolutely nothing I could do to help anyone else
in the aftershock of the carnage and cruelty committed by my son
at Columbine High School.

Concerned friends and clergy wanted to bring the families together, but the first lawsuit had been filed days after the tragedy,
and our attorneys rejected the idea of face-to-face meetings outright. I can't imagine anyone involved would have wanted to meet
with me so soon after the shootings, either.

People urged Tom and me to make a public statement through
the media. We did a few days after the tragedy, apologizing as well
as expressing our bewilderment and grief. Even so, I felt compelled
to communicate directly with the families of Dylan's victims, and

to the victims who had survived. I decided to handwrite letters of apology to each of the families.

I wasn't foolish enough to believe there were any words that could ever suffice. But I needed to let the families know the depth of my sorrow for what they had suffered at my son's hand. I had the idea that if I could extend some kindness, it might counterbalance Dylan's cruelty on that horrific morning. And, although there's nothing noble about it, I wanted them to know that although I had loved him, I was not my son.

Writing those letters remains one of the hardest things I have ever done. It took me a full month to finish them. How could I convey empathy, when even hearing my name would likely increase the suffering these families were feeling? How could I reach out, as a companion in sorrow, when my son—the person I had created and loved more than life—was the reason they were in agony? How do you say, "I'm sorry my child killed yours"?

The difficulty of writing the letters was compounded by the conflict it created within our own family. Tom was against the idea. He worried that sending an apology would be tantamount to accepting personal responsibility. Learning about the victims and how they died was excruciating for him, and he avoided it.

I felt differently. If hearing from me might bring some small measure of comfort and open the door for communication with the families, it was a chance I wanted to take. I had to do *something*. I hoped showing my own humanity might bring an iota of peace to people who would be forever tormented by the cruelty of what my son had done.

I had been deliberately avoiding news coverage, but in order to write to the families, I needed to know more about their loved ones. So I forced myself to read newspaper articles for information about the teacher and each of the children who had been killed. I never, ever wanted to dehumanize the individuals who had been killed or injured by thinking of them as a collective group—the "victims." In each case, I needed to know the particular, specific treasure that had been lost.

Sorrow piled on sorrow with every biographical detail I read.

Learning what each person had been interested in and what their friends and loved ones said about them broke my heart. The waste of it, the idea that Dylan had robbed innocent people of their precious lives, and of the futures they should have had, was intolerable. How could he have inflicted such pain? How could anyone, raised in our home, have done this?

At times, writing the letters felt like standing dangerously close to a fire, and sometimes I had to step back. Each day, I wanted to run as fast as I could from the task in front of me. But if I did, I knew I would lose my connection to what had happened. Columbine had already become the lightning rod it still is, a symbol in a single word for the hazards of bullying, mental illness, irresponsible parenting, guns. Like everyone else, I believed there were answers to be pursued, but I was not yet ready to take refuge in abstractions. Columbine wasn't "about" guns or bullying; it was about the fifteen people who were now dead, and the twenty-four who had been injured, some profoundly.

Yet even while I was trying to write coherent letters acknowledging my son's responsibility, I was clinging ferociously to my denial that Dylan could have been responsible for killing anyone. As I wrote them, I believed with all my heart that the people who sustained mortal wounds had been shot by Eric, not by Dylan. In the letters, I referred to the "role" Dylan played in the tragedy because I still didn't know what had really happened that day, only that people had been killed and wounded. I referred to a "moment of madness," because I believed Dylan had to have acted on impulse; it was inconceivable his participation could have been planned ahead of time. I could not yet believe my son was a murderer, because I did not accept that his intent had been to kill.

I feared that many of the families would be insulted by my presumption in reaching out. They would say—correctly—that I did not have the right even to utter their loved one's name. When I read the first drafts of the letters I had written, I almost threw them away. The words on the paper were shamefully, pitifully inadequate.

But writing them was all that I could think of to do. I could not undo what Dylan and Eric had done. I could not bring back the lives that had been lost, nor heal those who had been wounded physically or psychologically. I was powerless to dampen the aftershocks of the tragedy for myself or anyone else, and I understood I could not control how people would respond. I was not asking for forgiveness, or for understanding, or for anything, except the chance to say that I was sorry.

. . .

Read today that Mr. Rohrbough had destroyed Dylan and Eric's crosses. I don't blame him at all. No one should expect the grieving families of victims to embrace Dylan and Eric now. I'd feel the same way.

—Journal entry, May 1999

A week after the shootings, my brother, Phil, came to spend a few days with us. My sister couldn't join him: one of her teenage children, Dylan's cousin, had been so traumatized by the news of Dylan's role that she needed medical attention.

Phil had come to comfort us, but what could he say or do? We were shadow people, ghosts of ourselves, moving through a never-ending twilight characterized by discombobulation, shame, and sorrow. Our days were consumed with legal appointments and the paranoid measures we followed in order to avoid the media and those who might want to harm us.

Dylan's face was everywhere: *Murderer. Terrorist. Neo-Nazi. Outcast. Scum.*

Soon after the shootings, we received yet another terrible shock. It was reported that Robyn, Dylan's prom date, had bought three guns for the boys.

My first thought was, *Oh, no. Poor Robyn.* In a flash, I could see it: she had done it because they'd asked her to, because she liked them, because she was a nice person. She would never, ever, ever have done it if she'd believed it was unsafe. *She's going to have to live with this for the rest of her life,* I thought. Then, for the thousandth time: *Look how many people they've hurt.*

The aftershocks kept coming. Still mostly insulated from news and the outside world, I was only dimly aware of most of them. I didn't know until a year later that Marilyn Manson had canceled concert dates in our area out of respect, or that the NRA did not cancel their annual meeting, held at a hotel fifteen miles away from the school, just ten days after the shootings.

I did learn that school authorities and police had been told about Eric's website, the one Judy Brown had told me about on the terrible day of the shootings, and that he'd talked openly on the site about pipe bombs and killing people.

And I saw Dylan on the cover of *Time* magazine, next to the headline "The Monsters Next Door." Despite the monstrous nature of what he had done, it hurt me terribly to see that word used to describe him and utterly surreal to see his face under the iconic logo. It was still hard to believe Dylan had done something horrendous enough that the neighbors would know about it, let alone the entire world.

I read the article. The next day, I wrote:

Depression really kicked in when I read the Time Magazine *article yesterday. They made Dylan sound human, like a nice kid gone astray. This hurts more than the villain portrayal because it shows how totally senseless it all was. He didn't have to do any of this. He was so close to a life away from high school. If he was depressed, he didn't show us.*

A makeshift memorial had been erected in town, consisting of fifteen rough-hewn wooden crosses, one for each person who had died, including Dylan and Eric. Immediately, Dylan's and Eric's crosses were chopped down and thrown in a dumpster. A church group planted fifteen commemorative trees in a circle on their property, and police and congregation members stood helplessly by while two were felled.

Of course, I understood why people did not want Dylan and Eric to be mourned or memorialized, but this unchallenged display of anger frightened us. Within a few days of his arrival, my brother accepted an offer to sleep at a neighbor's house. He urged us to leave with him. "You're in such a state of shock, you can't see how dangerous this is."

We *were* in shock, but the bigger issue was that we just didn't care. One particularly bad night, Tom said wearily, "I wish he'd killed us, too." It was a thought we would have on many occasions over the years.

A reporter got ahold of our phone records and called everyone we'd communicated with over the previous months. Our friends and family members were already inundated, but now the press started showing up at the two apartment buildings we owned to question our tenants. We'd worked hard to build a family business, and the safety and comfort of our tenants was a priority, but they were being harassed simply because they'd had the misfortune of moving into one of our properties. We didn't see a way to protect them, so we moved forward to sell the buildings.

We considered leaving the area, but as hostile as the larger world was toward us, our own inner circle became an invaluable source of support. For more than a decade, our lives had been in Littleton, and the people we loved rallied immediately to our side. On days when I wasn't sure I would survive, friends materialized to keep me going.

If God sends us love on earth, I truly believe it is delivered through the actions of people. During that terrible time, we were sustained by the care of those around us. Friends and family members were stalwart with daily calls and hugs. Neighbors delivered home-cooked meals and returned empty serving dishes to their rightful owners. Our friends quickly learned to stop defending us in the press after so many of them saw their words distorted or put into a negative context, but they fiercely protected our property, not only from the media's intrusions, but from any stranger who appeared. In the early days, when our phone rang off the hook with interview requests and calls from strangers as well as friends—twenty or thirty calls a day—our closest neighbors bought us a caller ID device so we'd know when it was safe to pick up. After that, we screened every call.

On Mother's Day after the shootings, a friend who is a talented gardener scoured the bargain section at a local nursery. When I returned home, I was greeted by a profusion of spring color from the neglected pots on my porch: verbena, petunias, dianthus, lobelia, marigolds. It was a gift of beauty, and of herself, and it provided me with the surprising news that I could still appreciate such a thing.

In order to cope with our grief, and to piece together what had been going on in Dylan's mind, we needed to talk with people who'd known him, but I had no desire to put any of our friends in a position where they might be forced to testify in a trial. (We were not supposed to talk about anything with legal significance, but everything had legal significance.) I'm naturally forthcoming, and was used to sharing my thoughts freely with the people I cared about. Our lawyer told me I could talk about my own feelings, and so I did. The people around me were kind enough to listen, even when I told the same stories over and over again.

All I could do was take and not give back. I had never needed the kindness of others more than I did at that time, and I never did a poorer job of expressing my gratitude. This feeling added to my pervasive sense of guilt. My short-term memory had disappeared. I couldn't remember whom I'd thanked, or if I'd said anything at all to express my appreciation. I kept a notebook to help me remember what I had said and done, but I'm still convinced I failed to convey my gratitude to everyone who deserved it.

By the end of our first week back home, we knew we couldn't leave Littleton. The people who knew Dylan *before*—who remembered the day he pitched a victorious no-hitter, who could laugh about the time he ate an entire bucket of KFC by himself, or who'd been put into stitches by one of his dry asides—they were there, too, willing to share their memories of him. How would we survive without them?

Besides, could we ever truly run from this? There would never be a way to escape from the horror of what Dylan had done. No mere relocation could distance us from the truth, or from its stain. No matter where we went, this horror would follow.

• • •

Wandering around the house alone trying to function.
—Journal entry, April 1999

In the early 1970s, I worked as an art therapist at a psychiatric hospital in Milwaukee. One day I overheard Betty, one of our patients with schizophrenia, say, "I'm just sick and tired of following my face around." In the weeks and months after Columbine, Betty's phrase came often to my mind. As my state of shock began to lift incrementally, waves of negative emotions overwhelmed me, and I toggled among debilitating sorrow, fear, anger, humiliation, anxiety, remorse, grief, powerlessness, pain, and hopelessness.

The feelings weren't new; they'd been my constant companions since I'd gotten that first message at my office from Tom. Whatever protective shield had minimized their impact in the earliest hours was becoming ever less efficient, though. As more days passed, the insulation keeping me from fully experiencing the reality of what Dylan had done began to fall away, and my emotions, when they came, were searing. I could no longer distance myself from the community's pain, or pretend my son hadn't caused this agony. Seeing a photograph of a victim's funeral on the cover of the local paper would leave me unable to move under the crushing weight of my grief and regret. I could barely function.

I had always been hyper-organized and efficient, the kind of person who loves nothing better than sailing through her daily to-do list. In the weeks following Columbine, if I got a single thing done in the course of a day—the dishwasher emptied, a bill paid—it was a good day. I couldn't yet go back to work, but my career in disability services had at least provided me with a context. The symptoms of intense grief—memory loss, attention deficit, emotional fragility, incapacitating fatigue—are surprisingly similar to those resulting from traumatic brain injury.

Some days, I worried I was losing my link to sanity. One morning, I sat on the edge of the bed trying to get dressed. I put one sock on, then stared into space for an hour before I could put on the other. It took me almost four hours to get dressed. Another afternoon, a friend called to see how I was doing. "I do nothing. Why am I so tired?" I asked, genuinely bewildered. She spoke from her own experience with loss: "You're not doing nothing. You're grieving, and it's hard work." My grief for Dylan was at the heart of everything. It would have been crushing under any circumstances, but it was further compounded by my lack of comprehension, and by my feelings of guilt over the destruction he had wrought. My world had been rocked off its axis.

Friends who knew I often turned to art in times of trouble brought me art books and new sketchbooks to tempt me, but it was impossible for me to open them. Wearing bright colors made me feel physically ill. A life once filled with work and family activities and house maintenance and art and friends had come to a screeching halt. The long evening walks I took with our neighbors in the cliffs surrounding our home provided my only relief.

At the beginning of May, the school decided Dylan's closest circle of friends would not be allowed to attend their own graduation ceremony, scheduled for the end of the month.

At first, the unfairness of the decision aroused a real anger in me, and a sense of protectiveness for Dylan's friends. They were good kids and they were hurting, too. Most of them had reached out to us to offer their support, and to tell us they'd been as blindsided as we had been. A number of them had come over to our house, bearing photographs and videos of Dyl, and cards he'd given them. Zack's girlfriend, Devon, made a book for us of photographs and written memories, mounted on paper she'd made herself. There was Dylan—grinning while pushing Zack's dad into the pool; sporting a Hawaiian shirt and a bunch of leis at a costume party Devon had thrown; clowning around with Zack and making a hokey thumbs-up sign for the camera. I spent hours poring over these artifacts, desperate for confirmation that the sensitive, fun-loving kid Tom and I remembered had been real.

Upon reflection, my anger about graduation abated, and a grim resignation took its place. Who was I to be angry, even on someone else's behalf? These were extraordinary circumstances. There was no manual for how to proceed in the wake of the worst school shooting in history.

Afterward, Dylan's friends scattered like beads from a broken necklace. Not surprisingly, many of them suffered serious difficulties for years. Nate stopped by our house on his way out of town. He asked for an item to remember his friend by, a request that moved me, and I was happy to see him choose a pair of Dylan's sunglasses—they reminded us both of Dylan, in happier times.

But Nate had something to tell us, too. He'd seen Dylan give a large wad of money to a guy they worked with at Blackjack Pizza. When Nate pressed him, Dylan told him the money was for a gun.

We were dumbfounded by this news. Even Tom was willing to finally express anger toward Dylan for lying to us. We had been clinging to the belief that Dylan was an innocent victim, ensnared by Eric at the last minute—and yet here was evidence that he had taken an active role in buying a gun, more evidence that my son had not been the person I thought he was.

A month after the shootings, I sent the letters I had written to the families of the people who had been killed. Our lawyer watched the news for a response. (I still couldn't turn on the television.) As we had expected, the families' reactions were wildly diverse. Some appreciated the effort. Others were angry; at least one of the families tore my letter up, unread. There was no single point of view. In the weeks and months and years to come, when an individual or family acted aggressively, it helped me to remember they did not necessarily represent all the families involved.

I received two written responses from victims' families in the months that followed. One letter was from the teenaged sibling of one of the murdered girls. She said she did not blame us for the tragedy, and I wept with sadness and joy. Then, on my birthday eleven months later, we received a letter from the father of one of the boys who was killed in the school library. He reached out with compassion and said he wished he could help us in some way. The letter felt like a gift from heaven. We got permission from our lawyer to write back, but we did not meet for several years because of the many lawsuits against our family.

The small sense of accomplishment I'd gained from sending the letters to the victims' families was short-lived. There were far more losses than the thirteen who had been killed. I felt I also needed to write to the twenty-four others who had been injured. There were students who would never walk again, and those who would live in constant pain. After years of working with students living with disabilities, I had an idea of the hardships the injured students and their families would have to endure. I thought of the physical and psychological agony they must be experiencing, and the ongoing drain on financial resources. Some would have to adjust to new identities that would affect every aspect of their lives. Even if we were held financially responsible, there was not enough money in the world to relieve the suffering Dylan had caused.

The second set of letters—to the families of surviving victims— took many more weeks for me to write than the first. Again, I was struck by the inadequacy of my message, and by the flimsiness of mere words in the face of everything that had been lost. How dare I interject myself into their lives? But I felt I had to do something.

· · ·

I'm sick of waking up each day with a broken heart, of missing Dylan and wanting to scream loud enough to wake up from the nightmare my life has become. I want to hold Dylan in my arms again, to cuddle him as I did years ago, to hold him in my lap and help him with his shoes or a puzzle. I want to talk to him, and stop him from even considering this horrible act.

—Journal entry, May 11, 1999

There is a scene at the end of the movie *Raiders of the Lost Ark* where Indiana Jones is tied, back to back, to the heroine of the movie. They can do nothing but close their eyes as vicious flying spirits unleash a storm of destruction around them. Tom and I were similarly tied to each other, utterly exposed and unable to escape, and we did not know if there would be anything left of our lives when the hurricane passed. Our grief only increased with each revelation about Dylan.

Immediately after the shootings, we went to one of the therapists recommended in a letter from the county coroner. Tom and Byron went a few times but soon came to the conclusion that the sessions weren't helping. I stayed with it longer, though the therapist and I were barely scratching the surface of my pain. He seemed overwhelmed by our situation, and by the magnitude of what we were dealing with. He read the papers, watched the news, and surfed the Internet to gauge the world's reaction. When I walked into a counseling session, he would swivel away from his computer and allude to the threats made against us in the press or online. I was trying to insulate myself from that kind of fear and negativity, so these reports made me anxious. I'm sure the therapist was simply concerned about our safety, but at times he seemed considerably more preoccupied with the external factors around us than with my emotional state.

We did a few exercises to deal with grief, such as writing letters to Dylan, but Tom and I could not begin the hard work of facing the loss of a child. How could we? We were swept away by the madness engulfing us. Our grief for Dylan was buried under the difficulties of living with the life he had created for us.

It was becoming increasingly clear, too, that Tom and I were going in different directions with our pain. Tom's a born entrepreneur with none of my innate caution, always happy to dig into a new project without stopping to worry about how difficult or expensive it will be to complete. I'd fallen in love with his creativity, and had been enthralled by his risk-taking and lack of fear. We had always been strongly attracted to each other, and we shared the same sense of humor. Who you are dictates how you proceed through the grief process, though, and the extremity of the situation we were in began to highlight how different Tom and I really were.

Tom was looking for an explanation: bullies, the school, the media, Eric. None of that made sense to me. Although I was still maintaining some level of denial about the degree to which Dylan had been involved, it was easier for me to believe he had been crazy—or even evil—than to pretend anything he'd experienced could justify what he'd done.

While I took comfort from our visitors, Tom found it easier to be alone. It seemed to me that he wanted to control the lawyers working with us, whereas I was painfully aware we were out of our depth and felt grateful when a professional with expertise could tell us what to do.

Our marriage had been successful for almost thirty years because we complemented each other. But after Columbine, we couldn't seem to agree about anything. We were both riding the same roller coaster, but we were never in the same place at the same time. If Tom was sad, I was angry. If I was angry, he was sad. I'd always been able to brush off Tom's cranky moods, and to laugh at his colorful rants. When you're grieving in such an extreme way, though, your tolerance for stress is diminished. It was like the skin had been flayed right off me, leaving no layer of protection between me and overwhelming emotion. In my journal, I wrote:

Tom's words sound like a jackhammer to me, even those uttered most quietly. His thoughts are never aligned with mine. They always come from far away, and they're totally foreign to my thinking.

Our relationship with Byron was strained, too. He'd moved back home several weeks after his brother's death. By that time, he'd lived in his own apartment for two years and had grown used to being independent. Tom and I couldn't stop wringing our hands and prying into his personal life; we thought our failure to pry into Dylan's had caused Columbine. But we were barely rational, a point brought home to us one night when Byron went out to dinner with a friend.

The weather was bad, and Tom and I couldn't sleep for worrying about the treacherous conditions on the winding roads leading up to our house. We finally heard Byron's car pull into our drive around eleven, but he didn't come into the house as we expected. Instead, we heard strange clinking sounds from our garage, and then his car pulled out again at top speed.

We panicked. Our heads were filled with worst-case scenarios: weapons, drugs, suicide, theft, murder. Had Byron come home for a hidden gun or other contraband? Had he stashed illegal materials in our garage? Should we call the police?

Twenty minutes later, over the sound of our pounding hearts, we heard Byron's car pull in at a more leisurely speed. He was badly startled to find the two of us, wild-eyed in our pajamas, waiting for him at the top of the stairs. The proverbial hooves we'd heard had been a horse, not a zebra: on his way home, Byron had passed a car that had skidded off the slick road. He'd come home to get a chain from the garage so he could help the other driver out of the ditch.

After that night, I extracted a promise from him that he would never intentionally hurt himself or anyone else. I was surprised to find he needed the same reassurance from me. We were beginning to fall into the complicated pattern that would define our relationship in the years after the shootings, even as we became closer than we'd ever been. I'd encourage him to talk about his feelings, but when he confessed to despair (rational, under the circumstances), I worried he'd harm himself. It was a terribly unfair position to put him in. I was asking him to reassure me he was okay—really, I was asking him to *be* okay—when of course he was not. It would take us a long time to find a way to talk about our devastation while assuring one another we were still committed to life.

In reality, I am not sure we were. On many days, dying seemed easier than living. All three of us talked about death, ashes, epitaphs, the meaning of life. Tom said he knew what his last words would be: "Thank God it's over."

. . .

I read mail for five hours, crying nearly the whole time. Two boxes now, one from the post office and one from the lawyer. So many cards and letters of love and support, and yet one hate letter and I am shattered.

—Journal entry, May 1999

Much has been written about the need most people have, in the aftermath of a tragedy like Columbine, to assign blame. Whether it was the scale of the tragedy, or the senselessness, or a thousand other reasons I can think of, Columbine became—and remains—a lightning rod. People blamed video games, movies, music, bullying, access to guns, unarmed teachers, the absence of prayer in schools, secular humanism, psychiatric medication. Mostly, though, they blamed us.

To me, that made sense. If I had been sitting in my living room, shaking out the pages of the freshly delivered *Rocky Mountain News* with Dylan bagging up the kitchen garbage behind me and Byron happily and untidily ensconced in his apartment across town, I would have blamed us too.

Didn't I wonder about a criminal's family whenever I heard about a terrible act of violence? Didn't I think, *What on earth did the parents do to that poor child so he could grow up to do something like that? A child raised with love, in a loving home, could never have done such a thing.* For years, and without a second thought, I'd accepted explanations laying the blame squarely with the criminal's family. Obviously, the parents had been oblivious, irresponsible, secretly abusive. Of course the mother had been a shrew, a smotherer, a doormat.

That was why I was so surprised when people we'd never met began to reach out to our family, in sympathy both for our loss and for our predicament. It is also why I have such esteem and appreciation for the victims' families who reached out without blame. They cannot know, as I do, what it is to be the mother of a killer, yet they are able to operate from a place of compassion. That is remarkable to me. It is something I am not sure I would have been able to do.

Just days after the shootings, our lawyer handed us a cardboard box containing a hand-painted ceramic angel, a frozen dinner of creamed chicken and biscuits, and a few condolence cards—all gestures of sympathy from people we had never met. That trickle of consideration turned into a stream, and then a flood. People wrote from all over the country, and the world. All they needed was our name and "Littleton, CO" on the envelope, and their words and gifts found their way to us.

A lot of the mail came from people Tom and I had known at various times in our lives: elementary school classmates, teachers, coworkers, and former students. Some were from families in the area whose kids had known Dylan, sharing their memories of him. I read those many times. Lots of the letters were from strangers, though, and a great many of them were anonymous. We received prayers, poems, books, plaques, toys, children's drawings, and handmade objects. People made charitable donations in Dylan's memory. They sent cash and checks, which we returned.

People from all walks of life wrote to us: clergymen, attorneys, teachers, social workers, policemen, United States Marines, and prisoners. The generosity was astonishing. People offered legal services, confidential talks, massages, and private cabins where we could hide from the press.

A great many people wrote to tell us they were dismayed to see local memorials held for thirteen and not fifteen victims. They wrote to let me know their own religious organizations or social groups had remembered all fifteen—at concerts where Dylan's name had been read out with the names of the other victims, or masses where prayers had been said for his soul. I was grateful for those letters. For me, there had been fifteen victims. Although I understood the response in my own community, it was still hard for me to accept that Dylan's entire life had no value at all because of what he had done before he died.

It had been reported extensively in the media that Dylan and Eric had been bullied, and so we received letters from people of all ages who had been bullied in high school. I did not know Dylan had been bullied, and the shock of needing to readjust my image of him was extreme. Regardless, I was moved by the letter writers' descriptions of the blind rage, depression, and helplessness that result from feeling so powerless. "I'm not surprised it happened. I'm surprised it didn't happen at my school, too, and that it doesn't happen every day at schools across America," one young man wrote, after sharing his own high school experiences of being afraid to go to the bathroom or walk the halls. Young people wrote directly to Dylan, pouring out their sorrow and hatred for their own school culture, and I wondered if anyone around them knew of the grief they were carrying inside.

Many of the people who wrote shared personal experiences of loss. Some wrote about their own family's experience with mental illness and suicide. Those letters helped me tremendously, as did the ones where parents and grandparents shared stories about hardship and humiliation caused by a family member.

A minister wrote to share that his son was serving a life sentence for murder. I read that letter often. One of the (many) things I felt guilt about in the wake of the tragedy was my fear that I had failed to impart a proper religious education. I had taught Dylan right from wrong every minute of the day, but we hadn't regularly attended a church or a synagogue since the boys were small. It was silly—a single example was no kind of sample size—yet I took great comfort from knowing that in this one instance, at least, regular Sunday school hadn't been enough to stop a child from making a terrible choice.

Our lawyer assigned a member of his staff to go through and remove any hate mail or death threats. Despite his efforts to shield us, we did receive hate mail. And one negative letter obliterated the positive effects of hundreds of supportive ones.

One letter writer demanded in black marker: **"HOW COULD YOU NOT KNOW??!"**

It was, of course, the question I asked myself day and night. I had not imagined myself to be a perfect parent, by any stretch of the imagination. I did, however, believe my close connection (and not just to Dylan, but to both of my sons) meant I would be able to intuit if something was wrong, especially if something was very wrong. I would never have told you I had access to Dylan's every thought and feeling, but I would have said, with confidence, that I knew exactly what he was capable of. And I would have been wrong.

"There but for the grace of God, go I," one mother wrote. She was living with a violent, mentally ill child, and described eloquently how she woke up every day dreading a phone call bearing terrible news about her son, like the one I had received from Tom. It was a sentiment many others would echo over the years. One letter offered prayers of support, and was signed *From a Death Row Mom*.

We received a few letters from the families of victims of other shootings. One man's son was killed in junior high school, and he eloquently shared his initial feelings of outrage, pain, and numbness. That letter gave me a little insight into what the victims' families might be suffering. People wrote who had lost a child, like the young mother whose toddler suffered a fatal head injury when she fell within reach of family members. Those letters enabled me to connect to the part of me that was simply grieving Dylan. Of course, we heard from many people who had lost loved ones to suicide. I couldn't yet fully understand Dylan's death as a suicide, but those letters helped me to begin. I would later have the opportunity to meet many of the people who wrote.

Though we were isolated from our local community in many ways, these letters helped me to feel kinship with others on a global scale. Many more people than I'd ever imagined had experienced extreme hardships and loss. There was a devastating amount of pain out there in the world. It was as if we had tapped in to a deep wellspring of universal suffering. I wondered daily at people's compassion, and at their generosity. One card read simply, "God Bless Your Family," in the painstaking and shaky handwriting of a very elderly person, and I marveled at the enormous and possibly painful effort a stranger across the country had made—to get the card and the stamp, to write the note, to mail it—just so I would not feel so alone. These were people with an emotional bandwidth, a depth and breadth of understanding, that had come from pain in their own lives.

Unfortunately, it was still too early for me to take comfort from the stories of their survival. I still did not believe there would be an "after."

Like so many things that happened to us after the shootings, there was no way to respond normally to the mail we were getting. I responded personally to the first notes, and intended to continue, but the boxes of mail came, and came, and came. My grandfather had once written a thank-you note in response to a particularly

beautiful thank-you note he'd received, so this failure to acknowledge the generosity of people who'd reached out landed hard with
me. I hated the idea that people who had taken the time and made
the effort to express sympathy would go without thanks, but I simply couldn't keep up.

I stacked the letters around us, filling plastic bins to sort and
organize them, until they took over our family room. I developed a
triage system to prioritize those requiring a personal response, with
people who had shared their own despair and suicidal thoughts at
the top. I responded to many of the letters, but it was only a small
percentage. I stopped counting cards and letters when they reached
3,600, and they continued to arrive long after I was no longer
counting.

My guilt was amplified by the scathing criticism we were receiving from every quarter. We were pilloried daily in the press,
often for decisions I didn't even fully understand. For example, our
attorneys advised us to file our intent to put the sheriff's department on notice, a routine legal strategy to keep our options open if
new information about the case became available. Through it all,
we would maintain a positive working relationship with the sheriff's department, continuing to communicate and eager to help
in any way we could. But the stories in the media came quickly
after the decision, and made it seem as if we were going to sue
the sheriff's department for what our son had done. News stories
like this one drew an astonishing amount of vitriol. "Those parents are disgusting," one person seethed on a talk radio broad-
cast I accidentally heard while changing radio stations in my car.
People thought we should be jailed, hunted like animals, tortured, shot. I still can't look at comment sections of articles about
Columbine.

I was never able to escape the humiliation and fear that such
remarks left behind. I'd always thought of myself as a good citizen
and a good mother, and now I was being paraded through town as
the worst parent who'd ever lived. For the first time in my life, I
was living as an outcast, judged and rejected by others for circumstances over which I had no control. Dylan had unwittingly pro-

vided an opportunity for us to understand how he must have felt during the last years of his life.

We lived in a small psychological space following Dylan's death: one in which we were still attentive, well-meaning, loving parents who had lost our son. The only way we could survive was by minimizing our exposure to the negativity, and so we withdrew. Every time someone attempted to speak on our behalf, their words were twisted and misrepresented in the media. So we surrounded ourselves with friends and locked ourselves away from the rest of the world. We did not respond to even the most egregious accusations.

I am not sure refusing to engage was the best strategy. Our failure to speak up in our own defense made people believe we were hiding secrets. It felt, and still feels, wrong to let untruths stand—especially since many of the misconceptions about our family and how we raised Dylan are perceived to be true to this day.

· · ·

I'm tired of being strong. I can't be strong any more. I can't face or do anything. I'm lost in a deep chasm of sorrow. I have 17 phone messages and don't have the energy to listen to them. Dylan's room is just as the law enforcement people left it, and I can't face putting it in order.

—Journal entry, May 1999

During our first days back at home, we had made disjointed efforts to reclaim the house, but Dylan's room remained as the police had left it, with his possessions spilling out onto the mezzanine, and his stripped mattress leaning against the upstairs banister.

In the month after his death, I began to make daily forays into the room, putting a few things in order before the strength of my feelings overwhelmed me and I had to flee. I lingered in particular over Dylan's bathroom sink. Wisps of his blond hair remained in his comb, and his whiskers filled an electric razor we'd bought him.

It wasn't only the strength of my grief that held me back from doing more. Every time I disinfected a surface or laundered a hamper of dirty clothes, I was destroying traces Dylan had left behind. The idea of erasing him broke my heart, and I worried that with every emptied wastebasket I was losing opportunities to understand the last hours of his life. Of course, the investigators had taken everything they thought might be relevant, but I was still searching for answers in the wreckage left behind.

I was no closer to understanding what he had been thinking and feeling, or how the kid I loved and raised could have participated in an atrocity like this. What could possibly explain his state of mind? Had there been drugs in his system, undetected by the autopsy? Had there been outside influences? Organized crime, perhaps? Even if Eric had masterminded a plan and urged Dylan to participate, Dylan was a smart kid. He could have found a way to get himself out of it if he wanted to. Why hadn't he? Had Eric coerced or threatened him? Had Dylan been brainwashed? At one point, Byron asked seriously if Dylan could have been possessed. A month before, I would have laughed out loud at such a ridiculous idea, but in our new reality, demonic possession seemed as plausible an answer as any.

We had no gravesite, so I spent hours in Dylan's room trying to intuit the answers to the questions plaguing us. I was shocked to find a pack of cigarettes in one of his drawers. Not long before he died, I'd thought I smelled tobacco on him, and asked him outright if he was smoking. He gave me an exasperated look and said, "I'm not *that* stupid!" It seemed as if he had real disdain for the practice, and I'd believed him. The cigarettes in his drawer suggested he'd straight-out lied.

I was also saddened to find a nearly empty bottle of St. John's-wort in Dylan's medicine cabinet. I'd been in his bathroom lots of times in the previous months, to make sure he was keeping it clean, but I'd never looked inside the medicine cabinet. St. John's-wort is a natural antidepressant found at health food stores and drugstores. Here was bald, incontrovertible evidence that Dylan had been depressed enough to try to alleviate those feelings through medication. The expiration date on the bottle indicated he'd had it a long time.

I was beginning to appreciate how gullible I had been. Our mail was filled with letters from people, mostly adults, confessing the illicit activities they'd hidden from their parents when they were themselves teenagers: sexual exploits, drug use, theft. A few of the stories were funny—foolish adolescent decisions with happy endings. (One letter writer had been apprehended by the police on the roof of his childhood home without any pants on.) But most were tragic, and represented years of painful silence.

This collective unburdening was taking place in our own circle of friends, too. Almost everyone who visited told me something they'd hidden from their parents during their teenage years: drinking and drug use, a road trip to Vegas, years of drugstore shoplifting, a much-older boyfriend. Prompted by the events at Columbine, one friend finally admitted to his father (and to us) that as a young boy he had been sexually molested by their neighbor over a period of years. I caught myself silently wondering what everyone in the world was wondering about me: *How could his dad not have noticed something so huge?*

We also received a letter, postmarked April 27, 1999, which I reprint here with permission of the author, although I have changed names and places to protect the privacy of those involved. It came from Cindy Worth, a woman of about our age. Tom had known her family growing up, and had stayed in touch with them through the years. We both admired the Worths; they were successful and happy, pillars of their church—*good* people—and I was always struck by how loving and close they were to one another.

With real sadness and alarm, we read the following:

Dear Tom, Sue and Byron,

Forgive me for the length of this letter, but there is so much to say. I hope that by sharing my story with you, you will find some comfort and peace and better understand why Dylan didn't talk to you about the pain and anger he was suffering.

Mom and Dad moved to Colorado [when] I was 14 years old. Almost from the start, I was harassed by a group of boys who called me "Flipper" because my nose is long. They would walk behind me in the school hallways and sing the theme song to the Flipper TV show. They hung used tampons and kotex in my locker, and stole letters from my notebook. They read unmailed letters to my friends back home in the boy's locker room before football practice.

The culmination to the harassment occurred when I was raped by a football player. He boasted to his friends that it would have been "better" had he not looked at my ugly face.

I never told Mom and Dad—not until a couple of days ago. I wanted them to know—and I want you to know—why I didn't tell them. It might help to understand why Dylan didn't talk to you about his problems.

I felt a tremendous amount of shame about being a target of harassment and assault. I can tell you from first-hand experience that young people blame themselves for the pain they suffer. I believed there must have been something wrong with me for people to treat me this way.

I wanted Mom and Dad to think the best of me. I assumed that if I told them what happened, they would think of me as I thought of myself—flawed and ugly.

I was too young and confused to recognize that what had happened was a crime. I thought that if I told anyone, the taunting would get worse.

I suffered in silence for about 3 months, all the while becoming more and more depressed. I was contemplating suicide when I met someone who, literally, saved my life.

Ken was a funny-looking, outgoing, joyful kind of guy, somewhat of an outsider himself, but it didn't seem to bother him. He sought me out and became my friend. After several weeks I felt safe enough with him to tell him what happened. This sweet, gentle 14-year-old boy had enough wisdom to listen and hug me while I shed gallons of tears. Ken grew up to become a minister. He was and always will be MY minister.

This is what SHOULD have happened for Dylan. A friend, a peer, should have been there for him. A friend who could guide Dylan away from anger and depression, not feed it.

Please know this. This friend could not have been you, Tom and Sue, as his parents. Or you, Byron, as his brother. The process of growing up and separation makes it *extremely difficult* for children to seek out their parents and siblings for help with these hidden, painful problems.

I believe with every fiber in my body and stirring in my soul that Dylan is with the Lord and that we will see him and rejoice with him again.

I love you. We love you. We are lifting you up.

Cindy

Tom and I reread this letter many times. Tom had known Cindy her whole life; I'd known her more than twenty years. Our children had celebrated their birthdays together. Neither of us would ever have imagined she'd experienced anything such as she described— either the bullying or the rape—or that she'd been so close to suicide. We spoke to her devastated parents a week or two later. They had also been utterly shocked by what they'd learned.

Among other things, Cindy's letter validated for us how a child's personal devastation could go undetected by the most watchful parents, teachers, and peers if they chose to keep it concealed. I had been a teacher at the college level for most of my career, and knew well that young adults snuck around, hiding six-packs of beer and furtive smooches in the parking lot. Still, I would not have thought it possible for a kid to hide an event as earthshaking as rape, or thoughts and feelings as serious as suicidal ideation, especially from parents like the Worths. Each day brought a new shock to illuminate how painfully naive—and dangerous—this belief of mine had been.

More than anything, Cindy's letter made me long to talk with Dylan. A running dialogue with him played in my head like background music in a constant, exhausting loop. In the earliest days at Ruth and Don's house, my doctor had written me a prescription for anti-anxiety medication. I took it only once. The tamping down of my anxiety sent my grief surging full-force to the surface. I was unable to stop crying, as if a tap had gotten stuck in the "on" position. After that, I had decided to live with my emotions without medication.

There was no point, I was beginning to realize, in trying to avoid or outrun the confusion or the grief. The best I could do was simply try to survive it—and, in the months and years to come, to do everything in my power to understand all the things I had not known about my son.

CHAPTER 8

A Place of Sorrow

This library had been a place for innocent children, a place where they should have been safe, and now they were all dead.

—Journal entry, June 1999

In early June of 1999, we read in the newspaper that family members of the victims were being invited to visit the school library, where many of their children had died, before renovations gutted the room.

I knew Dylan could never be considered a victim of Columbine, and we understood why we had not been contacted. Yet we needed to see the place where Dylan had taken his own life, and the lives of so many others. Our lawyer spoke to the sheriff's department and arranged a visit. We had been living more or less in hiding since the shootings, so we met the lawyers in the parking lot of a hardware store in order to switch cars. The cloak-and-dagger routine, for once, did not feel absurd.

The school was still a crime scene. As soon as I saw the yellow tape, my heart thundered in my chest. As we walked through the corridors, we saw construction workers repairing the damage Dylan and Eric had caused. Patches of black soot on the carpets, walls, and ceilings showed where they had tossed small explosives as they walked through the school. Ceiling tiles had been removed, and sections of the carpets. Sheets of clear plastic covered shattered windows. Not for the first or last time, I was dumbfounded by the magnitude of the damage my son had caused. Workers looked down at us from ladders, and I wondered if they knew who we were.

The library door was locked, covered with a sheet of plastic, and swathed in yellow police tape. Before we entered, the sheriff's department told us we were there to see where our son had died, and that was all. I felt grateful for the professionalism of the police, and for the respect they showed to all the victims.

I was trembling when we entered. Always looking for answers, I wanted to believe that seeing where Dylan and the others had died would provide me with a revelation, some insight. I hoped I would walk into the room and understand something vital about the events of that day, and about Dylan's state of mind, and I tried to set my sorrow aside so I could receive any truth occupying the space.

The moment I walked into the room, everything fell silent. I could no longer hear the repairs being made in the hallway. I sensed only two things before I was overtaken by tears. I felt the presence of children, and I felt peace.

The police led us to the place where Eric and Dylan had shot themselves. My heart caught when I saw the long, lean, angular shape marked out on the floor. Of course that was Dylan; it looked just like him. My tears splashed the floor. Byron's gentle hand was on my back as I knelt beside the shape resembling my son and touched the carpet that held him when he fell.

CHAPTER 9

Life with Grief

Quote in the paper about cancer patients. It said "The people who do well create a place in their mind and their spirit where they are well, and they live from that place." This is what we are doing. Tom's analogy is that a tornado has destroyed our house, and we can only live in one part of it. This is what living with grief is like. You dwell in that small place where you can function.

—Journal entry, August 1999

The theologian C. S. Lewis begins *A Grief Observed*, his beautiful meditation on the death of his wife, with these words: "No one ever told me that grief felt so like fear."

Years later, those words still hit me with the full weight of the unassailably true. Any loved one's death, especially the death of a child, shakes you at your very foundation. As Iris Bolton, a suicide loss survivor and author, has written, "I thought I was immortal, that my children and my family were also, that tragedy happened only to others." We need to believe this in order to survive, and the truth laid bare can be terrifying. For me, the incomprehensibility of the way Dylan died magnified these feelings of instability at the foundation of my identity by throwing everything I believed to be true about the life I'd lived, about my family, and about myself into question.

One of the students I worked with when I was still at the community college shared with me one of the most difficult things about living with her disability.

"Everyone sees the disability first. To them, I'm an amputee before I'm a person," she told me.

At the time, I was grateful to her for the insight because I knew it would help me in my work. After Columbine, though, I knew exactly what she meant. I was certain I would always be seen as the woman who raised a murderer, and that no one—including me—would ever see me as anything else.

. . .

Though I was fifty years old, in the months after Columbine I felt keenly the loss of my own parents. I was grateful they hadn't lived to see what my life had become but longed, childlike, for the simple reassurance of their presence.

My father died when I was eighteen, but I was thirty-eight when I lost my mother, and I relied on her long after I became an adult. At her funeral, my siblings and I referred to her as the North Star, a tribute to her unerring gift for helping us to find our bearings in life even in the most turbulent of circumstances. I suspect that is why, in the months and years after Columbine, I dreamed about her almost as often as I dreamed about Dylan.

In one dream I had soon after the tragedy, it was night and a cold wind was blowing. I was searching for my car in an enormous parking lot while clutching Dylan, about two years old, in my arms. I tried to wrap a blanket around him to keep him warm as I walked up and down the rows looking for the car in increasing desperation, but huge, heavy shopping bags filled with papers hung from my arms. These made it so difficult to carry Dylan that I worried I would drop him onto the pavement.

Just as he was beginning to slip from my grasp, my mother stepped forward. She said, "Give me the bags. You take care of your son." One by one, she lifted the heavy handles cutting into my wrists and arms, allowing me to hold Dylan tightly, and wrap the blanket securely around him. I found our car and placed Dylan safely in his car seat while my mother stood by, holding the bags she'd taken from me. Then I woke up.

The dream revealed the path I needed to follow. The papers in the bags represented everything pulling me away from my grief:

worry about the lawsuits, money concerns, fear of seeing my name in the newspapers, the thousands of letters and bills and notices and legal documents taking over our den in enormous drifts of fear and obligation. It was easy for me to get overwhelmed by the constant media assault, the world's hatred and blame, not to mention my constant anxiety that something terrible would happen to Byron. Our financial situation emerged as completely disastrous, and so complicated that it seemed we would never dig ourselves out of the hole.

But my mother was right. I had to focus on grieving for Dylan and his victims, and let go of everything else.

That was difficult. Even if I hadn't been incapacitated by grief, the sheer administrative weight of what we were dealing with would have overwhelmed me. A month after the tragedy, Tom and I were still wandering the rooms of our empty house like ghosts, dazed by loss and remorse, haunted by the same circular thoughts. *I miss Dylan. How could he do such a horrible thing? I can't believe I'll never see him again. How could someone I loved so much murder people in cold blood? Other children? If only I'd known, said the magic words, done whatever it took to stop him. How could he have done such a thing?*

And then, always, always, the impossibility and permanence of the loss: *How can it be possible I will never again feel his scratchy cheek against mine?*

Periodically, we'd be jolted back into a kind of frenetic energy—if not by a renewed realization of what Dylan had done, then by the myriad ways the ramifications of his actions would destroy the home and the life and the family we'd spent twenty-seven years building. Though Gary Lozow significantly discounted his legal services, the first bill we received shocked us into reality. We had absolutely no idea how we would pay it. In that instance, my mother stepped forward from the grave to help us. Before she died in 1987, when the boys were small, she bought life insurance policies for both of them. Dylan's two policies were paid out to us after his death, and they exactly covered the amount of that first bill.

It was only a drop in the bucket, though, and there would be years of legal bills ahead. Tom tried to find consulting work in the oil field, but there were few opportunities, and those that did come up disappeared quickly when potential investors learned he was the father of one of the shooters in the Columbine tragedy.

Our insurance company took some time to decide whether they would cover our legal expenses at all. When they finally agreed to, we learned they wouldn't cover our working with Gary. This was devastating, as he'd come to feel more like a trusted friend than an attorney—an oasis of sanity in the madness. Starting over with outsiders was emotionally difficult, but our new attorneys, Frank Patterson and Gregg Kay, were compassionate and patient with us as we showed them family photos and talked about our lives with Dylan. I needed to feel they knew us as a family, that they knew Dylan. Before long, we grew comfortable with them.

Even with their help, each day brought a mountain of incomprehensible paperwork and decisions made more distressing because we couldn't fully understand their implications. Everybody was suing somebody else. There were lawsuits against Dylan's friend Robyn, who'd bought three of the four guns; and Mark Manes, who'd sold them the other one. There were lawsuits against the companies that manufactured the guns, and against the company that made Eric's antidepressant medication. There were lawsuits against the sheriff's department, the county, and the police. Thirty-six lawsuits would ultimately be filed against us. Our lawyers were meticulous, and did their best to explain what was going on, but the complexity of our legal situation was far beyond my ability to grasp it.

To be honest, although the lawyers were exercised about it, my own feeling was: *Who cares?* To the extent that the lawsuits would provide a parent with the money to take care of a grievously wounded child, I was glad for them. But the lawsuits wouldn't give parents their children back. They wouldn't return Dave Sanders, the teacher who had been shot, to his family. Lawsuits wouldn't give us the opportunity to do a thousand things differently, or provide us with an explanation of how the unthinkable had happened. And they wouldn't bring Dylan back.

· · ·

Yesterday was terrible. After it took me 4½ hours to get up, the rest of the day wasn't much better. I cried and cried and just couldn't get it together. I talked to S. in the afternoon and told her I couldn't go back to work, after I'd just told her I could.

—Journal entry, May 1999

A month after Columbine, I was on the phone with Susie, my supervisor from work. She'd been terrific about checking in with me on a regular basis, occasionally delivering a meal, or a plant tied with good wishes from my coworkers. (Years of accumulated sick leave and unused personal days within the state community college system were the only reason I still had a job at all.)

I was crying, as usual. Susie listened for a while, and then she said: "I think you should come back to work."

The idea startled me into silence. Returning to work would be impossible, preposterous. How in the world could I think about anything else but Dylan and the disaster he created? How could I leave the safety of my home, and face people who never knew Dylan the way I'd known him, the way I'd loved him?

"I can't do it," I said.

Gently, she persisted. Yes, we'd have to work out the details, but it would be good for me, and my colleagues could use my help. "What if I gathered a project you could do from home? Something with no deadline you could work on at your own speed?" I didn't have the energy to protest. It was easier to agree than to push back.

The innocuous package Susie sent later that week sat untouched for days. Once I began, I could maybe get an hour's worth of work done in a day—and on many days I couldn't even do that. Returning to work for real seemed utterly hopeless.

But I needed to reconnect to a part of my identity that had nothing to do with being Dylan's mother, and tackling a project that could be completed also appealed. Our personal lives felt monumental, unscalable. Nothing would ever be resolved, understood, or finished. A work project, even in my severely compromised condition, could be done, and done well. So I kept at the little project, even on days when it took me an hour to write a coherent sentence.

Eventually I realized I couldn't do it properly without collaborating with the members of my team. As my supervisor had hoped, the small project hooked me back into life, and I began to make plans to return to work, part-time.

I did so with trepidation. This was a relatively new job for me, and while I enjoyed cordial relationships with my new coworkers, I didn't know any of them well. I worried that they didn't have an image of my son to counter the image of him blaring from every news channel. As for me—well, I was the mother of a murderer.

I couldn't stand thinking that the very fact of my presence would re-traumatize my colleagues. The community had suffered dreadfully, and tendrils reached into my workplace. The children and family members of some of my colleagues had been in the school and narrowly escaped with their lives. One coworker's husband, a teacher at the school, had almost been shot. His close friend Dave Sanders died that day. An administrator's daughter was in intensive therapy with post-traumatic stress disorder (PTSD). Each day brought a new headline about the investigation, the lawsuits, or the many conflicts brewing over access to information. Even if a coworker hadn't known anyone in the school, how could they be expected to know what to say when we bumped into each other getting coffee in the break room? How could they know how to work with me?

Fortunately, the community college system I worked for had an outstanding leader at the helm, a president who understood the complexity of the situation. She wanted to help me to be comfortable, while simultaneously ensuring my presence would not be unduly troubling for anyone else. A week before I returned, she sent a memo to all system office staff. Anyone concerned about working with me, she wrote, should come to her. A policy was already in place to help employees deal with the torrent of media inquiries, and a counselor would be made available to anyone who needed support. While it was difficult to be the subject of such a memo, I greatly appreciated the wisdom of it.

I met with a staffer in the human resources department to make arrangements for my privacy and safety. I was amazed that she spoke about the accommodations as if my experience had been an ordinary setback, like a chronic illness or a parent with Alzheimer's. We asked the receptionist to screen my calls, and to erase my schedule from the whiteboard. An administrator offered me her office so I could make personal calls behind a closed door. I slid my nameplate out from its bracket on my cubicle wall and tucked it away in my desk drawer.

A day or two before my return, the president sent one more memo, graciously hinting that my coworkers should give me enough personal space to find my equilibrium. She gently cautioned people not to overwhelm me with attention, though they might wish to offer their condolences. I was grateful for this wisdom, too.

Even with so much accommodation, my first day back at work was one of extreme emotional fragility. There was no room in my mind for anything but Dylan, and the horror of what he and Eric had done. I prayed I wouldn't see anyone in the elevator on my way in—not so much because I felt ashamed, but because a single kind word or touch would make me cry, and I sensed that if I lost control so early in the day, I'd never be able to regain it.

Several of my associates had worked from my cubicle in my absence, answering calls and doing their best to sustain the momentum of ongoing projects. I was an intruder in the space. Papers I didn't recognize were stacked in the corner; my computer's password had been changed. Worse was the black telephone on my desk, monstrous to me. For many months afterward, a wave of anxiety would sweep over me when I found the red message light flashing on my phone. But there were no messages that first morning.

Before long, people began to pass by. Some offered words of welcome and sympathy. Others gave me a quick hug.

I arrived late to our large monthly staff meeting. All the chairs were taken, so I joined the people leaning against the back wall. For the first time since the tragedy, I was in a room filled with people, some of whom I did not know. It was hard not to feel that everyone was focused on me, although they were scrupulously careful not to stare.

My stamina was still poor in those early days, and simply standing proved to be too much. A few minutes into the meeting, I found myself short of breath and too weak to stand. I worried that sitting on the floor would look unprofessional, and the last thing I wanted to do was draw attention to myself, but I was going to pass out. So I slid down the wall to the floor, rearranging my skirt over my knees as best I could.

I ended up sitting cross-legged behind a row of chairs. One of my colleagues made eye contact and offered his seat. It was a lovely gesture—minimal enough not to embarrass me, but telling me I was noticed and cared about. I shook my head. *No thanks; I'm okay. You stay where you are.* I spent the rest of the meeting on the floor, present but not present, watching the backs of people's knees and listening although I was unable to see who was speaking.

Small victories, as they say. I wanted to hide, but I was there.

. . .

I was at work from 9–2:30 and made it through 4 meetings. I fought the whole time to look and act normal. I was slumped down and exhausted. By the end of the day I was beaten. I have huge, looming thoughts, and trying to get out normal words and thoughts and actions are like trying to push an elephant through the eye of a needle. No one can understand what I've been through or am going through. It's all I can do to even attend or listen. When I got to my car after work, I shut the door and sobbed.

—Journal entry, June 1999

Although I did not realize it at the time, returning to work provided an essential framework for my recovery on many levels.

First of all, it allowed me to experience directly the compassion and sympathy other people were capable of. It made me cry to be hugged, but I learned to welcome the tears and not resist them. It was easier to allow myself to feel the sorrow than to suppress it. My colleagues walked the fine line of giving me my privacy while still showing compassion and myriad small kindnesses whenever they could. I doubt they will ever know how much they helped me.

In July, one of my coworkers came to my cubicle, representing the rest of the staff. In her arms was the most exquisite bouquet of dried flowers I had ever seen. We didn't know each other well, and her manner was formal when she said that no matter what my son had done, he was still my baby and everyone with children related to my loss. I could see she had no love lost for Dylan, and she probably couldn't understand why I had loved him either, but she was trying to find common ground. Gratitude overwhelmed me, and I was unable to speak.

Later in the fall, there was a craft sale in the break room, and I bought a couple of ornamental Christmas-themed pins to give to friends. I wrote a check and opened my wallet to show identification, but the woman working the cash box assured me it wasn't necessary. "Right," I said, putting my driver's license away. "Because who on earth would pretend to be me?" It was the kind of black humor that sustained me in those days; in my awkward way, I was trying to put her at ease. But there was genuine heartbreak on her face.

Nobody I worked with spoke to the press, although the calls were constant. One reporter tricked the receptionist into connecting him with my supervisor. Frustrated, he confronted her: "Why hasn't anyone there been willing to talk about Sue Klebold?"

"They're not talking because they're good people," Susie told him sharply, and it was true.

My first weeks back, I could only think about Dylan. I would cry for most of the long drive downtown in the morning, appreciating the private time to connect with my memories before trying to put him out of my mind so I could function for the day. The last thing I did each morning before leaving my car was look in the mirror and wipe off the salt marks on my cheeks left by tears.

Despite the patience of my colleagues and my best efforts to behave professionally, I was a wreck. I was paralyzed by self-consciousness in a way I remembered from my own adolescence. Because I was having chronic intestinal issues as a result of the stress, I was scared to eat in case I suffered an attack without a bathroom close by. I did what I could to reduce my anxiety level—I even stopped setting an alarm clock because the sound would leave me jangly for an hour afterward—to no avail.

A friend told me once that the brain "on grief" is like an older-model computer running a program drastically too complex for its capacity—it grinds and stutters and halts over the simplest calculation. It took great effort just to hear what others said. My powers of concentration were nowhere near restored, and racing thoughts about my personal situation and about Dylan kept me in a world of my own.

I took copious notes, but no productivity trick could compensate for the deficit. My face still burns when I remember the first meeting I led after the tragedy. I asked everyone to go around in a circle to introduce themselves and say a little about what they did. When the room fell silent, I unwittingly invited them to go around the circle and introduce themselves—again. The sideways glances and uncomfortable seat-shifting alerted me to my mistake, but there was nothing to do but stumble through my apology.

It took a long time for me to return to a full schedule. In the same way my evening walks were helping me to rebuild my physical strength, so did I have to regain the emotional capacity to be around others. Work was a rehabilitation of sorts, a safe environment where I could rebuild my identity and work through my unique grief experience. The families of the victims were always on my mind, especially how difficult it must have been for them to try to resume some semblance of a normal life after what Dylan had done.

As time went by, my constant anguish began to feel almost comical. Stashed handkerchiefs dropped out of notepads, calendars, sleeves, and my pockets when I stood up. I could always be relied upon to provide a Kleenex pack. Seasonal allergies? Ask Sue.

I hoped for kindness, and for the most part I got it, more than I felt I deserved. But not everyone was kind and understanding, and that was okay too. The denial I had been living in—especially the belief that Dylan had been coerced into participating, or that he hadn't directly committed any of the violence—was a natural response, but it was no longer appropriate. Being back in the world meant confronting the enormity of what Dylan had done.

I sensed judgment and anger and pain from some of the people I worked with. Friends told me when someone spoke unkindly behind my back. Some people avoided me, or confronted me indirectly. One of these incidents stands out in my mind, not because it was the worst confrontation, or the most devastating comment anyone made, but because it articulated exactly what I feared everyone was thinking, not to mention my own worst fears about myself.

I went along on a monitoring visit of a vocational program our office had funded in a small rural high school outside Denver. Being in a high school was difficult for me, and I fought tears the entire visit, especially when we stepped into a large computer lab where a group of happy, productive kids were working.

We introduced ourselves to the computer teacher, a young man not much older than his students, and congratulated him on the thriving program. When I said my name, he stared into my face with intensity. When one of our team members complimented his ability to keep so many machines in good working order, he said, "Well, you get to know the machines. After a while, it's like being a good parent." At that, he turned away from the person who'd asked the question so he could make searing eye contact with me. "When you're a good parent, you just sort of know what your kids are up to."

Those experiences hurt, and I hated them. But as much as I wanted to flee whenever the topic of Columbine surfaced, I could not spend my life walking out of meetings to avoid comments I did not want to hear, or not going to them at all so I'd never encounter a situation that might cause me distress. Despite the horrendous maelstrom of emotions I was living with, I wasn't the only one hurting. I had to face the magnitude of Dylan's actions, and accept how his terrible, violent choices had affected others. Each time I recovered from an uncomfortable encounter, I took another step toward accepting the totality of what Dylan had done. Whether people supported or judged me, being back to work put me shoulder to shoulder with the community my son tried to destroy.

I'd always been conscious of the opinions of others; suddenly, their approval was paramount. I felt sure my own behavior was being evaluated and judged and used to explain how Dylan could have killed and maimed. Always mildly obsessive about my work, I entered a period of intense perfectionism. I would make no errors, commit no miscommunication. I would catch every typo; do every project better than I needed to do it and with time to spare. It wasn't enough to be competent, or normal; I had to convince others I had not caused the craziness exhibited by my son. If I did make a small mistake, I'd often become too upset to continue working. Whenever someone asked me a question, I felt criticized. Driving, I worried I'd accidentally injure or kill someone in my distraction, cementing the world's conviction that I didn't deserve to draw breath.

I looked at photographs of other people's happy families on their desks and wondered: *What did they do, that I didn't?* At the same time, I felt defensive and desperate to show people Dylan had been loved, that I'd been a good mother—and that, despite our closeness, I'd had no idea what he was planning or the slightest suspicion he was capable of such a barbaric act.

Of course, I was assigning to others all the negative feelings I had about myself. I had raised a murderer without knowing it, a person with such a faulty moral compass that he'd committed an atrocity. I was a fool, a sucker, a dolt. I hadn't even been one of those cool parents who smokes pot with their kids or introduces them to their groovy boyfriends. No, I'd been an "everybody sits down for family dinner" kind of a parent, an "I want to meet your friends *and* their parents before you spend the night at their house" kind of a parent. What good had it done?

I remembered driving a kindergarten-aged Dylan back to the grocery so he could return a piece of penny candy he'd taken without paying for it, and how grateful I'd been when the manager soberly accepted Dylan's apology and took the candy from his small hand instead of rewarding his theft by allowing him to keep it. I thought of all the times I'd called the mom hosting a sleepover to find out what movie she was planning to show. More than once, I'd asked for a less violent selection. Why had I bothered trying to establish a contextual framework for violence, when the whole world could see how miserably I failed to protect my son and so many others from it?

For twenty years, signing permission slips and designing elaborate Easter egg hunts and making sure my boys had sneakers that fit had been the touchstones of my life, around which I had fit my work and my art and my marriage. Now I had to ask: What had the point of any of it been?

It's probably impossible to raise a child without having regrets. After murder-suicide, the guilt and second-guessing are constant, intolerable companions. When I went home from work at night, I paged obsessively through our family photo albums. There were the trips to the dairy farm, the natural history museum, the park—the ordinary stuff of a happy middle-class childhood. I was relieved to see how often in the photos Dylan was hugged, tickled, cuddled, or otherwise touched with love. I daydreamed about buttonholing strangers on the street and showing them the albums. *There*, I wanted to say. *See? I'm not crazy. Look at how happy we were!*

But the sight of Dylan's arm, casually slung around Tom's neck while he grinned and called out to me behind the camera, would once again tap in to that seemingly endless river of sorrow.

In the old movie *Gaslight*, the Charles Boyer character is trying to drive his wife, who is played by Ingrid Bergman, insane. He moves artwork and jewelry, and plants items he claims she's "stolen" in her purse. It works: when his wife can no longer trust her own perceptions of reality, she begins to break down. I thought of *Gaslight* often in those days, as I tried to reconstruct an identity for myself. I had thought I'd been a good mother. I had loved and been proud of my son. Nothing I saw when Dylan was alive made me think he was suffering from problems of any real magnitude. Nor, looking back, could I see any obvious, screaming signs. The cognitive dissonance was intense.

When you're a good parent, you just sort of know what your kids are up to. The teacher's comment stung me more than hateful invective would have—not because I didn't believe it, but because I did.

• • •

Tom mostly wonders if we will ever be reunited with him. This is on
Tom's mind constantly. He says he'd feel comforted if he knew he'd
see him again. I think a lot about where Dylan is and whether his evil
actions prevent him from resting in peace, in God's care. I hope there
is a forgiving God who will recognize that he was a child.

—Journal entry, May 1999

My friend Sharon lost a child to suicide, and she urged me to find a
suicide loss survivors' support group.

I was desperate to be among people who would listen and sym-
pathize and not judge, but I could not imagine walking into a room
filled with strangers and talking about what Dylan and Eric had
done. More to the point, as Gary Lozow had pointed out, if our lawsuits went to trial, another support group participant might have to
serve as a witness. I felt I had caused enough damage already.

The isolation was terrible. My anxiety levels were sky-high, and
I felt very disconnected. We were not in communication with the
Harrises. The one person in the world who might have been able
to understand what I was going through was Tom, but the divide
that had sprung up between us in the earliest days after the tragedy
continued to widen.

This is not unusual, of course. Although the statistics you've
heard about the likelihood of divorce after the death of a child are
probably inflated, most marriages do suffer immense disruption.
One often-cited reason is that women and men may grieve the loss
differently: men tend to grieve the loss of the person the child would
have become, while women tend to grieve the child they remember.

That divide was true for us. I incessantly reviewed memories of
Dylan as a baby, a toddler, a child, and a teenager, while Tom focused on everything Dylan would never do because he was dead.
This focus on Dylan's lost future chafed me, as if Tom were pressur-
ing Dylan posthumously to fill his fatherly expectations. The things
we fought about seem unimportant to me now. We were lashed together, back to back, at the center of this terrible storm, but sometimes it felt worse to be with someone than to be alone.

Our coping mechanisms were often in conflict, too. I had always been more social and extroverted, while Tom preferred solitude. The tragedy exaggerated our respective orientations. As stressful as it was to expose myself to hatred and judgment, my reemergence into the world at large exposed me to kindness and generosity, too. Interacting with other people also meant my denial could not become entrenched. An unpleasant conversation might hurt my feelings and set me back temporarily, but ultimately I believed engaging with the outside world was helping me to come to terms with reality.

While I was pushing myself to get back out in the world, though, Tom was becoming increasingly private. I wanted to throw open the doors, and Tom wanted to circle the wagons. More and more, I found I was leaving him to it.

• • •

I sang sad songs and cried all the way to work. I could barely walk. I moved in slow motion. The words "Sometimes I feel like I'm almost gone" described how I felt. I got to work, sat at my desk and cried. I thought I might go home because I didn't feel like working, then realized that home would be worse. Somehow, I eased into my work day and eventually the weight lifted and I began to concentrate on work.

—Journal entry, August 1999

My life split into two hemispheres: the grinding tumult of my personal life, and the quiet order of work.

My concentration grew. Every once in a while, for a minute or two or five or fifteen, I'd become absorbed enough to forget what I was grappling with. Those moments, when they happened, were a gift. Not only did they provide me with respite, but they connected me with the person I'd been before the tragedy: a reliable, capable person who could make a difference.

Just as our friends were opening up to us about their own adolescent traumas and transgressions, so did my coworkers begin to share their personal experiences of shame and loss. Once again, I realized there was a vast wellspring of pain and suffering in the world, one I was now irrevocably tapped in to.

One coworker's son was serving a prison sentence for attempted murder. Another shared her firsthand experience with depression, suicidal thoughts, and psychiatric hospitalization. Hearing these stories was both an honor and a lesson. When my associates entrusted me with their own painful histories, it reminded me that my crisis, as enormous and inescapable as it felt, was just *my* crisis. Other people suffered. They endured terrible things, and they went on.

It was good to be able to offer comfort, too, however meager. I didn't have anything profound to say, and anyway, who wanted advice from the mother of a murderer? But I could give, just by listening.

As I wrote in my journal,

> *I've learned two important things. One, that there are many good, kind people out there. And two, there are many people who have suffered greatly and who keep going with strength and courage. These are the ones who can eventually support others. I hope I can be of use to someone some day.*

It would be a long road.

The stripping away of my identity showed me how tied up I had been, my whole life, with ego. I had always wanted to be liked, and had reveled in being a productive member of my community. I chose work through which I could help others; feeling good about what I was doing had always been more important than making tons of money. I had taken great pride in my sons, in the family Tom and I had built, and in being a good mother. After Columbine, none of that could be true anymore. I wasn't just a bad mother, but the worst mother who ever was, openly hated on the front page of my local paper. Far from being liked and respected, the best I could hope for was that the people around me could find some measure of compassion along with their horror and judgment.

The challenge for myself was even steeper. I would never really be able to move beyond what Dylan had done. Like a cattle brand, the events at Columbine High School and my son's role in them had become an indelible part of who I was. To survive, I would have to find a way to live in this new reality.

Short of ending my own life, there wasn't anything I could do about what the rest of the world thought. My new and greatest hope was simply integration: the old Sue with the new.

CHAPTER 10

The End of Denial

Right now all I want to do is die. Tom keeps saying he wishes he had never been born. Dylan was so loved, but he didn't feel loved. I don't think he loved anyone or anything. How did it happen? I didn't know the boy I saw [on those tapes] today.

My relationship with Dylan in my head and heart has changed.

—Journal entry, October 1999

In October, six months after Columbine, the sheriff's department agreed to share the evidence they'd collected. They invited Tom and me to come in for a presentation of the material.

My reaction to this news was complicated. After months of speculation and rumor and misinformation, it was a relief to know we would finally have the truth. At the same time (and for the same reason), I was petrified. As I wrote the week before: *The meeting will take more courage than I can muster. I can only have my own little construct of what really happened until I speak with the investigators. I don't want them to destroy the Dylan I am holding on to in my mind.*

Two days before we were scheduled to go in, Gary Lozow called. The sheriff's department had told him they would be presenting video evidence as part of their report, and wanted to warn us that seeing it might well be "more painful than April twentieth."

Gary assumed they were referring to surveillance tape. Tom said he'd refuse to watch footage of the massacre. I couldn't believe we were even discussing such a thing. If I had to see Dylan killing people, I'd go mad.

The night before the meeting, Tom and I compiled a list of

questions. We were still convinced that Dylan had either been a reluctant participant or accidentally become entangled in something
bigger than he understood at the time. We'd heard a rumor that
military training materials on brainwashing techniques had been
found in the Harris home, which had refueled our belief that Dylan
had been another victim of the tragedy. It was plausible; Mr. Harris
did have a military background. I entertained fantasies that we'd be
able to hold a public memorial service.

But that was only a moment. I was coming to understand how
fragile a construct we had created. Denial had been a necessary—
indeed, perhaps a lifesaving—defense mechanism for me. As time
went on, though, it was becoming more difficult to sustain. Much
of what was reported in the media was wrong, which reinforced our
skepticism. But we knew that Dylan had participated in the purchase of guns, and there were many credible eyewitness reports of
Dylan shooting kids, and of the hateful things he'd said. The cracks
in my cobbled-together belief system were beginning to widen.

As I suspected, the meeting at the sheriff's office would blow
them wide open.

. . .

*Today is really like the end of my life as I knew it before. If I learn
horrible things tomorrow that I must carry with me from now on, I
will look back on today and remember it as the end of a better time. We
worked on our questions tonight. Byron gave me a long hug to help me
face tomorrow. I hope tomorrow does not destroy the memory of the
boy I loved. I don't know what this video is they want us to see.*

—Journal entry, October 1999

On the morning of October 8, we went to the sheriff's department.
We had met the lead investigator, Kate Battan, and another investigator, Randy West, when they had questioned us in our lawyer's
office not long after the shootings. They'd been with us for our visit
to the Columbine High School library. They were kind and pro-

foundly professional in their interactions with us, and I was never more grateful for this than on that day.

After our initial greeting, Tom and I sat on two of the chairs arranged in rows in a room set up for a formal presentation. I thought about the Harrises, and about the other Columbine families. Sitting on the same chairs at different times seemed to be as close as we could be to each other.

Pointing to various locations on the diagram of the school they'd set up on an easel, Kate and Randy began to tell the story of what Dylan and Eric had done on the morning of April 20, 1999. It was the first time Tom and I learned from an official source what had happened that day, and in the days leading up to it.

The material that follows is graphic, and making the decision to include it here was not an easy one. The victims of this tragedy and their families have endured sorrows and hardships beyond measure, and I don't want a description of the event itself to reinvigorate the trauma they have already experienced. There is also evidence to suggest that describing how these crimes are committed may provide a road map for other disturbed individuals to follow, although eliminating graphic images and dramatic language and minimizing details mitigates the likelihood of contagion.

That said, it is important to me to acknowledge the heinous acts Dylan and Eric committed prior to their deaths. Because so much of this book is focused on my love for Dylan, it is essential for me also to own the viciousness of his final moments on earth. As a practice, I do not minimize the magnitude of what Dylan did in order to comfort myself, and I never, ever forget how I would feel if Dylan was one of the innocent people slaughtered or maimed that day. My intention here is to honor the precious children and the beloved teacher who were.

Kate began to speak. The massacre had been carefully planned. The boys placed a small decoy bomb in a field about three miles away from the high school, hoping the explosion would distract emergency personnel from the events at the school. They drove to the school and entered the building around 11:15 with two duffel bags containing propane bombs. Outside, Eric ran into Brooks Brown, who reminded him about a test he'd missed. "It doesn't matter anymore," Eric said. "Brooks, I like you now. Get out of here. Go home." Dylan and Eric placed the bombs inside the cafeteria and headed back to their cars to wait. When the bombs in the cafeteria did not explode as planned, the boys came back together, climbed to the top of the steps outside the school's west entrance and began shooting.

Kate did not share with us the horrible details of what the boys said, how cruelly they treated some people, or where bullets or fragments of debris entered the bodies of the victims. She did her best to reduce the visual and auditory imagery, adhering instead to the chronological facts of who shot whom, which weapons had been used, and where at the school each individual had been injured. Intentional or not, I perceived this as an act of mercy, and I was grateful for it.

Eric shot Rachel Scott, killing her instantly, and Richard Castaldo, who was hit multiple times and paralyzed below the chest. Eric then shot at Daniel Rohrbough and Sean Graves and Lance Kirklin, who were climbing the hill toward them, killing Daniel and wounding the other two. Five students were sitting on the grass opposite the west entrance. Eric shot at them. Michael Johnson was hit, but he ran and escaped with his life. Mark Taylor was also shot multiple times but survived by pretending to be dead. The other three students ran.

Dylan walked down the steps toward the cafeteria. He shot Lance Kirklin and stepped over Sean Graves on his way into the building. Eric, still outside, shot at several students sitting near the door to the cafeteria, paralyzing Anne Marie Hochhalter. Without shooting at anyone or investigating the bombs in the cafeteria, Dylan rejoined him, and together they shot at a distant group of kids who had escaped over the chain-link fence to the soccer fields. They did not hit anyone.

Patti Nielson, a teacher, headed outside from the second floor to stop what she thought must be a video project or a prank. As she approached the doors of the west entrance, the boys shot out the glass in the doors, injuring a student, Brian Anderson, with flying glass and hitting Nielson in the shoulder. Nielson ran into the library and told the students there to get under the tables. She hid under the library counter and called 911.

Columbine's armed school guard, Deputy Neil Gardner, arrived in the parking lot. Eric shot at him, and Gardner shot back, but Gardner did not hit him. Gardner and another deputy from the Jefferson County Sheriff's Office also exchanged fire with Eric a little later, but no one was hit.

The boys entered the building. Eric had shot his rifle forty-seven times. Dylan had shot three times with his handgun and two with his shotgun. The boys had also thrown pipe bombs.

Eric and Dylan moved through a hallway, throwing pipe bombs and shooting at random. Stephanie Munson was injured by a bullet. Then Dave Sanders, who taught business at the school, and who had evacuated a huge number of students from the cafeteria and personally seen them to safety, came around the corner, looking for more people to warn. He and another student saw Dylan and Eric and turned to warn some others. Both boys shot down the hallway toward Dave Sanders; it's still not known whose shots killed him. Rich Long, another teacher, dragged him into a classroom, where two students, Aaron Hancey and Kevin Starkey, administered first aid for three hours. Despite their efforts, he died later that afternoon, still waiting to be evacuated.

Dylan and Eric threw two pipe bombs over the railing into the cafeteria below; these exploded. They threw a pipe bomb into the library hallway that also exploded. Then they went into the library. Eric shot at a desk where Evan Todd was hiding; Evan was hit but not seriously injured. Dylan fatally shot Kyle Velasquez, who was hiding underneath a computer workstation. The boys reloaded and then began shooting out the window at the rescue workers helping the students outside. Dylan then shot at a table, injuring Daniel Steepleton and Makai Hall. Eric shot under a desk without looking, fatally wounding Steven Curnow, and then injured Kacey Ruegsegger. He walked over to another desk and killed Cassie Bernall. Dylan shot Patrick Ireland as he was helping Makai Hall.

Underneath another set of tables, Dylan found Isaiah Shoels, Matthew Kechter, and Craig Scott, Rachel Scott's younger brother. Dylan hurled racial epithets at Isaiah before Eric shot and killed him. Dylan then shot and killed Matthew Kechter. Eric threw a CO_2 cartridge at the table where Makai, Daniel, and Patrick were. Makai managed to throw it away before it exploded.

Eric began to shoot randomly. Dylan shot at a display case and then at the nearest table, where he hit and injured Mark Kintgen. He shot again, injuring Lisa Kreutz and Valeen Schnurr. Then he killed Lauren Townsend.

Eric bent to taunt two girls under a table, then fired at Nicole Nowlen and John Tomlin. When John tried to move away, Dylan killed him. Eric then shot Kelly Fleming, killing her instantly. He hit Lauren Townsend and Lisa Kreutz again, and wounded Jeanna Park.

The boys went to reload their weapons at a table. Eric noticed John Savage, a boy Dylan knew. John asked Dylan what they were doing, and he said, "Oh, just killing people." John asked if they were going to kill him. Dylan told him to leave. John fled.

Eric shot and killed Daniel Mauser. Both Dylan and Eric then fired under another table, injuring Jennifer Doyle and Austin Eubanks, and fatally wounding Corey DePooter. The two of them found and taunted injured Evan Todd.

Eric had broken his nose with his own shotgun's recoil and was bleeding heavily. The boys made their way to the library entrance. Dylan shot into the library break room, hitting a TV. He slammed a chair down on top of the library counter where Patti Nielson was hidden.

Then the two boys left the library. After they were gone, thirty uninjured survivors and ten injured survivors evacuated the area. Patrick Ireland and Lisa Kreutz remained in the building; Patrick was unconscious, and Lisa could not move. Patti Nielson, another teacher, and the two library staff members locked themselves into rooms adjoining the library.

For the next thirty-two minutes, Eric and Dylan wandered through the school, firing their guns at random and setting off pipe bombs. Kate Battan pointed out to us how many people, probably between two and three hundred, were still left in the building. Many teachers and other staff had stayed in the building to warn and protect the remaining children. During the presentation, Kate reiterated how remarkable it was no one else had been killed. The boys went back to the cafeteria and tried to detonate the propane bombs they'd left there earlier. They looked through classroom windows, making eye contact with kids hidden there, but did not go into the rooms or shoot. They did not cause any further injury at all. They went back to the cafeteria and into the school kitchen. Then they returned to the library, where they again shot through the windows at police officers outside before killing themselves. They left behind the biggest bombs of all in their cars, set to go off around noon. These did not detonate.

Patrick Ireland regained consciousness and crawled to the library windows, where he fell into the arms of two SWAT team members standing on the roof of an armored truck. Lisa Kreutz, who sustained multiple gunshot wounds, was evacuated later in the afternoon, along with the four people hidden in the break room.

One teacher, William "Dave" Sanders, was dead, along with twelve students: Cassie Bernall, Steven Curnow, Corey De-Pooter, Kelly Fleming, Matthew Kechter, Daniel Mauser, Daniel Rohrbough, Isaiah Shoels, Rachel Scott, John Tomlin, Lauren Townsend, and Kyle Velasquez. Twenty-four other students had been injured, three hurt as they tried to escape the school.

I went completely numb as detailed information about the massacre rained down on us. It was like a documentary so violent and depraved that I would never, ever, under ordinary circumstances, have watched it.

A single fact had emerged, without any ambiguity at all: *Dylan had done this thing.*

The event had been planned a long time in advance, and Dylan had participated in the planning. The attack had been carefully timed and strategically constructed. Dylan had deliberately killed and injured people. He had derided them as they begged for their lives. He had used racist, hateful language. He had not shown mercy, regret, or conscience. He had shot a teacher. He had killed children in cold blood.

I was, and will always be, haunted by how those lives ended.

For the first time in months, my eyes were dry. Not only could I not grasp what I had just heard, but I couldn't feel anything at all. Every belief I had created in order to survive had been shredded. The notepad filled with our questions sat unopened on my lap.

As the details began to sink in, so did one of the most shocking and terrifying revelations of that morning: the destruction intended was of a far greater scope. The attack was really a failed attempt to blow up the entire school. The large propane bombs the boys had placed in the cafeteria had been timed to go off when the room was full of students. Because of a miscalculation, they did not explode. Kate said that if they had, a wall of fire would have enveloped the crowded cafeteria, trapping hundreds of students. The ceiling might have collapsed, bringing the whole second floor crashing down into the cafeteria.

The horror of what happened, then, paled in comparison with what the boys had planned. I could barely breathe, thinking about it. As catastrophic as the tragedy was, it could have been much, much worse. Indeed, that was what my son had intended.

Gathering himself, Tom pressed for more information. The greatest mystery still had not been explained: What was Dylan's state of mind? Why was he there? What thoughts and feelings would cause him to take part in this atrocity?

We believed Dylan had left absolutely no trace behind to explain his actions. The investigators had already told us he'd erased the hard drive on his computer, and they had taken from his room everything that might have given us insight into Dylan's frame of mind. We had searched and searched for a note. I'd asked his friends to look when they visited; they'd opened CD cases and rifled through books. None of us had found anything.

So Tom and I were still clinging to one last shred of hope. It was obvious that Dylan had fully participated in the massacre, but had he done so willingly? Was it not possible he might have been brainwashed, drugged, or otherwise coerced? Kate shook her head and told us the police were sure Dylan had participated willingly. When we asked how she could be sure, she told us the boys had left behind a videotape.

This was the video evidence we'd been warned about. Although the boys had taken video production classes together, it had never occurred to me that Dylan and Eric might have created a videotape of their own. The news that they had done so sent a jolt of terror and dread through my gut. Still, there was no way I could possibly have been ready for what I saw when Kate inserted the tape and hit Play.

. . .

Once again, my life broke apart. If I hadn't seen it I wouldn't have believed it. My worst fears have come to pass. I keep thinking about his crazy rage and his intent to die. He lied to us and to his friends. He was so far removed from feeling. I keep trying to understand how that sweet, beloved child got there. I'm so furious with God for doing this to my son.

—Journal entry, October 1999

The "Basement Tapes" were videos of Dylan and Eric talking to the camera in various places and times in the weeks before the shootings. Many of them were shot in Eric's basement bedroom, which explains the name they were given by the media.

We'd had no idea these videos existed, but as soon as the tape started to play, I realized I was going to have to let go of every one of my assumptions about my son's life, and about the actions leading up to his death and the atrocities he committed.

My heart nearly broke when I first saw Dylan and heard his voice. He looked and sounded just as I remembered him, the boy I had been missing so much. Within mere seconds, however, the words he was saying came into focus, and my brain reeled. I stood up from my chair, wondering if I'd have time to get to the restroom before being sick to my stomach.

He and Eric were preposterous, posturing, giving a performance for each other and their invisible audience. I had never seen that expression of sneering superiority on Dylan's face. My mouth gaped open when I heard the language they were using—abominable, hate-filled, racist, derogatory words, words never spoken or heard in our home.

The dynamic between the boys was laid bare, and it was a revelation. Adrenaline coursed through me, making it hard to concentrate, though the information on the tapes felt so important I didn't even want to blink.

On the first recording, we saw Eric act as emcee, introducing topics he wants memorialized on the tape, while Dylan adds contemptuous support. At first glance, Eric seems like the calm, sane one, while Dylan rages in the background. It is obvious that Dylan's rage is a crucial component in the dynamic. Over and over, Eric urges him to "feel the rage," and Dylan obliges by pulling out anything he can to lock himself into a state of anger and hold himself there. The lengths he goes to are ridiculous, as when he recalls slights from his preschool days.

The psychologists who reviewed the tapes would come to a similar conclusion: that Eric relied on Dylan's slow-burning, depressive anger to fuel and feed his sadism, while Dylan used Eric's destructive impulses to jolt him out of his passivity. It would take years for me to filter what I heard on the tape and to understand the role of anger in Dylan's self-destruction.

Through the appalling bravado, and the shocking, hateful words spilling out of his mouth, I could see Dylan's familiar adolescent self-consciousness, the same awkward embarrassment he displayed whenever Tom brought out the video camera to make a home movie. I wanted to both leap through the screen and beat him with my fists while screaming at him—and, in the same moment, to reach back in time, to hold him and tell him that he was deeply loved, and not alone.

I no longer remember the order in which the segments played.

In one, the two boys sit in two chairs facing the camera, eating and drinking alcohol from a bottle. They list the people they want to hurt, and describe what they would like to do to them. (As Kate pointed out, none of the people mentioned on the tapes were injured in the attack.) In another segment, Dylan holds the camera while Eric plays dress-up and shows off weapons. They talk about keeping the plan a secret. Eric shows how carefully he hid the weapons so his parents would not find them.

Kate inserted a side comment here for our benefit. This portion of the video was a real eye-opener, she said, even for those who worked in law enforcement. Investigators had failed to discover one of Eric's hiding places in their initial search of the Harrises' home; they'd had to go back after seeing the tape. She added that people on the team went home and searched their own children's rooms as they had never searched before.

Dylan talks about sneaking his newly purchased shotgun into our house. He had sawed off the end, making it smaller and easier to conceal—not to mention illegal to own. He describes his tension as he held the gun inside his coat and slipped up to his room without being suspected. We've never learned whether the gun was stored inside our home or elsewhere. It might have been kept inside his box-shaped headboard; the inside could not be accessed unless the bed was taken apart. Watching, I felt hopeless. Even if we had continued to search his room, as we did regularly for six months after his arrest in junior year, we probably would not have looked there.

At one point on the tape, Dylan makes a derogatory comment about my extended family, and another about his older brother, Byron. We had been grieving for six full months, and nobody had borne the brunt of the world's venom more bravely than Byron had. Our older son had stepped up and shouldered the terrible responsibilities that had landed on him with astonishing grace and courage. It was ironic. Dylan had so little to complain or be angry about that he was reduced to grasping at straws like his relationship with his brother or rarely seen relatives in order to stoke the rage Eric needed him to sustain.

In another snippet of tape, Dylan complains to Eric that I am making him participate in a Passover seder. On the weekend they made the video, I had decided to make a traditional Passover dinner and invite a neighbor to join us, and I asked both of my sons for their work schedules so I could plan accordingly. Dylan responded in a way I found immature and self-centered. He didn't want to participate. The youngest person at the table has to read part of the service, and he found it embarrassing.

I asked him to reconsider. "I know this holiday means nothing to you, but it means something to me. We'll have a good dinner. Do it for me?" When he said he would, I thanked him and told him I appreciated it. Then there he was on the video, complaining to Eric about his obligation to attend.

Eric, who is playing with a gun while Dylan talks, becomes very still and silent when he hears the word "Passover." He hadn't known my family was Jewish. When Dylan realizes what he has let slip, he starts backpedaling. He seems afraid of Eric's reaction, and tells him I'm not really Jewish—just a quarter, or an eighth. I couldn't tell if he was worried about being judged, or being shot.

Eric finally breaks the tension by offering a word of consolation to Dylan. Watching it, I thought, *You stupid idiots! All this talk about hating everyone and everything, and you don't even know what you're talking about. It's all something you've invented in your minds to sustain your anger.* The heartbreaking thing was that, for a moment there, it seemed like Dylan had almost realized it.

At one point on the tapes, Eric suggests they each say something about their parents. At that, Dylan looks down at his fingernails and says, almost inaudibly, "My parents have been good to me. I don't want to browse there." Neither one of them acknowledges a connection between the actions they are planning and the pain they will cause the people who love them. In another recording, they go so far as to announce that their parents and friends hold no responsibility for what is about to happen, as if tidying this minor detail will make everything fine for their families when it's all over.

The last segment was the shortest one. It was also the most difficult for me. In it, the boys pause to say a few words of farewell before going over to the school to carry out their plan. Supplies are piled around them, as if they are heading out on an expedition. Eric tells his family how they should distribute his possessions.

Dylan does not utter an angry word or speak of hatred or vengeance. He makes no mention of the death and destruction to come. There is none of the braggadocio of the previous tapes. He does not cry, either; his affect is flat, resigned. Whatever else he intends to do, he is going to the school to end his own life. He looks away from the camera, as if speaking only to himself. Then he says softly, "Just know I'm going to a better place. I didn't like life too much. . . ."

Watching this, I had to bite my lip to stop myself from screaming, *Stop! Stop! Don't go. Don't leave me! Don't do this. Don't hurt those people. Give me a chance to help you! Come back.* But wherever he was, Dylan couldn't hear me anymore.

. . .

Tufekci: "I can see no benefit whatsoever to releasing those tapes, only the possibility for great harm."

—Notes from a conversation with sociologist
Zeynep Tufekci, February 2015

Years later, Tom and I would fight to make sure the so-called Basement Tapes were not released to the public.

We encountered a lot of resistance. People believed we were hiding something, or protecting Dylan's reputation. (As I drily commented to Tom the first time we heard that particular accusation, "I think that horse has already left the barn.") I was even challenged by some survivors of suicide loss: "Don't you think making the tapes public would help people to understand why this happened?"

The answer was *No, I don't.* I still don't—and my reasons are closely interwoven with many of the broader, global issues surrounding suicide and violence at the heart of this book: specifically, the real fear that another disturbed child would use the tapes as a blueprint or a model for their own school shooting.

Dylan and Eric had already been, in certain quarters, heralded as champions for a cause. Tom and I had received chilling letters from alienated kids expressing admiration for Dylan and what he'd done. Adults who had been bullied as children wrote to tell us they could relate to the boys and their actions. Girls flooded us with love letters. Young men left messages on our answering machine calling Dylan a god, a hero. An acquaintance working at a youth correctional facility told me some of the imprisoned boys cheered as they watched television coverage of the destruction at the school. A video project Dylan and Eric had made, leaked to the media, had become a rallying cry for bullied kids.

These communications made me sadder and sicker than the most castigating hate mail. If the tapes were made public, we would never be able to control who could see them. (Even writing about the timeline of the events at the school and describing the tapes, as I have done in this chapter, makes me nervous, and I would not have done so without getting an explicit go-ahead from people who study these issues.) We could not, in good conscience, release the tapes. Enough harm had been done.

This wasn't mere superstition on our part. As the years went on, our fears that Dylan and Eric's actions would provide inspiration to other disturbed kids were confirmed over and over again. Columbine-related materials were found among Virginia Tech shooter Seung-Hui Cho's possessions, and in the Sandy Hook Elementary School shooter Adam Lanza's belongings. An investigation by ABC News published in 2014 found "at least 17 attacks and another 36 alleged plots or serious threats against schools since the assault on Columbine High School that can be tied to the 1999 massacre."

We know, without a doubt, that exposure to suicide or suicidal behavior can influence other vulnerable people to make an attempt. Over fifty studies worldwide have powerfully connected news coverage of suicides to an increased incidence of similar, or copycat, suicides. This effect is called "suicide contagion." It's also known as the Werther effect, a term coined by sociologist David Phillips in the 1970s. The name itself highlights how long we've known about the phenomenon: in the eighteenth century, a host of young men imitated the protagonist of Goethe's novel *The Sorrows of Young Werther*, dying by suicide dressed as he did, in yellow pants and a blue jacket.

The media's acknowledgment of the Werther effect has unquestionably saved lives. Perhaps you've noticed that suicide deaths, especially those of teenagers, are rarely reported in the news. That's not accidental; it's because media outlets are following guidelines endorsed by the Centers for Disease Control and the National Institute of Mental Health, both of which suggest that limiting and dampening coverage may save lives.

The guidelines recommend that media outlets avoid repetitive, glamorizing, or sensational coverage, and should not offer simplistic explanations for suicide. Methods should not be graphically discussed. Final notes should not be reprinted. Photographs of the location of the death, of memorial sites, and of grieving family members may be inflammatory, and should be avoided.

By agreeing to report on suicides not as if they were high-profile crimes, but as part of a massive public health problem, members of major media outlets have saved lives. The two areas of exception are death by suicide of a high-profile celebrity, and murder-suicide. Now, I'm not naive enough to believe I will ever see a world where there is no coverage surrounding the death of a well-known figure like Robin Williams, or of an event like the shootings at Sandy Hook Elementary School. As tragic as these events may be, they are also news stories. But there are many ways even these events can be covered more responsibly, and there is a strong argument for doing so. I believe, in particular, there is a compelling argument for changing the way we cover murder-suicide.

A growing body of research suggests that the rising number of mass shootings in the United States is inextricably linked— along with the easy availability of high-capacity guns, and a lack of knowledge about and support for brain health issues—to the way the media cover these events. And if such media coverage can either contain or instigate contagion, then I agree with media experts like Drs. Frank Ochberg and Zeynep Tufekci that it is imperative to institute a new set of guidelines for reporting on murder-suicide.

There is, of course, already a material difference between the way these events are covered by legitimate mainstream news organizations and what happens in the deepest, darkest corners of the Internet—or even on cable news, with twenty-four hours of programming to fill. Meg Moritz, a journalist and professor who has looked closely at the media coverage of Columbine, reminded me that the journalists in question are often making split-second decisions under less-than-optimal circumstances. Even so, it's not unreasonable to expect legitimate news organizations to follow best-practice guidelines.

Many of these guidelines are "don'ts." Don't show images of the shooter, particularly ones of him with weapons, or in the outfit he chose to carry out the massacre. Don't show the weapons used, or other evidence. Don't endlessly repeat the name of the shooter; instead, refer to "the killer" or "the perpetrator." Don't give airtime or publish the videos they make (like the Basement Tapes) or manifestos posted to their social media accounts. Don't compare the killer to other killers, particularly by putting emphasis on how many people they have killed. Tufekci believes that numbers—how many dead and injured, the number of bullets fired—and photographs are particularly inflammatory, as they provide a benchmark for competition. Don't sensationalize the violence or the body count—"the most people killed and injured in the country's history!" Don't oversimplify the motivations behind the act.

Most important, don't inadvertently make heroes out of the killers. It seems obvious, and yet when an event like this happens, you can't avoid detailed (and, I would argue, fetishistic) descriptions of the weapons used, how the killers hid their arsenals, what they did and ate on the fateful day, exactly what they wore. Their names become household names. We know their favorite foods, video games, movies, and bands. These details may eventually emerge, of course; leaks happen, and the Internet is the Internet. But if these images and details accelerate and inspire violence, then they should not be endlessly repeated on CNN.

Dr. Frank Ochberg is a psychiatrist, a pioneer in trauma science, and the chairman emeritus of the Dart Center for Journalism and Trauma at Columbia University. When he educates journalists about trauma, he advises them to broaden the discussion around traumatic events instead of sensationalizing them. Which details will genuinely help us to unravel the events that have taken place? What resources can we point people to? How can we set this tragedy in a larger context of mental health?

One of the biggest improvements would simply be to refrain from jumping to conclusions, especially by oversimplifying root causes. School shooters don't kill people "because" of violent video games or techno music, and people don't die by suicide because they've lost a job or been dumped by a girlfriend. Many articles I read in the wake of Robin Williams's death expressed shock that a man so wealthy and beloved could feel he had nothing to live for. Of course, money and popularity don't protect people from brain illness any more than they cause it.

When we oversimplify the cause of a suicide, we create risk by suggesting that a romantic rejection or a setback at work is a reason to consider death. A firing or a breakup might contribute to someone's despondency, but people get dumped and fired all the time; these events by themselves cannot explain why someone dies by suicide. Similarly, violent video games have been shown to desensitize kids to the reality of violence, and they are likely particularly dangerous for vulnerable kids who are struggling with brain illness or other cofactors. But school shooters don't go on rampages because they played *Grand Theft Auto* or *Doom*.

It's my hope the recommendations I have made here won't be seen as pro-censorship or a threat to free speech, but as a call for ethical reporting. (In an act I respect greatly, the novelist Stephen King asked his publisher to withdraw his novel *Rage* after a number of school shooters quoted from it.) The iconic Columbine photograph is a still from the surveillance tape showing Dylan and Eric in full paramilitary garb, brandishing their weapons in the school cafeteria. Whenever I see it—especially when it accompanies an article that purports to be taking a more constructive approach—I have to stop myself from throwing the magazine across the room.

Certainly there is precedent for changing the way the media report events with an eye to the greater good. A good reporter would never dream of publishing a sexual assault victim's name, or specific troop movements. Perhaps it will soon become similarly unthinkable to publish a killer's mug shot over the number of people he killed and injured in bright, blood red.

Some news organizations have begun to listen. In 2014, a conservative Canadian network made the decision not to name or show a photograph of the perpetrator who shot five police officers, two fatally. The editorial they ran explained the decision: "It's easy to report on the life of the killer, to scour his deranged Facebook page, to speculate about motive, but doing so could actually encourage the perception that his heinous acts are somehow justified." I don't feel as strongly about hiding the names of the killers as many media analysts do; I'm happy to leave that recommendation to someone better qualified. However, it's notable that the station's in-depth coverage of the event was in no way compromised because they did not report those details.

In many countries in Europe, national news councils monitor coverage and penalize infractions. This is probably impossible in the United States, and may not be desirable (although I wish there had been an avenue to discipline the *National Enquirer*, which published leaked crime-scene photographs from Columbine, including a photograph of Dylan and Eric dead in the library). There are conversations happening in the best newsrooms every day about sensitivity and contagion and trauma. I believe that, in time and with education, news agencies will adopt these guidelines voluntarily, for the simple reason that it is the right thing to do. In the meantime, when you see coverage you feel is irresponsible, you can (as I do) write an e-mail to the news organization, or make your objections heard on social media.

The fear of contagion was the main reason Tom and I fought so hard to keep the Basement Tapes sealed, but it was not the only one. Aside from whatever destructive behaviors another alienated kid might learn, I was horrified to think the friends and families of people who had suffered losses might be re-traumatized unwittingly, simply because they happened to be flipping through a magazine in a grocery store line, or sitting underneath a television at a sports bar.

I was also concerned that releasing the tapes would continue to feed the comforting fantasy that evil will present itself in a way only a fool could fail to recognize. For me, the tragedy at Columbine was proof of how dangerous this fantasy can be. When you watch Dylan on the videos, you think: *That kid is insane, practically boiling over with rage. He is planning to commit real violence, and to die by suicide. Those parents must have been complete idiots. There's no way they could live in the same house with that person and not know he was dangerous.*

All I can say is it's what I would have thought, too.

There was no way to release the tapes responsibly. Nor was there a convincing reason to do so. An army of professional investigators and psychologists had studied the tapes, and they had been unable to reach agreement regarding why Dylan and Eric had committed this atrocity. What on earth was the general population going to learn?

I often think it would be far more instructive—and frightening—to show the video we took of Dylan on the afternoon of his prom, three days before the massacre, smiling and playfully tossing tiny snowballs at his dad behind the camera. To my mind, the expertise with which desperate people can mask their true feelings and intentions is the far more important message.

The tapes stayed private. Conspiracy theorists raged, but there was no cover-up. There just wasn't anything worth seeing.

. . .

My relationship with Dylan in my head and heart has changed. I'm so angry with him right now. I wonder what I did as a Mom to make him feel so hurt, so angry, so disconnected.

—Journal entry, October 1999

Leaving the sheriff's office after seeing the Basement Tapes, I was in a whole-body state of shock. In the parking lot I staggered toward the car, slurring my words like a drunk. The horror of what we had just heard—not to mention that the tragedy could have been so much more severe, and the violence perpetrated so substantially worse—practically brought me to my knees.

In the days and months after that meeting, my entire world broke open all over again. Viewing the Basement Tapes finally forced me to see my son the way the rest of the world saw him. No wonder they thought he was a monster.

There's a miniature gyroscope in each one of us, searching for equilibrium and maintaining our orientation. For months after seeing the Basement Tapes, no modulation was possible. I could barely tell which way was up.

Once I emerged from a state of shock and started to feel something again, I was consumed with fury. I was reeling from what Dylan had done to so many innocent people, and what he might have done to so many more. I had kept his loving memory alive in my heart all those months, but he had destroyed that memory, and everything else. At Thanksgiving, the only thing I could think of to be thankful for was that the bombs hadn't gone off. Dylan's empty chair was a reminder of the other families, mere miles away, with empty chairs of their own. I held Byron's hand while he graciously gave his thanks for the food and for us, but there was no possibility of further conversation, or of eating more than a perfunctory bite. When Byron excused himself from the table after a miserable fifteen minutes and stood up to carry his dishes into the kitchen, Tom and I both started crying.

My digestive issues worsened that fall. When my annual gynecological checkup rolled around, my doctor was genuinely freaked out by the way I looked and sounded. I'd known him for years; he'd delivered Dylan, in fact, and I'd been pregnant at the same time as his wife, so we'd been in the same new baby care class. As a medical professional and as a friend, he was adamant: I needed to find a therapist.

It was truer than he knew. Because of the legal restrictions, I'd never joined a support group. And while my friends and colleagues had been wonderful in allowing me to share my memories of Dylan and my grief and my questions, how on earth could I talk about what I'd seen on those tapes? The lawsuits made it impossible, first of all. And now that some of my questions had been answered, my shame and anger eclipsed everything else.

Desperate, I made an appointment with the therapist I'd seen in the immediate aftermath of the attacks. I'd always suspected he didn't have the right training to handle the complications of my situation, and that appointment was the final straw. After I'd told him what we'd seen and heard on the tapes, he could only sit in stunned silence. Finally, he confessed he was in over his head, and didn't know how to help. He asked if I would be willing to allow him to consult with another counselor. Though I was grateful to him for his honesty and his help, we agreed to part ways.

I asked for recommendations from my doctor, from friends, and from a pastor and a rabbi. Gary Lozow helped me to vet the candidates. It was a dispiriting process. One therapist couldn't wait to get off the phone when she heard who I was. She didn't want to become entangled in the many lawsuits swirling around our family. Some displayed a prurient interest in the details of the case, while others confessed they simply weren't up to the task. We kept at the search, and I found someone who had also lost a child, which made a world of difference. When I looked into her eyes, I felt I'd come home.

In truth, I was only blindingly angry with Dylan for a few days after seeing the tapes. I had to let it go. Anger blocks the feeling of love, and the love kept winning.

. . .

It was my new therapist who helped me to see why that day at the sheriff's office had devastated me so entirely. I'd had to start the grieving process all over again. The Dylan I had already mourned was gone, replaced by someone I didn't even recognize.

Like Dorian Gray's portrait, the picture I had of Dylan in my mind grew uglier every time I looked at it. The buffer I'd clung to all those months—believing he'd been an unwitting or coerced participant, or acting in a moment of madness—was gone. The evil face

I'd seen on the tapes was a side of him I did not recognize, a side I'd never seen during his life. After seeing the tapes, it was really hard not to say, *That devil—that is who he was.*

With my therapist's help, I would find there was no lasting comfort in casting Dylan as a monster. Deep down, I couldn't reconcile that characterization with the Dylan I had known. The rest of the world could explain away what he had done: either he was born evil—a bad seed—or he'd been raised without moral guidance. I knew it wasn't nearly so simple.

After we saw the Basement Tapes, I opened a small box in my desk drawer where I keep a few treasured keepsakes. Among them was a tiny origami horse. I checked and rechecked the box for the little horse, periodically taking it out to examine it as if its folds held the answer to the questions I was asking.

When Dylan was about nine years old, I contracted a nasty eye infection that persisted despite several trips to the doctor. Dylan had been concerned, checking my eyes often to see if they had improved. He was always a physically affectionate child, and I can still summon the sense memory of his hand on my shoulder as he peered anxiously into my eyes. While I was still healing, I discovered a tiny winged horse made of folded paper carefully placed on my desk, along with a note in his childish handwriting. The note said, "I hope my get well Pegasus makes you well. I made him espessially for you. Love, Dylan."

How could I reconcile the cherub with the halo of golden hair who used to giggle while smashing kisses into my face, and the man—that killer—on screen? How could the person who had made me this get-well Pegasus possibly be the same person I'd seen on that tape? I needed to synthesize my own experience of mothering that boy while acknowledging the person he'd become at the end of his life.

There was no longer any way to avoid the horrific fact that my son had planned and committed nightmarish acts of cruelty. But the gentle-hearted kid who'd made me that Pegasus; the lovely, shy boy who couldn't resist helping with a thousand-piece jigsaw puzzle; the young man whose characteristic bark of a laugh punctuated the

Mystery Science Theater 3000 episodes we watched together—he had been real, too. Who was it I had loved, and why had I loved him?

A friend once e-mailed me the following quotation, and it struck me as so apt that I dug up the book to read more: "Have patience with everything that remains unsolved in your heart," Rainer Maria Rilke writes in his fourth letter to a young poet. "Try to love the questions themselves, like locked rooms and like books written in a foreign language. Do not now look for the answers. They cannot now be given to you because you could not live them. It is a question of experiencing everything. At present you need to live the question. Perhaps you will gradually, without even noticing it, find yourself experiencing the answer, some distant day."

A time would come when my heart would fully open once again to my son—when I could weep not only for his victims, but also for him. I would learn of the deep suffering Dylan experienced, perhaps for years, of which I had been totally unaware. The anxiety disorder and PTSD I would experience myself after Columbine would provide me with firsthand experience in the ways that a crisis in brain health can distort a person's reasoning. None of this would excuse or lessen what Dylan did. Yet my greater understanding of the brain illness I now believe gripped him enabled me to grieve for him again.

That process would take years. First I had to live the question, and everything unsolved in my heart. Seeing those tapes was the first step. As terrible as the experience was, I had to accept that Dylan had been an active and willing participant in the massacre. Going forward, I would need to piece together the contradictory fragments I had collected in order to understand how Dylan could have hidden a side of himself so entirely from Tom and me, as well as from his teachers, his closest friends, and their parents.

And I was determined to do so, not simply so I could have a context for my own grief and horror, but to understand what I could have done differently.

PART II

Toward Understanding

Dylan, age fourteen, playing poker with my brother and sister.
The Klebold Family

CHAPTER 11

The Depths of His Despair

These days, when I introduce myself at a conference, I say, "My son died by suicide." Then I say, "He was one of the shooters in the Columbine tragedy."

I'm accustomed by now to the jaw drop. Almost invariably, the person says, "I never thought about it that way, but I guess it *was* a suicide, wasn't it?"

It never surprises me that people have this reaction. Of course they do; I was Dylan's mother, and that was my reaction, too. Both the realization that Dylan had died by suicide and the implications of that understanding came in increments, but the import of the realization continues to be felt.

As you've probably gathered by now, I have long since given up hoping for a single puzzle piece that will drop into place and finally reveal why Dylan and Eric did what they did. I wish the vectors propelling the boys toward catastrophe had been unambiguous. I am also wary of the many pat explanations that sprang up in the wake of the tragedy. Did school culture and bullying "cause" Columbine? Violent video games? Negligent parenting? The paramilitarization of American popular culture? These are pieces in the greater puzzle, to be sure. But none of them, even in a combination amplifying their individual effects, has ever been enough for me to explain away the kind of hatred and violence the boys displayed.

I am even wary of talking about "the boys" in this way, as if their motivations were necessarily shared. Dylan and Eric planned the massacre together, and they acted together, but I believe—as most of the investigators who examined the evidence do—that they were two different people, who participated for very different reasons.

So while there is likely not a single answer, there is one piece of the puzzle that reveals more for me of the overall picture than any other: that Dylan was experiencing depression or another brain health crisis that contributed to his desire to die by suicide, and his desire to die played an intrinsic role in his participation in the massacre.

I realize this is a controversial statement. I certainly do not mean to imply that Dylan's brain health issues made him capable of the atrocities he would eventually enact. To do so would be to insult the hundreds of millions of people around the world living with depression and other mood disorders. Stigma and ignorance mean that many people who are struggling do not pursue the help they desperately need. The shame attached to getting help for a crisis in brain health is not only tragic but deadly, and I have no desire whatsoever to contribute to it.

Nor do I believe a crisis in brain health is necessarily an explanation for what Dylan did. The automatic conflation of violence and "craziness" is not only painful for people who are suffering, it is incorrect. According to Dr. Jeffrey Swanson, who has spent his career studying the intersection between mental illness and violence, serious mental illness by itself is a risk factor for violence in just 4 percent of incidents. It is only when mental illness appears in combination with other risk factors—primarily drug and alcohol abuse—that the numbers increase. (Dylan was drinking at the end of his life, something Tom and I did not know.)

Most people living with mood disorders are not dangerous to others at all. As Swanson also points out, though, there *is* some overlap between mental disorders and violence, and I cannot believe it's productive for anyone when we take the conversation off the table.

There is, in particular, an overlap between brain health issues and mass shootings. In 1999, prompted by the shootings at Columbine High School, the US Secret Service and the Department of Education launched the Safe School Initiative, an examination of thirty-seven school attacks, in the hopes of preventing others in the future. The researchers found that "most attackers showed some history of suicidal attempts or thoughts, or a history of feeling extreme depression or desperation." Access to brain health screening and treatment, then, is critical in preventing violence—as well as suicide, eating disorders, drug and alcohol abuse, and a host of other dangers threatening teens. Better access to these resources may not be "the" answer, but it's pretty close to one.

You will notice that I use the terms "brain illness" and "brain health" throughout this book, as opposed to the more commonly used "mental illness" and "mental health." That decision was the result of a conversation I had with Dr. Jeremy Richman, a neuroscientist whose daughter, Avielle Rose Richman, was one of the children murdered by Adam Lanza at Sandy Hook Elementary School in Newtown, Connecticut. Dr. Richman and his wife, Jennifer Hensel, a scientist and medical writer, founded the Avielle Foundation in their daughter's honor, hoping to remove the stigma for people seeking help, to develop the concept of a "brain health checkup," and to identify behavioral and biochemical diagnostics to detect those at risk of violent behaviors.

In our conversation, Dr. Richman explained: " 'Mental' is invisible. It comes with all the fear, trepidation, and stigma of things we don't understand. But we know there are real, physical manifestations within the brain that can be imaged, measured, quantified, and understood. We need to move our understanding to the visible world of brain health and brain disease, which is tangible."

The emphasis I place in this chapter on Dylan's suicide may sound insensitive, as if I believe his death was more important than the deaths he caused—which is not the way I feel at all. I simply mean that coming to understand Dylan's death as a suicide opened the door to a new way of thinking for me about everything he had done. I truly believe Dylan lost access to the tools allowing him to make rational decisions, and I hope in this chapter to discuss some of the reasons with thoughtfulness and sensitivity. I am endlessly grateful to the world-class experts who made themselves available in order to help me understand.

Were there signs I missed that Dylan was going to commit a crime, especially one of such devastating magnitude? No. Even now, I do not believe there were. Both boys did "leak" their plan by making disclosures of varying accuracy and specificity to their friends. But they did not leak to us.

That doesn't mean I was powerless, however, because there *were* signs that year that Dylan was depressed. I now believe that if Tom and I had been equipped then to recognize those signs, and been able to intervene as far as his depression was concerned, we would at least have had a fighting chance to prevent what came next.

Understanding Dylan's death as a suicide came almost as an afterthought for me. But for Dylan, the desire to die by suicide was where it all began.

· · ·

One afternoon, a few months after the tragedy, I was leafing through a journal over a cup of tea in the break room. Our office received a number of higher-education journals, and looking through them helped me feel connected to a larger world not devastated by my son. I had stopped reading mainstream newspapers and magazines, lest I run into a quote about our family from a "trusted friend" I'd never met, or a scathing editorial about our overindulgence of Dylan, or our family's lack of moral values. Whatever news about the investigation or the lawsuits or the victims I needed to know came through our lawyer, or from friends and family members.

I came across an article on youth suicide prevention. In the first paragraph, the author said something like, "There is a temptation to look to outside influences like violent video games and lax gun control laws for an explanation of the tragedy at Columbine. But among all the other deaths and injuries, two boys died by suicide that day."

Those words stopped me in my tracks. Because I had been so single-mindedly focused on the murders he had committed, I had strangely not considered the significance of Dylan's death by suicide.

Intellectually, of course, I knew Dylan had died by his own hand: the autopsy report had said so. I had taken another short step toward conceptualizing Dylan's death as a suicide in the wake of a short-lived but popular conspiracy theory in the aftermath of the shootings: that Eric had killed Dylan. (It's alive and well online.) Whenever anyone raised the issue with me, I told them it didn't matter. Whether Dylan had pulled the trigger or had been killed by Eric (or by a cop, per another conspiracy theory floating around in those days), Dylan was responsible for his own death.

And yet, until I saw that journal article, I was sure his suicide had been an impulsive act, a response to this "prank gone awry"— not part of any long-standing plan.

After reading the article, I wasn't so sure. It wasn't quite an "aha" moment—the situation was far too complex, and I was far too horrified and confused. Still, something in me shifted. That random journal article created an aperture in me, an opening to an understanding I had not allowed myself to have: whatever else he had intended, Dylan had gone to the school to die.

. . .

My former boss and close friend Sharon, a suicide loss survivor, had treated Dylan's death as a suicide right from the start. Since I couldn't join a support group, she brought me stacks of books. For her, Dylan's intent to die by suicide was a given, and she saw, long before I did, that it was an important piece in the overall puzzle.

Sharon's presence and conversation were a solace, but the pile of books and pamphlets about suicide she brought me sat unread for months. Even if I could have concentrated long enough to read more than a sentence or two, I couldn't yet focus on Dylan's intention to hurt himself, but only why and how he had gone to the school to hurt others. My ignorance was huge, and so I could not imagine that Dylan had been depressed, or suicidal. Those words had nothing to do with us, or with our situation. Devon had told me that after dancing with her at the prom, Dylan had dropped a kiss on the top of her head. Was that the behavior of a depressed person?

After seeing the article in the break room, I started into the stack of books that Sharon had brought me, and what I found there surprised me a great deal. I believed myself to be an educated person, and a sensitive one. But, like many people, I had unthinkingly bought into many of the most prevalent (and damaging) myths about suicide. Opening those books was the first step in a lifetime's work of educating myself and others—and of coming to terms, in a real way, with what had gone wrong in our own home and family.

Survivors often comment about how remote suicide seemed to them before they lost a loved one to it; the real question is why we persist in believing it's rare, when it is really anything but. Someone in America dies by suicide every thirteen minutes—40,000 people a year. That is anything but insignificant.

According to the CDC, suicide is the third leading cause of death among people aged 10–14, and the second among people aged 15–34. So, besides accidents and homicide, nothing kills more young people in this country than suicide—not cancer, not sexually transmitted disease. A 2013 study looked at almost 6,500 teens. One in eight had contemplated suicide, and one in twenty-five had attempted it, yet only half of them were in treatment.

More than a million people in the United States attempt suicide each year—which means three attempts *every minute*. Many of them do so without raising any red flags, an indication that our standard assessment practices may be of limited use.

Even after more than ten years as a suicide prevention activist, I still find those numbers—and the general public's ignorance about them—staggering. I taught Dylan, as I had taught his brother before him, to protect himself from lightning strikes, snakebites, and hypothermia. I taught him to floss, to wear sunscreen, and the importance of checking his blind spot twice. As he became a teenager, I talked as openly as I could about the dangers of drinking and drug use, and I educated him about safe and ethical sexual behavior. It never crossed my mind that the gravest danger Dylan faced would not come from an external source at all, but from within himself.

In my deepest self, I believed that those close to me were inoculated against suicide because I loved them, or because we had a good relationship, or because I was an astute, sensitive, caring person who could keep them safe. I was not alone in believing that suicide could only happen in other families, but I was wrong.

Almost everything I knew about suicide was wrong. I thought I knew what kinds of people tried to kill themselves, and why—they were selfish or too cowardly to face their problems, or captive to a passing impulse. I had bought into the cultural cliché that people who died by suicide were quitters—either too weak to handle the challenges of life, or attention-seeking, or trying to punish the people around them. These, I learned, are myths that are born out of thinking about suicide without really trying to inhabit the suicidal mind.

Suicidal thought is a symptom of illness, of something else gone wrong. Most suicides are not impulsive, spur-of-the-moment decisions at all. Instead, most of these deaths are the result of a person losing a long and painful battle against their own impaired thinking. A suicidal person is someone who is unable to tolerate their suffering any longer. Even if she does not really want to die, she knows death will end that suffering once and for all.

We know there is an incontrovertible correlation between suicide and brain illness. Studies from all over the world suggest that the overwhelming majority—from 90 to 95 percent—of people who die by suicide have a serious mental health disorder, most often depression or bipolar illness.

Many of the researchers I have talked to believe that (barring chronic illness–related end-of-life decisions), suicidality is fundamentally incompatible with a healthy mind. Dr. Victoria Arango is a clinical neurobiologist at Columbia who has dedicated her career to studying the biology of suicide. Her work has led her to believe that there exists a biological (and possibly genetic) vulnerability to suicide, without which a person is unlikely to make an attempt. She is currently working toward identifying specific changes in the brains of people who have died by suicide. "Suicide is a brain disease," she told me.

Dr. Thomas Joiner, whose books are both meticulously researched as well as beautifully compassionate and personal, writes as both a psychologist and a survivor of his father's suicide. His theory of suicide, a Venn diagram with three overlapping circles, has redefined the field.

He proposes that the desire to die by suicide arises when people live with two psychological states simultaneously over a period of time: thwarted belongingness ("I am alone") and perceived burdensomeness ("The world would be better off without me"). Those people are at imminent risk when they take steps to override their own instinct for self-preservation, and therefore become capable of suicide ("I am not afraid to die").

The desire for suicide, then, comes from the first two. The ability to go through with it comes from the third. Over the years, this insight would prove important to me.

. . .

I finally started to read some of his journal pages. He was expressing depressed and suicidal thoughts a full 2 years before his death. I couldn't believe it. We had all that time to help him and didn't. I read his writings and cried and cried. This was like the suicide note we never got. A sad, heart-wrenching day.

—Journal entry, June 2001

From the day the tragedy occurred, we had been desperate for information about Dylan's state of mind when he died. He had purposely left nothing behind, and law enforcement had emptied his room of anything of relevance, so there was little to study. After nearly two years, we had come to accept we would never know what he had experienced during the last months of his life. Then, in 2001, Kate Battan's office called. The sheriff's department had pages of Dylan's writing in their possession, and offered to share copies with us.

These writings are always referred to as "journals," but really these were scattered pages, compiled by the investigators after the fact. Most of them were taken from Dylan's school notebooks, although some of the bits and pieces of paper he wrote on were old advertising flyers or other scraps, which he then tucked into various binders and books. The stack of photocopied pages was about half an inch thick. Some entries were a sentence long, while others went on for pages.

What I found in Dylan's writing was a revelation. I had not known he had expressed his thoughts and feelings in writing at all, as I did, and it made me feel close to him. The entries themselves broke my heart. I know how deceptive self-recording can be. I often spill pages and pages when I am sad or scared or angry, whereas better times rate only a breezy line or two. I also know that people can say things in their diaries they don't have any real plans to act on: *I swear, I'm going to kill Joe if he doesn't return my weed whacker.* Even with that caveat, Dylan's anguish—his depression, perceived isolation, longing, and desperation—jumps off the page.

He talks about cutting himself, a sign of severe distress. He writes about suicide in the very earliest pages: "Thinking of suicide gives me hope that i'll be in my place wherever i go after this life— that ill finally not be at war w. myself, the world, the universe—my mind, body, everywhere, everything at PEACE—me—my soul (existence)" and often afterward: "oooh god I want to die sooo bad . . . such a sad desolate lonely unsalvageable I feel I am . . . not fair, NOT FAIR!!! Let's sum up my life . . . the most miserable existence in the history of time." He talks about dying by suicide for the first time a full two years before Columbine, and many more times after that.

There is despair and anger but little violence, especially in the pages before January 1999. Besides sadness, the most common emotion expressed throughout Dylan's journals—and by far the most prevalent word—is "love." There are pages covered in huge, hand-drawn hearts. He writes, heartbreakingly and sometimes eloquently, about his unfulfilled, excruciating desire for romantic love and understanding. "A dark time, infinite sadness," he wrote. "I want to find love." He fills pages with details of a passionate, painful infatuation with a girl who does not even know he exists.

The two psychological states Joiner points to as components in the desire to die—thwarted belongingness ("I am alone") and perceived burdensomeness ("I am a burden")—are painfully apparent, although he kept both his hurt and his infatuation closely guarded. I pushed back for years against the public perception of Dylan as an outcast, because he had close friends (not only in Eric, but also in Zack and Nate), and because he participated in a wider circle of boys and girls. But—and it is vital for every survivor of suicide loss to understand this about the person who has died—the journals revealed a vast chasm between our perception of his reality and Dylan's own perception of it.

He had friends, but he did not feel as if he belonged. In one journal entry he lists his "nice family" among the good things in his life, but the hugeness of our love for him could not penetrate the fog of his desolation. He understood himself as a burden, although we never once felt he was. (Tom and I did worry aloud about how we would pay for his college tuition, which haunts me to this day.) He expresses anger at a world where he does not fit, is not understood. At the beginning, the anger is directed mostly at himself. Gradually, it turns outward.

· · ·

I thought it might be helpful to have a distillation of a few points.

1. Nothing you did or didn't do caused Dylan to do what he did.
2. You didn't "fail to see" what Dylan was going through—he was profoundly secretive and deliberately hid his internal world not only from you, but from everyone else in his life.
3. By the end of his life, Dylan's psychological functioning had deteriorated to the point that he was not in his right mind.
4. Despite his deterioration, his former self survived enough to spare at least four people during the attack.

—E-mail from Dr. Peter Langman, February 9, 2015

That Dylan was seriously depressed is not up for debate. A posthumous diagnosis is, of course, impossible, yet some experts believe the problem may have been more serious.

His journals are difficult to understand, and not simply because Dylan's handwriting was so poor. Toward the end of his life, he wrote things like "When I'm in my human form, knowing that I'm going to die, everything has a touch of triviality to it." A statement like this implies that, at least part of the time, he did not feel human. It was as if being human was out of his reach: "made a human, without the possibility of BEING human."

Dylan was intelligent and educated, and a better-than-average writing student. Yet in the journals he often made strange word choices. Sometimes the words he used weren't real words at all, but neologisms—words he'd made up, like "depressioners," and "perceivations." The way he constructs his sentences is unusual, too—as in the passage I've already quoted: "such a sad desolate lonely unsalvageable I feel I am." This isn't the shorthand of a jour-naler; there's almost a singsong quality to many of the iterations that recalls Dr. Seuss.

This was one of the first things Dr. Peter Langman noticed. Dr. Langman, a psychologist, is an expert on school shooters and the author of a number of books, including *Why Kids Kill: Inside the Minds of School Shooters*. Our conversations in the course of writing this book have been difficult for me; they have also brought me in-sight and some measure of relief. With his permission, I have relied heavily on his interpretations to make sense of Dylan's writing.

Dr. Langman told me he had originally intended to leave Dylan out of *Why Kids Kill* because he was unsure about Dylan's motives. There were too many contradictions: How did this kid, widely reported to be shy and gentle, turn into a vicious killer? Then, in 2006, the sheriff's department released some of Dylan's writings to the public, offering a window into the disparity between how Dylan presented himself to the world, how he behaved when he was with Eric, and how he seemed to himself.

Dr. Langman believes that the early descriptions of Dylan as shy, extremely self-conscious, and self-critical may mean he suffered from a mild form of avoidant personality disorder. People with APD are shy past what we consider to be normal introversion. As Dylan en-tered adolescence, the stressors in his life became unmanageable for him, and he progressed to schizotypal personality disorder.

Schizotypals often seem "odd" to other people. (Dylan was often described as goofy by people who did not know him well.) They may be paranoid, or especially sensitive to slights, as Dylan was. They often use strange, rambling syntax and unusual words, as Dylan did in his writings. They withdraw into a world where reality and fantasy are not always distinguishable. These are not full-on delusions, but a fuzziness in the boundary between what is real and what is not. This fuzziness is increasingly evident in the journals: in reality Dylan felt profoundly inferior, and so, according to Dr. Langman, he created a fantasy where he was a godlike being. Toward the end of his life, that fantasy predominates.

I do not myself know what to make of Dr. Langman's diagnosis. I'm not sure what's worse—knowing Dylan was suffering from a serious impairment, or knowing I did not recognize such a serious impairment while he was living under my roof. There is little succor in either.

With the help of Dr. Kent Kiehl, who studies the brain structures of criminals at the University of New Mexico, I had Dylan's journals analyzed independently. The reviewer found no evidence of a formal thought disorder, but points to

> persistent and unrelenting themes of depression, suicidality, and alienation. . . . and increasing dissociation from his sense of himself prior to the onset of his depression. As his inner pain and sense of alienation worsen so too does his dehumanization of others. . . . This grandiose identification, dehumanization of others, loss of emotive capacity other than the experience of pain, and the promise of a release from pain, form the context of a delusional inner world that lead to the suicidal and homicidal plans discussed in the journal.

The reviewer also points to "prominent borderline themes" throughout the journal.

The report ends,

> With only the journal to go on it is not possible to make a definitive diagnosis but major depression with transient psychotic episodes and/or borderline personality disorder with transient psychotic episodes are the most compelling diagnoses based on this journal.

In the end, it doesn't really matter what Dylan's particular diagnosis might have been. Nobody disputes Dylan's depression, or its ability to confuse a person's decision-making process. In fact, nine out of the ten school shooters Dr. Langman profiles in his recent book, *School Shooters: Understanding High School, College, and Adult Perpetrators*, suffered from depression and suicidal thoughts. Even if serious depression was the only thing going on, Dylan was not, as Dr. Langman put it to me, "in his right mind."

. . .

Kay Redfield Jamison, in her masterful book about suicide, *Night Falls Fast: Understanding Suicide*, writes: "Most suicides, although by no means all, can be prevented. The breach between what we know and do is lethal." In Dylan's case, of course, the decision to die was lethal not only to him, but to many others.

Even if a person does not discuss their intention to die by suicide, there are often warning signs that they are in trouble. Certain events, such as a previous suicide attempt or trouble with the law, can put people at higher risk. There are often behavioral indications as well, like social withdrawal and increased irritability.

If those warning signs are noticed and recognized for what they are, treatment can help. Because—and this was hard for me to hear when my loss was recent, although I derive great hope from it now—*suicide is preventable*. Every expert I have talked to emphasizes the wealth of successful treatments for mood disorders, if people can only be convinced to take advantage of them, and stick with them.

Not every suicide is preventable—yet. (Ed Coffey, a physician and vice president at the Henry Ford Health System in Detroit, pioneered a program called Perfect Depression Care, which made a goal of zero suicides in the program. When asked if reducing suicide death to zero is realistic, he's known for shooting back: "What number would you choose? Eight? Does that include my mother, or your sister?") Brain health disorders can be pernicious. Sometimes they progress, and win. We can say the same thing about cancer, though: even with gold-standard treatment, some people will die from the disease. Does that mean we throw our hands up in despair? Or do we commit ourselves to early detection and prevention, and to better and more personalized treatment—to catching these diseases at Stage I or II, instead of Stage IV?

I sometimes feel envious of families who did everything they could to obtain effective treatment for a loved one, even if they ultimately lost that fight. My son struggled alone with his illness. I did not suspect Dylan was depressed until I was shown his writings and learned he thought about suicide and longed for the peace and comfort of death. His closest friends, boys he hung out with every day for years, did not know how depressed he felt. Some of them refuse to accept that characterization to this day. But I was his mother. I should have known.

Dylan might have died by suicide later in his life; that I cannot know. Eric might have hatched and executed a version of the plan to destroy the school by himself, or with another kid. He might have gotten through the crisis without violence, or gone on to commit an act of terror in another place and time.

What I *do* know is that Dylan did show outward signals of depression, signs Tom and I observed but were not able to decode. If we had known enough to understand what those signs meant, I believe that we would have been able to prevent Columbine.

CHAPTER 12

Fateful Dynamic

*Definitive statement: "I do not think that Columbine would have hap-
pened without Eric."*
—Note from a conversation with Dr. Frank Ochberg, January 2015

Dylan's journals also shed light on his relationship with Eric—
and, in particular, the terrible interdependence fatal to them
and to so many others.

In the summer of 1997, Dylan's friend Zack started dating Devon,
who became his girlfriend. Nate also started dating a girl. To us, this
was hardly noticeable—Dylan still spent time with Zack one on one,
and Zack, Devon, and Dylan all hung out together. He spent time
with Nate and other friends, too. Yet Dylan experienced Zack's new
relationship as a betrayal. This is another example of the marked
separation between Dylan's reality and how he perceived that reality.

The summer Zack met and fell for Devon, Dylan and Eric
started spending more time together. Eric's name appears more frequently. Dylan writes about suicide many times that summer, as he
did many times previously, but there are no homicidal comments in
his journal until that fall. Even after the boys have begun making
plans, Dylan reveals a secret in these most private pages: he believes
he will be dead by his own hand before they have a chance to carry
them out. After talking about the temptations of suicide for close
to two years, Dylan finally says good-bye in June 1998. "This is
probably my last entry. I love my self close second to [redacted] my
everlasting love. Goodbye."

The next entry, dated January 20, 1999, begins with his dismay at finding himself still alive. "This shit again. Back at writing, doing just like a fucking zombie." Later in that entry, he mentions the plan with Eric as a possible solution to the way he feels. "I hate this non-thinking stasis. I'm stuck in humanity. Maybe going 'NBK' (gawd) with Eric is the way to break free." (NBK—for Natural Born Killers, after the Oliver Stone movie of the same title—was the name the boys used to refer to their plan to attack the school.)

After that, the journals become noticeably darker and more hopeless. Dylan's thoughts are more scattered and difficult to understand as he comes to believe that Eric's plan represents a way out. His ambivalence is present right up until the shootings.

At the end of his life, Dylan was connected to only two emotions: anger and hopelessness. Any feelings that might have connected him to others in a positive way were beyond his reach. He believed death was the only possible escape from his pain; there simply wasn't anything else left in his emotional toolbox. To use Joiner's language, he perceived himself to be profoundly alienated from everybody on earth. To use mine, Dylan was loved, but he did not feel loved. He was valued, but he did not feel valuable. He had many, many options, but Eric's was the only one he could see.

. . .

One night, probably during his junior year, Dylan told me, "Eric's crazy."

I responded, "You're going to meet people all your life who are difficult, and I'm glad you have enough common sense to recognize it when you see it." I told him his dad and I had a lot of confidence in his ability to make good choices, with or without his friends.

Our confidence was misplaced, but neither did we have any idea of what Dylan was dealing with. I had no inkling that the situation might be truly dangerous. Nor did I have any conception of what Dylan meant by "crazy." Eric was higher-maintenance than

Dylan's other friends, and I'd seen evidence of his volatile temper at a soccer game. The problem, though, was much more serious.

Like Dylan, Eric kept journals—private writings where he reveals his innermost thoughts and feelings. They are almost unreadably dark, filled with sadistic images and drawings, fantasies of rape, dismemberment, and scenes of massive destruction, including, in more than one place, the wholesale extinction of the human race. Dr. Langman writes, "[Dylan's] journal is markedly different from Eric's in both content and style. Whereas Eric's is full of narcissistic condescension and bloodthirsty rage, Dylan's is focused on loneliness, depression, ruminations, and preoccupation with finding love. Eric drew pictures of weapons, swastikas, and soldiers; Dylan drew hearts. Eric lusted after sex and fantasized about rape; Dylan longed for true love."

Based on his journals, many of the experts I've spoken to feel comfortable saying that Eric displayed the traits and characteristics of a psychopath. As with Dylan, a true posthumous diagnosis is, of course, not possible. (In any case, because the adolescent brain is still developing, a formal diagnosis of psychopathy is only possible after the subject turns eighteen.) Even so, Eric certainly satisfies a great number of the diagnostic markers associated with this personality disorder.

Psychopathy is characterized by diminished empathy and provocative behavior. Most important, psychopaths (also called sociopaths; some experts differentiate between the two, the majority do not) don't have a conscience, the part of the mind that enables us to feel guilt. They lie without compunction and are often highly skilled manipulators. There are some psychologists and psychiatrists who believe that psychopaths can be successfully treated. The ones I spoke to are not convinced. Not every psychopath is a criminal or a sadist, but if they do move in that direction, as Eric did, they can become highly dangerous.

A 2001 study of adolescent school shooters, prompted in part by the massacre at Columbine High School, resulted in two interesting findings. The first is that 25 percent of the thirty-four teenage shooters they looked at participated in pairs. This is different from adult rampage killers, who most often act alone. Dr. Reid Meloy, a forensic psychologist and expert on targeted violence and threat assessment, authored the study. He told me that these deadly dyads mean it's absolutely critical for parents to pay attention to the dynamics between kids and their friends. The second finding from his study: typically, one of the two kids was a psychopath, and the other one suggestible, dependent, and depressed.

This appears to have been the dynamic between Dylan and Eric. In Eric's yearbook, Dylan gloats about bullying kids, but in the privacy of his journals, he reveals his shame and guilt, and promises himself he won't do it again. It's very like the posturing on the Basement Tapes. There were distinct gaps between what Dylan felt, how he behaved around Eric, and what he did.

Dr. Langman believes Dylan's ambivalence may have extended up to the massacre itself. On at least four occasions at the school—always out of Eric's earshot and line of sight—Dylan let people go. The physical evidence suggests two incidents during the rampage when Eric went to retrieve Dylan, perhaps to make sure he was still on board. I take no comfort from this—Dylan committed atrocities, end of story. But learning about his ambivalence devastated me. In my notes after a conversation with Dr. Langman, I wrote:

> *Crying too hard to take any more notes. . . . I had made myself accept Dylan as a sadistic killer, but I had not yet come to grips with a Dylan who was trying to counteract his own "evil" with moments of goodness. I think I met this Dylan for the first time when Langman talked about it, so it gave me a different Dylan to grieve for.*

Dylan's ambivalence also made me feel even more culpable than I did already. Dr. Marisa Randazzo directed the Secret Service's research on school shootings, and (as Marisa Reddy) was one of the authors of the landmark federal study of school shootings conducted jointly by the US Secret Service and the Department of Education. Dr. Randazzo and Dr. Meloy both told me that when troubled kids learn they have other options besides homicide and suicide to solve the problems plaguing them, they generally take advantage of those other options.

Dylan did make efforts to extricate himself from the relationship with Eric. My guilt about this, in particular, fills me with despair. After the two boys got into trouble in their junior year, Dylan made an attempt to distance himself, and he asked for my help. We developed an internal shorthand: If Eric called to ask Dylan to do something, he'd say, "Let me ask my mom," and shake his head at me. I'd say, loudly enough to be heard on the other end of the line, "I'm sorry, but you can't go out tonight, Dylan. You promised you'd clean your room/do your homework/join us for dinner."

At the time, I was simply happy that Dylan wanted distance. I had told both my sons they could always use me as an excuse in an emergency. I was thinking particularly of drinking and driving, but I meant any unsafe situation. So I was pleased, not only that Dylan had taken me up on my long-standing offer, but that he'd found a way to separate from his friend without hurting Eric's feelings.

After I saw the dynamic between Eric and Dylan on the Basement Tapes, I found myself revisiting this episode in a new light. If Dylan didn't want to go out with Zack or Nate or Robyn or any of his other friends, he simply told them so: "Nah, I can't this weekend. I need to write this paper." Only with Eric did he need me to bail him out. I never wondered about that or thought to ask Dylan: "Why can't you just say no?" Asking for my help seemed like a sign of his good judgment, but afterward I realized that it was a portent of something much more disturbing. It was a sign I had missed until it was too late.

During one of our conversations, Frank Ochberg said, "Dylan did not have the profile of a killer, but he had vulnerability to become enmeshed with one." FBI investigators found that Eric had tried to interest other boys in a plan of mass destruction, including Zack and Mark Manes.

They didn't bite. Dylan did.

. . .

Randazzo: "There is often a fine line between people who are suicidal and homicidal. Most suicides are not homicidal, but many who are homicidal are there because of suicidality."

I believe this is what happened to Dyl.

—Annotated note from interview with
Dr. Marisa Randazzo, February 2015

Criminal justice specialist Dr. Adam Lankford, author of *The Myth of Martyrdom*, studies the suicidality of suicide bombers and mass shooters. He writes that rampage shooters, like suicide bombers, share three main characteristics: mental health issues that have produced a desire to die, a deep sense of victimization, and the desire to earn fame and glory through killing.

In one study, he looked at almost two hundred rampage shooters involved in events from 1966 to 2010. Almost half of them died by suicide as part of their attacks. Others may have intended to die, but were restrained or taken into custody before they had the chance. Truly suicidal or not, rampage shooters have less than a 1 percent chance of escaping the consequences of their actions. To plan an event with such a disastrously low chance of escape or survival implies what Lankford calls "life indifference."

According to threat assessment experts, mass shooters almost always follow a discernible path to the shootings they commit. Recognizing the signposts on that path is the key to preventing these events. The pathway often begins with the desire to die.

For a long time, murder-suicide was viewed as a subset of murder, not of suicide. Some murder-suicides do correspond to the murder model, where suicide is a "plan B" turned to only when other escape options have failed. But a shifting understanding of suicide and a closer look at the data have revealed that many murder-suicides, if not the vast majority, have their genesis in suicidal thoughts. In other words, as Dr. Joiner writes, "If it can be shown that suicide is fundamental in murder-suicide, then suicide prevention is also murder-suicide prevention."

In the case of Columbine, at least, I believe that is true. For years I searched for the missing integer, the piece of Dylan's character that allowed him to do what he did. From what I've learned, I now believe the third segment of Dr. Joiner's Venn diagram—the capability to die by suicide—provides part of the answer.

In his writings, Dylan takes comfort from the idea of death. But he does not seem to have the capability for suicide by himself.

As Dr. Joiner points out, people have to become desensitized to the violence and the fear of pain in order to be able to harm themselves. (He posits that this is why suicide rates are higher in populations routinely exposed to—and therefore inured to—pain and horror, such as doctors, soldiers, and people with anorexia.) Our natural instinct for survival is hardwired, and most people have to work themselves up to ignoring it over time.

Dylan couldn't—by himself. He talks about suicide, but he does not by himself come up with a plan to do it. His writing about it, as it is about most things, is abstract. That paralysis is reflected throughout the journals. He wants a job working with computers, but he can't get one or keep the one he gets. He talks over and over about the girl he has a crush on, but there is no evidence he made any advances toward her. He agonizes over the letter he writes to her, but doesn't deliver it. In fact, there's no evidence they ever spoke.

The same thing appears to be true for suicide, and he turns to Eric for help: "Soon. . . . either ill commit suicide, or I'll get w. [redacted girl's name] & it will be NBK for us." Dylan appears to have "needed" Eric's homicidal plan in order to be able to do what he most wanted to do: die by suicide. Dr. Joiner suggested to me that planning with Eric for the rampage may have been part of the way Dylan rehearsed his own death. The preparations helped him to desensitize himself.

For years after the attack, I resisted blaming Eric for Dylan's participation. I believed, as I still do at some level, that whatever hold Eric might have had over him, Dylan was still accountable for the choices he made. At one point, at least, he was separate enough and objective enough to tell me Eric was "crazy," and ambivalent enough to try to get help to distance himself from the relationship.

Given what I have learned about psychopathy, I now feel differently. I find the violence and hatred seething off the page in Eric's journals almost unreadably dark, but his writing is clear, whereas Dylan's was not. As Dr. Langman puts it, "Dylan's writing is jumbled, disorganized, and full of tangled syntax and misused words. Eric's *thoughts* are disturbing; Dylan's thought *process* is disturbed. The difference is in what Eric thinks and how Dylan thinks."

We know Eric was overwhelmingly persuasive. His Diversion counselor, dismissing him early from the program, said at the end of her final report, "muy facile [*sic*] hombre," which my Spanish-speaking friends translate as an affectionate characterization along the lines of "super-easy guy." Eric's perceived halo may have extended to Dylan, whose own grades weren't good enough to justify his early dismissal from Diversion. A number of the psychologists I have spoken to have told me how scarily charismatic and charming psychopaths can be—how quick they are to find the wedge, and how masterfully they work the lever. I am not sure that Dylan, especially in an impaired state, was in a position to extricate himself from that relationship.

Dr. Randazzo has interviewed a number of would-be school shooters, intercepted before they could execute their terrible plans. She describes both their ambivalence and their tunnel vision. "When they reach that point of desperation, they're looking for a way out. They can't see any other options. They just don't care." Knowing this does not for a moment lessen Dylan's culpability, but it may get us closer to an explanation of how he came to be there. Dr. Dwayne Fuselier, a clinical psychologist and the supervisor in charge of the FBI team during the Columbine investigation, told me, "I believe Eric went to the school to kill people and didn't care if he died, while Dylan wanted to die and didn't care if others died as well."

CHAPTER 13

Pathway to Suicide

Dylan's Junior Year

Dylan with family at a local restaurant, about three weeks before Columbine.
The Klebold Family

Four-hour lawyer appt was upsetting. The more we talked the more we saw how this "perfect" kid was not so perfect. By the time we were done we felt that our lives had not only been useless, but had been destructive. . . . We wanted to believe that Dylan was perfect. We let ourselves accept that and really didn't see signs of his own anger and frustration. I don't know if I can ever live with myself. I have so much regret.

—Journal entry, May 1999

In his junior year, Dylan got into trouble. Not once or twice, but a few times, in a series of escalating events.

That makes this the hardest chapter in this book for me to write, because I know most people reading it will say: *Hey, Sue: this kid was falling apart, and you just stood by and did nothing. What the hell were you thinking?* The signs that Dylan was struggling were not overt or glaring, but we observed them—and misinterpreted them.

Now, the overwhelming majority of children, even if they are facing brain health challenges, are not going to commit a school shooting. If you live with a teenager, though, there's a reasonable chance he or she is struggling with a brain disorder. An estimated one in five children and adolescents has a diagnosable mental health condition. Only 20 percent of those kids are identified. That is why parents too often learn or think about brain health issues in teens only after those issues result in violence, crime, or self-harm. Despite its prevalence and the danger it poses, brain illness in teenagers too often goes unrecognized, even by caring teachers, well-meaning counselors and pediatricians, and the most vigilant parents.

Left untreated, even the mildest brain health impairment can derail a young person's life, and stop a child from reaching his or her full potential, a tragedy in itself. A disease like depression can also have much more serious consequences, as it sets many of the traps that snag children in adolescence: drug and alcohol abuse, drunk driving, petty crime, eating disorders, cutting, abusive relationships, and high-risk sexual behaviors among them.

In 1999, I did not know the difference between the sadness and lethargy I had always called depression, and *clinical* depression, which many sufferers describe as a feeling of nothingness. I had no idea that about 20 percent of teenagers experience a depressive episode, or that experiencing one episode puts them at higher risk of another. (A recent CDC report puts that number closer to 30 percent.)

I did not know that depression manifests itself differently in teenagers than it does in adults. Where adults may appear sad and low-energy, teenagers (especially boys) tend to withdraw and show increased irritability, self-criticism, frustration, and anger. Unexplained pains, whininess, sleep disorders, and clinginess are common symptoms of depression among younger children.

Neither did I know that the symptoms of depression in adolescents are often masked by the many other developmental and behavioral changes they're going through, which may be one of the reasons diagnosis often comes too late. Parents may not be alarmed by a teenager who sleeps late into the weekend, or a good eater who pushes away his plate—"ugh, gross"—although changes in sleep and appetite can be symptoms of depression. Diagnosis is further complicated because many depressed children show none of these signs.

Dylan's depression remained undiagnosed, and untreated. In this he was not alone. The vast majority of depressed teens do not get the help they need, even as their condition interferes with their relationships with friends and family and with their schoolwork, and dramatically raises the risk they'll get into trouble with the law or die by suicide. In Dylan's case, of course, it was both.

Tom and I did know Dylan was going through a rough patch. That year, the whole family was plagued by health problems and money worries. Tom and I spent quite a bit of time worried about Byron, who had moved into his own apartment. The overall difficulty of the year contributed to our failure to see what was right in front of us.

There is another reason Tom and I did not react with greater purpose when Dylan's life went off the rails in junior year, and that is *because he seemed to get himself back on track.* At the end of that year, and throughout his senior year, after the damage and disappointment of the previous months, Dylan seemed intent to prove to us he was getting his life together.

I mention this not to make an excuse, but because it is such a common refrain among parents who have lost children to suicide. "He was so much better!" those shocked parents say—as Dylan seemed better to us.

To borrow a cliché, we thought he'd been scared straight by the gravity of the trouble he'd gotten into the year before. Unfortunately, the finish line he was moving toward with such clarity was not, as we believed, an independent life in a dorm room at the University of Arizona while earning a degree in his beloved computer science. Instead, it was a plan that would end in his own death, and those of so many others.

. . .

Things have been really happy this summer. . . . Dylan is yukking it up and having a great time with friends.

—Journal entry, July 1997

The summer between Dylan's sophomore and junior years was low-key. There was, however, one disturbing incident, and it involved Eric Harris.

Dylan hadn't played soccer since kindergarten, but he decided to join the team Eric played for that summer, and they gave him a shot although he had no experience and few skills. We were pleased to hear he was joining the team, as soccer wouldn't strain the arm he'd injured pitching. Plus, we admired his willingness to try a sport he hadn't played in years.

Dylan wasn't a great athlete—he was strong, but lacked agility and the coordination to manage his long, gangly limbs. He did not play soccer particularly well, but he attended practice faithfully. When the team made the playoffs, Tom and I came out to watch. Dylan played poorly, and the team lost.

Still sweaty, Eric and Dylan came over to where we were standing with the Harrises. Before we could congratulate them on a good effort, Eric began to scream. Spittle flying from his mouth, he lashed out at Dylan, ranting about his poor performance. Chattering parents and boys from both teams fell silent and stared.

Eric's parents flanked him and guided him off the field as Tom, Dylan, and I drifted slowly, in stunned humiliation, toward our own car. I couldn't hear what the Harrises were saying to Eric, but they appeared to be trying to settle him down. Dylan walked between Tom and me, silent and impassive.

I was shocked by the sudden inappropriateness of the display, and by the extremity of Eric's rage. Dylan's utter lack of affect alarmed me too; he had to be wounded, though he revealed nothing. My heart ached for him. I wanted to hug him, but he was fifteen years old and surrounded by his team. I couldn't embarrass him further.

As soon as we got inside the car, though, I said, "Man! What a jerk! I can't believe Eric!" As Tom started the car, Dylan stared out the window with a blank expression on his face. His calm in the face of Eric's freak-out seemed unnatural, and I hoped he'd allow himself to acknowledge anger or humiliation as we drove away, but he did not.

I pressed him, wishing he'd blow off steam. "Didn't it hurt your feelings, to have him act like that? I'd be incredibly upset if a friend treated me that way." Dylan was still looking out the window, and his expression didn't change when he answered me: "Nah. That's just Eric."

Tom, I could tell, was fuming. Dylan, on the other hand, appeared detached, as if he'd already shrugged it off. How fragile must Eric's ego be, to be that upset about losing a dumb soccer game? I was more embarrassed for him than I was for Dylan; the tantrum had made Eric seem like a much younger child.

Over the course of the drive home, I kicked into my Mom Rescue Mode. As if I knew anything about it at all, I suggested various ways Dylan could fix his soccer game. I thought I was probably making his humiliation worse, but I couldn't stop myself. I told him that if I'd learned anything in my years of being chosen last for every team in high school, it was that the best players tended to go after the ball as if their lives depended on it. The people who won were usually the ones who wanted it most.

Dylan said nothing, and I wound down. At the next game, the last of the season, he surprised us by playing better than he'd ever played before, charging to gain control of the ball. They lost, but Dylan's coach praised his improvement, and he seemed more at ease with himself. Foolishly, I thought my advice might have helped a little, and Tom and I were both pleased to see that Eric showed no more evidence of poor sportsmanship.

Tom was furious with Eric for screaming. He never did entirely forgive him, but did not forbid the relationship. Dylan, we thought, could handle himself. In hindsight, of course, I wish we had been brutal in our separation of the two boys.

. . .

> *Losses and other events—whether anticipated or actual—can lead*
> *to feelings of shame, humiliation, or despair and may serve as trig-*
> *gering events for suicidal behavior. Triggering events include losses,*
> *such as the breakup of a relationship or a death; academic failures;*
> *trouble with authorities, such as school suspensions or legal difficul-*
> *ties; bullying; or health problems. This is especially true for youth al-*
> *ready vulnerable because of low self-esteem or a mental disorder, such*
> *as depression. Help is available and should be arranged.*
>
> —American Association of Suicidology

As soon as Dylan's junior year started, the whole family was bom-
barded by problems.

The first few months of Byron's experiment in independence
were hard to watch. I reassured myself by thinking about Erma
Bombeck's statement about her own boys: they lived like hamsters.
Still, I worried. At least I knew he was getting two or three decent
meals a week. He came to us most Sunday evenings for dinner, and
always left with a bag of hearty leftovers.

Byron's diet and housekeeping abilities were the least of our
worries about him. That fall, he weathered one crisis after another.
First, a car sideswiped his while he was waiting at an intersection.
His injuries were minor; nevertheless, it was scary, and his car was
totaled. He continued to cycle through a succession of menial jobs.
He'd often quit them for trivial reasons, like not wanting to get up
early, or to wear the uniform. When he could afford to pay his bills,
he'd sometimes forget.

I had a fundamental belief in Byron's goodness, as I did in
Dylan's. "He'll get it together," I often reassured Tom. But when
every phone call brought news of a fresh setback, even I couldn't
help wondering if Byron was ever going to settle down.

I was going through changes of my own. In September, after an
extended period of political upheaval at the college where I worked,
I started a new job, coordinating a small grant to help people with
disabilities in the community college system acquire computer
skills. I only had to go to the office four days a week, but I took a
fairly significant pay cut. The grant was also time-limited, which

added a degree of uncertainty. My commute was almost an hour longer than it had been, and I found it a little unsettling to know it would take me so long to get to my kids if they needed me.

The biggest stressor in our lives, though, was the rapid and alarming decline in Tom's health. For years he'd complained of joint pain: stiff knees, a sore neck, sharp shooting pains he described as ice picks in his toes. He experienced periods of unexplained weakness, and a series of crippling migraines like little strokes, which left him temporarily unable to see or to speak. A diagnosis of rheumatoid arthritis, right about the time Dylan entered high school, explained the chronic pain. RA is degenerative, so Tom was afraid his health would continue to worsen, leaving him disabled and unable to work.

One morning at breakfast, while he was lifting a carton of orange juice, a tendon snapped in his arm. The two of us stared dumbly at his thumb, which was no longer a working digit, but dangled loosely from his hand. Tom is a bull for whom no project is too daunting, a man who'd think nothing of working an eighteen-hour day swinging a sledgehammer, who'd lay concrete until his knees bled—and he'd been vanquished by a half-gallon of Tropicana. He was falling apart.

The constant pain, combined with his uncertainty, meant he couldn't work the long days expected of a geophysicist. This added to our financial anxiety, especially with Dylan's college tuition looming ahead of us. He cut back on projects around the house, although our fixer-upper still needed a lot of fixing up. And he couldn't go for his beloved evening runs, which had been his primary means of staying in shape, and a way for him to relieve stress.

We all could have used a better stress-relief valve. Between our money worries, Tom's increasingly serious illness, my new job, and Byron's instability, I felt like a captain keeping a ship on course through a storm while reassuring my panicking crew. Most nights, I would fall into bed so exhausted I could barely manage to brush my teeth, and often lay awake worrying that our family wouldn't be okay at all.

Disruptions like these—especially money worries, and a parent undergoing a health crisis—are risk factors for depression and suicide in teens, and a combination of them significantly increases risk.

We did notice Dylan was crankier with us than usual. We had a gentle household, overall. We weren't door slammers or yellers, and our boys weren't allowed to talk back, or to use bad language in front of us or any other adult. Even during the worst of our struggles with Byron, I was proud that we were always able to talk civilly with each other. Being a teenager, Dylan managed anyway to convey his sullenness and irritation. If I asked him to slow down when he was driving, he'd reward me with a long, slow sigh, and he'd drive like a granny for a couple of miles to make sure I got the point. "Would you please change your sheets before you go out?" I'd ask, and he'd roll his eyes almost imperceptibly as he was turning away to go do it.

I didn't enjoy this behavior, but took it in stride. Lots of other moms were dealing with much worse in the disrespect department. With Dylan, there were still flashes of sweetness to keep us from worrying too much. When I worried about his mood swings or his irritability, he'd cheerfully run an errand with me, or join Tom and me for dinner and keep us laughing until we forgot our concerns. He wasn't the kind of kid you could stay worried about for long.

Until he was. Because that year, as if everything going on with Tom and Byron and our finances weren't enough, the one family member who had always seemed to get through life without much trouble began to have problems of his own.

. . .

Dylan turned sixteen in September. When Tom and I suggested a party, he demurred: "Guys, I don't want to make a big deal out of this." But a sixteenth birthday is a milestone, and Tom and I wanted to mark it for Dylan.

Our family tradition was to go to a restaurant of the celebrant's choice. That year, Dylan chose a barbecue restaurant with a 1940s classic movie theme. Byron couldn't get anyone to cover him at work. While we hated for him to miss his brother's birthday celebration, we were pleased to see evidence of his work ethic and supported his decision not to attend. Plus, Tom and I had a surprise planned: although Dylan's friend Zack also had to work that night, we'd arranged for Eric and Nate to meet us at the restaurant.

Dylan was genuinely surprised to see his friends. So surprised, it took him half the evening to loosen up and start enjoying himself. I was sympathetic. He was attuned to the slightest of social discomforts, though Nate and Eric found us much less embarrassing than he did. Dylan knew of our intolerance for rudeness and picky eaters as well, and was probably worried about how his friends would behave. Over the course of the night, though, he relaxed, and with good humor he thanked us for overriding his protests and surprising him. But the roller-coaster ride was about to begin.

Later that month, he woke up in the middle of the night with terrible stomach pains. We were concerned enough to take him to the emergency room, where they ruled out appendicitis and everything else. Puzzled, the doctors released him, and he appeared to recover completely. I would later learn that unexplained somatic symptoms, particularly abdominal pain, may be a marker for depression.

Then, two days later, at the beginning of October 1997, Tom received a call from the school. Dylan had been suspended. The news was a shock. It was the first time either of our boys had been disciplined at school.

Dylan's interest in server maintenance and network administration had led one of the teachers to ask if he and his friend Zack would help maintain the Columbine High School computer system. Digging around in the system, the boys discovered a list of locker combinations. Dylan opened and closed one or two locker doors to see if the list was current, then transferred the data to a disk and shared it with Eric. Zack took it a little further and left a note in the locker of his girlfriend's ex-boyfriend. The boys were caught, and an administrator at the school informed us that Dylan was to be suspended for five days.

Tom and I thought the punishment was unnecessarily harsh. Dylan deserved a disciplinary consequence for his involvement; he had no right to dig into school records. But he'd only opened the lockers to see if he could, and closed them without touching anything. Tom in particular felt the punishment failed to show the boys why the offense was wrong, and alienated them from their school when it would be better for them to feel connected to it. We both hoped the school would consider a warning or probationary period instead of banishment, and arranged to meet with the dean.

It was not a good meeting. There was nothing in the rulebook to cover what the boys had done. In the absence of written policy, the administration had decided to treat the boys as if they had brought a weapon to school.

I was shocked. What they had done seemed closer to sneaking into the girls' bathroom, or an act of academic dishonesty like plagiarism or cheating. I wasn't minimizing the offense (nor would I have thought it was okay to sneak into the girls' bathroom). But the boys *hadn't* brought a weapon to school, or done anything like it.

We asked if the administration might consider other consequences. The boys could donate extra time to maintain equipment, or clean out a storage room. The dean told us that the district superintendent was aware of the incident and wanted it to be handled with a high level of severity; we could speak with the computer teacher if we had additional questions. An administrator myself, I recognized the dean's need to get the papers signed so she could move on to the next problem.

While we waited for the computer teacher, I got a moment alone with Dylan. I wanted him to understand the consequences of what he had done. He was fond of the teacher, and I told Dylan he could have gotten him fired, or caused the elimination of the program altogether. There was no defiance or cynicism on Dylan's face, just sadness. I was satisfied to see he understood. The teacher, when he joined us, seemed shaken but kind, and primarily concerned about Dylan. There were apologies all around. What came next, however, was more painful for Dylan than the suspension: the teacher told Dylan he could no longer help with the school's computers.

As we drove away from the school, Dylan seemed numb. I asked him if he thought he'd be okay; he told me he would. He was taking accelerated chemistry, trigonometry, world history, fourth-year French, computers, and composition—a fairly heavy workload of difficult classes, and I asked how he would keep up during his suspension. He said he could get the assignments from his friends. When Dylan asked what I was thinking, I told him the truth. "I don't understand the decision, and I don't agree with it, but I'm going to support it. This will be resolved quickly if we comply with the ruling, and I don't want to make a bad situation worse by alienating you from the people running the school." He nodded, to show he understood.

Tom was home with Dylan most of the time during the suspension. During one conversation, Dylan complained that the school's administration favored athletes, making excuses for them while coming down hard on others for lesser offenses. In Dylan's mind, school was a place where things were "not fair." Yet he seemed to take the suspension in stride, and after the five days were up, all three of us smoothed our ruffled feathers and moved on.

In October, Dylan got his driver's license. I was nervous about him driving around without an adult in the car, but he was relieved not to have to depend on us or on his friends for rides. Tom's hobby was finding beat-up old cars at bargain prices. As soon as he felt Dylan could handle a car responsibly, he bought a black BMW for $400. It had a broken window and some interior damage, not to mention it was light-years away from being able to pass Colorado's emissions tests, but the two of them weren't daunted by the amount of work it needed, and they both got a kick out of the fact that the car was sixteen years old—exactly Dylan's age. Dylan agreed to help pay for gas and insurance.

After Dylan got his license, I told my sister it was as if he'd grown wings. Most of his friends were still in the suburb we'd left behind when we'd moved out to the foothills. From a safety standpoint, we'd rather he stay overnight with them than drive home late on the canyon road, but I didn't like feeling so separate. Tom reminded me I had to let him grow up.

He and Nate and Eric and Zack went bowling, played pool, or went to the movies. Occasionally there were supervised parties.

Raising teenagers was not new to us, and Dylan faced the usual barrage of questions when leaving the house: "Where are you going? Who's going to be there? Who's driving? Will there be drinking? Will the parents be home? Leave us a phone number." We checked often, and Dylan was always exactly where he said he'd be. The only time he ever came home late for curfew, he'd gone to the rescue of a friend stranded after a fender bender.

Tom and I did feel Dylan was withdrawing from us that year. He'd quit Blackjack Pizza so he could look for a job working with computers, but he hadn't found one, and he wasn't doing sound for any school productions that fall. It was nice to have him home at night, though I worried he had too much time on his hands, and thought he spent too much time on his computer. Withdrawal, of course, can be a sign of depression in adults and teens, but Tom and I didn't identify Dylan's desire for privacy as a red flag. When he was in his room, he was either talking to friends on the phone or interacting with them on the computer. He wasn't withdrawing from others; if anything, his social life had taken off.

The unsettled feeling with which we'd begun the fall continued as the days grew cooler. One of my favorite teachers at the Art Students League died suddenly of a heart attack. My brother's wife was hospitalized, and my sister, who had struggled for years with health problems, was unwell again. Tom's health continued to deteriorate. In November he had surgery to fix the broken tendon in his arm, and he scheduled a shoulder surgery for January. He still couldn't work much, and our financial concerns intensified.

A friend consoled me with the Winston Churchill chestnut: "If you're going through hell, keep going." But the bad news kept coming. We got a call from Byron in the emergency room; he needed stitches in three places after standing up to a racist ex-skinhead. That night, I finally allowed myself to acknowledge my despair over Byron's situation. Of course, I was proud of him for standing up for his beliefs, but his decisions kept getting him into trouble, and nothing we did—therapy, support, tough love—seemed to help.

Thanksgiving was a rare bright spot in that dark season. Eight of my extended family members came to stay, a hectic change from the quiet life we usually led. My brother and my sister and I have always been close. We all talk too fast and laugh loudly; getting a word in is like merging onto the autobahn. Dylan found the chaos a little overwhelming, but I loved having my family around.

My dad owned neighborhood movie theaters—my first job was selling popcorn at a concession stand—and we're passionate about old movies. We all love books and music, too. Not surprisingly, we like to play charades. Dylan usually preferred to play poker with the adults, but that year he gave in to the begging and joined us for a round or two of charades. I was so proud of how funny and clever he was, and delighted that his innate shyness hadn't prevented him from joining in.

There was no way to know that, within a few short months, everything would fall apart, and Dylan would once again rise to the top of our family's worries.

• • •

In early January of 1998, Dylan told Tom about his frustration with a couple of kids at school who were "really asking for it." The kids were freshmen, and Tom resisted the temptation to laugh: Dylan was six feet four inches tall, and a junior. Dylan told us he wanted to get some guys together to confront the boys. Tom and I told him not to give them the satisfaction of a response. I was worried someone would be hurt, and Tom was worried Dylan would embarrass himself by engaging with freshmen.

Dylan could not let it go. Without our knowledge, he and Eric rounded up some friends. They confronted the kids and told them to meet them at a spot away from school, but the younger boys never appeared. Tom and I found out about the planned rumble after the fact. Dylan believed he had handled the situation effectively, but we were upset and told him so. At least, I thought, no one had been hurt.

Later that month, I got a phone call from Judy Brown, the mother of Dylan's friend Brooks. Brooks and Eric had gotten into a fight at school, and Eric had thrown a snowball at Brooks's car, damaging the windshield. Judy was furious and launched into a tirade against Eric, which perplexed me. It seemed to me that the boys shared responsibility for the incident, and I didn't understand her impulse to get involved when they'd resolved it themselves. The ferocity of her hatred for Eric seemed like an overreaction to me.

Not long after the call from Judy, Tom got another call from the school. Four months after his suspension for hacking the locker combinations, Dylan had deliberately scratched the face of someone's locker with a key. He was given an in-school suspension for a day and owed the school seventy dollars to pay for a new door. Tom went over to write the check. He asked the dean about the freshmen, certain that Dylan would not have lashed out without being provoked. The dean acknowledged they had a particularly "rowdy" group of freshmen, acting as if they "owned the place," but assured Tom that the administration was dealing with it.

We talked with Dylan that night. Tom was irritated with him for destroying property and irritated with the school for charging so much money to repaint a locker door. Dylan gave Tom the cash he had on hand and promised to work off the rest of the debt by doing extra chores. I told Dylan he couldn't allow the obnoxious behavior of others to upset him.

I don't know whose locker Dylan scratched, or if it was simply the one in front of him when the destructive urge hit. I have read in the years since that the scratch read "Fags"—a slur I have also read was frequently leveled against Dylan and Eric in the hallways at Columbine—but we did not hear that from the school.

It is, of course, not ridiculous that a younger boy could bully an older one. I simply never imagined anyone would bully Dylan. My idea of the type of kid targeted by bullies was as unrealistic a stereotype as my idea of the kind of person who dies by suicide. The way he dressed and wore his hair was intended to set him apart from the preppy, affluent, suburban mainstream, but it was not outrageous. We also believed Dylan's height would be intimidating, because he told us it was. Once, during sophomore year, Dylan said something to Tom about "hating the jocks." Tom asked him if they were giving him a hard time, and Dylan answered with confidence: "They don't bother me. I'm six four. But they sure give Eric hell."

Since the tragedy, much has been written about the school culture at Columbine High School, and Dylan's place in it. Regina Huerter, director of Juvenile Diversion for the Denver district attorney's office, compiled a report in 2000, and Ralph W. Larkin independently confirmed many of her findings in his exhaustively researched 2007 book, *Comprehending Columbine*. Both researchers found Columbine High School was academically excellent and deeply conservative; that much we knew. But they also describe a school with a pervasive culture of bullying—in particular, a group of athletes who harassed, humiliated, and physically assaulted kids at the bottom of the social ladder. Larkin also points to proselytizing and intimidation by evangelical Christian students, a self-appointed moral elite who perceived the kids who dressed differently as evil and targeted them.

This research lines up with the many anecdotal stories we heard after the tragedy from kids who suffered physical and psychological abuse at the hands of their classmates at the school. One story in particular stands out. When Tom went to the sheriff's department in the fall of 1999 to retrieve Dylan's car from the impound lot, a county employee offered his condolences and told him how his own son's hair had been set on fire by some other students while he was attending Columbine High School. The boy, who sustained fairly serious burns to his scalp, refused to allow his father to go to the administration because he was afraid it would make the situation worse. Shaking with anger as he spoke, though the incident was no longer recent, the outraged dad told Tom he had wanted to take the school apart "brick by brick."

About five years after the massacre, I spoke with a Columbine High School counselor. He told me that, after an earlier, publicized bullying incident, the high school had implemented closer supervision of the student body, including teachers in the hallways between classes, and in the cafeteria at lunch. But we agreed it's impossible to control what two thousand students are doing on a campus—or to know what those kids are doing to one another in the Dairy Queen parking lot. Despite the administration's claim that steps were taken to stem conflict among students, their efforts fell short. For many people, Columbine High School was a hostile and frightening place even if you were one of the most popular kids, and Dylan and his friends were not. One of our neighbors told us her grown son's reaction to the tragedy, a refrain we heard many times: "I'm just surprised it didn't happen sooner."

Both Huerter and Larkin claim teachers turned a blind eye to harassment and even violence in the hallways, either because they did not take it seriously—"kids will be kids"—or because they sided with with the popular athletes doing the bullying. They cite instances where school administrators declined to take action, even after being informed of specific incidents. This isn't as surprising as it would be now. Bullying wasn't on the cultural radar in 1999: there weren't federal laws against it or mandated school guidelines or *New York Times* bestselling books about queen bees and sticks and stones. Peer cruelty certainly wasn't seen as the serious public health issue we now understand it to be.

Tom believes, as Larkin does, that the culture at Columbine was toxic, and a desire for revenge motivated the attack the boys launched on the school. Many experts disagree: despite Larkin's claim that the propane bombs Dylan and Eric placed in the cafeteria were put under the tables where the jocks typically sat, they did not target popular kids or athletes during the attack, or anyone at all. (Of the forty-eight shooters profiled in Dr. Langman's book *School Shooters: Understanding High School, College, and Adult Perpetrators,* only one of them specifically targeted a bully.) Furthermore, there is almost no mention of bullying in Dylan's journal. If anything, he appears to have envied the jocks for their social comfort and ease with girls.

I personally fall somewhere in the middle. Bullying, however severe, is not an excuse for physical retaliation or violence, much less mass murder. But I do believe Dylan was bullied, and that along with many other factors, and perhaps in combination with them, bullying probably did play some role in what he did. Given Dylan's temperament and core personality traits, it's easy to understand why being bullied would have been especially hurtful to him. He hated to be wrong, and didn't like to lose. He was extremely self-conscious and critical of himself. (Relentless self-criticism is, incidentally, another sign of depression.) He liked to feel self-reliant, and wanted to be perceived as someone who was in control. This sense of himself would have been badly eroded with each incident. Apparently, they were common.

One day, Dylan came home, his shirt spotted with ketchup. He refused to tell me what had happened, only that he'd had "the worst day of his life." I pressed, but Dylan downplayed it, and I let him. *Kids have disagreements,* I thought. *Whatever it is, it'll blow over— and if it doesn't, I'll know.* There has been reporting that the incident was more serious than I could ever have imagined: a circle of boys taunting Dylan and Eric, shoving them, spraying them with ketchup, and suggesting they were gay. That incident alone may not explain the deadly kinship forged between the boys, but it is the kind of shared humiliation in which a bond is formed.

Tom and I were aware of another incident. Junior year, Dylan had a parking space in a remote lot next to the school grounds. A few weeks after he confronted the freshmen, he told his father his car wasn't running well. Tom found the hood flattened as if someone had stood on it, leaving an indentation deep enough to damage the fuse box. Dylan said he hadn't noticed the dent. Tom asked him outright if the freshmen had intentionally damaged his car. Dylan said he didn't know when or how it had happened, although he was certain it had happened in the school parking lot. The car was old, and we'd never expected it to survive high school without a few dings. But our failure to find out what happened to it is one thing I regret.

Tom and I did not perceive Dylan as being unpopular; he simply had too many friends for us to see him that way. Unfortunately, we did not have the slightest idea what his daily life was really like at school. Larkin cites a video Dylan made. He and a few other boys are walking down a hallway, filming nothing in particular. Four students approach from the opposite direction. One of them, wearing a Columbine Football sweatshirt, drives an elbow into Dylan's side as he passes, causing him to cry out and the video camera to swing wildly. The athletes laugh, and Dylan's friends mutter something inaudible. Larkin correctly sums up what's so chilling, which is that Dylan and his friends continue down the hallway after the hit as if nothing out of the ordinary has happened. "Apparently such behavior was common enough to be accepted as normative," Larkin writes. This observation was supported by a number of interviews he did with students.

It mirrors our own conversations, too. One of Dylan's friends told me he'd never seen any examples of students mistreating other students—and then, in the very next breath, told me about kids hurling a soda can full of tobacco spit in his direction at a school sporting event. Another of Dylan's friends told us a car full of kids threw glass bottles and other trash at their group as they drove by. (Larkin reports that throwing trash from moving cars at lower-caste students was common.) A resigned Dylan tried to comfort a horrified newcomer to the group: "You get used to it. It happens *all* the time."

It hurts that it was so easy for Dylan to hide what his life was like at school. I still have dreams in which I discover his hidden pain. In one, I am undressing him, still a toddler, for a bath. I pull his shirt off and see a bloody network of concealed cuts across his torso. Even writing about it now makes me cry.

Dylan's struggles may have been hidden from us, but they were not uncommon ones. A 2011 study by the Centers for Disease Control found that 20 percent of high school students nationwide reported they had been bullied on school property in the thirty days before the survey; an even higher percentage reported they'd been bullied on social media. Anti-bullying advocates suggest the number may be closer to 30 percent.

A tremendous amount of research has been done on the effects of peer harassment, and there is unquestionably a correlation between bullying and brain health disorders that stretches all the way into adulthood. A Duke University study found that, compared with kids who weren't bullied, those who were had four times the prevalence of agoraphobia, generalized anxiety, and panic disorder as adults. The bullies themselves had four times the risk of developing antisocial personality disorder.

There is also a strong association between bullying and depression and suicide. Both being a victim *and* bullying others is related to high risks of depression, suicidal ideation, and suicide attempts. Researchers at Yale found that victims of bullying were two to nine times more likely to report suicidal thoughts than other children.

The connection between bullying and violence toward others is more complicated, although again there's a correlation. Bullied kids often become bullies themselves, which appears to be what happened with Dylan and Eric. Larkin cites a student who claims they terrorized her brother, a student with special needs, so badly he was afraid to come to school. Researchers call students who both bully and suffer bullying "bully-victims," and find that these bully-victims are at the greatest psychological risk. "Their numbers, compared to those never involved in bullying, tell the story: 14 times the risk of panic disorder, 5 times the risk of depressive disorders, and 10 times the risk of suicidal thoughts and behavior."

The humiliation and degradation Dylan experienced at the hands of his schoolmates likely did contribute to his psychological state. At some point his anger, which had for years been directed toward himself, began to turn outward, and the idea of personal destruction he found so comforting began to include others. Repeated incidents of disrespect at school, an environment that should have been safe, may very well have constituted the pivot point.

Of course, even if Dylan did endure humiliation at the hands of his classmates, it cannot absolve him in any way of responsibility for what he did. At the same time, I have deep regrets I wasn't more in tune with Dylan's feelings about the place he spent his days. I wish I had spent much more time and energy on determining the climate and culture of the school (and how appropriate it was for Dylan) than on assessing it academically.

Once in a while, I allow myself to fantasize about the thousand ways the story could have ended differently, and all of those fantasies begin with a different school. My biggest regret, though, is that

I did not do whatever it would have taken to know what Dylan's internal life was really like.

. . .

At a suicide prevention conference I attended, a father described how he'd failed to recognize signs of depression in his twelve-year-old daughter. He'd noticed she'd been whinier and clingier than usual, sure, and complaining of invisible ailments, even after her pediatrician had found nothing wrong. *My stomach hurts. My head hurts.* She'd been more reluctant than usual to go to bed, too. *Just to the end of this chapter. Five more minutes, I swear.* But he had no inkling these were all potential signs of depression in a child of that age.

I hadn't either. Years later, I mentioned this to a friend with an eleven-year-old daughter. She was sufficiently alarmed to conduct an informal poll of the experienced parents she knew. Would they have recognized clinginess, hypochondria, and sleep disturbances as possible symptoms of depression in their own kids? Not one of them would have. Would you?

More disturbingly, the father I met at that conference told me his daughter's pediatrician had also not recognized these signs—never mind that she was at an elevated risk to die by suicide. In approximately 80 percent of completed suicides, the individual has seen a physician within the year before their death, and almost half have seen a doctor within the prior month. Dylan went to our family doctor with a sore throat weeks before he died.

It is essential for physicians to routinely screen for symptoms of depression and suicidal tendencies in their patients. Teachers, school counselors, coaches—these people can be powerful bystanders. Gatekeeper programs (like ASIST, the Applied Suicide Intervention Skills Training program by LivingWorks) teach participants to identify people struggling with persistent thoughts of suicide. The interventions they make can save lives.

Dylan's high school grades had never been particularly great, despite his intelligence, but they slipped far enough in the last few weeks of his senior year for two teachers to express concern. His hair was clean, but long and untrimmed, and it stuck out from the backwards baseball cap he always wore, and his facial hair was patchy and grizzled. Everyone in his life, including Tom and me, attached a value judgment to what we observed, instead of wondering if there might be something wrong.

This is one of the paradoxes we must confront. Of course it would be easier to help depressed teens if they were nicer to be around, or more communicative about their thoughts. If only they looked like the kids in the pamphlets do: clean-cut and attractive, staring out a rainy window with a wistful expression, chin propped on a fist! More commonly, though, a disturbed teenager will be unpleasant: aggressive, belligerent, obnoxious, irritable, hostile, lazy, whiny, untrustworthy, sometimes with poor personal hygiene. But the fact that they're so difficult, so dedicated to pushing us away, does not mean they do not need help. In fact, these traits may be signals that they do.

. . .

The next incident during Dylan's junior year was the most catastrophic of all.

On January 30, a few days after Dylan scratched the locker at school, he and Eric were arrested for breaking into a parked van and stealing electronic equipment.

Dylan had agreed to go with Zack to an activity at his church that night, and the two of them planned to come back to our house for a sleepover afterward. Tom and I were listening to music together in the living room when the phone rang around 8:30 p.m. It was Zack's dad, audibly upset. Zack had quarreled with his girlfriend and left the event with her. He'd gotten hurt, possibly after stepping out of a moving car, and wasn't making much sense. It was all very confusing, but Zack's parents wanted us to know the plan had changed. Dylan wasn't with Zack; he'd left the church with Eric.

I thanked Zack's dad for the update and immediately called the Harrises, who were as concerned as we were not to know where the boys were. Both sets of parents promised to get in touch immediately if we heard from the kids. Within minutes, our phone rang again. It was the county sheriff. Dylan and Eric had been arrested for criminal trespass.

Tom and I drove to the local sheriff's auxiliary office; the Harrises were already there. The offenses included First Degree Criminal Trespass and Theft, both of which were felonies, and Criminal Mischief, a misdemeanor.

My mouth hung open when I heard how serious the charges were. I could not believe that our Dylan, who had never done anything really wrong in his life, could do something so terrible. This was the kind of trouble that might seriously impact his future. Neither of us had ever been arrested, so we called one of our neighbors, a lawyer, for advice. He told us Dylan should "spill it," tell the complete truth. Before he hung up, he reassured us. "Boys do dumb stuff. He's a good kid. He'll be okay."

We waited for what felt like an eternity. Mrs. Harris wept. Then a deputy followed the boys through the substation office door. I practically threw up when I saw Dylan paraded past me in handcuffs.

We waited hours to learn whether our children would be sent to a detention facility or allowed to return home. Finally, the officer who arrested them recommended they be considered for a Diversion program, an alternative to jail for first-time juvenile offenders accused of minor crimes. The program would provide supervised counseling and community service, and allow the boys to avoid criminal charges and placement in a detention facility. The boys were released into our care.

Our drive home was silent, as all three of us contended with our various emotions: fury, humiliation, fear, and bewilderment. We arrived, emotionally and physically exhausted, around four o'clock in the morning. Tom and I needed to discuss how we wanted to respond. There would be consequences, we told Dylan, but we would talk about them after we got some rest. Exhausted as I was, the sun was up before I was able to close my eyes and sleep.

Tom woke before I did. When Dylan got up, they took a long walk. Afterward, Tom told me Dylan had been very, very angry—at the situation, the cops, his school, the unfairness of life. He was so angry that he didn't seem to accept or acknowledge the wrongness of what he had done.

I was still mad myself, and didn't want to talk to Dylan until I could be calm. Later in the day, the two of us sat together on the stairs. The master bedroom was on the ground floor, and Dylan's room was upstairs, so we often sat on the stairs between them to talk. I recounted our conversation verbatim in my journal that night, and have relived it in my mind countless times since his death.

I began, "Dylan. Help me understand this. How could you do something so morally wrong?" He opened his mouth to answer, and I cut him off. I said, "Wait. Wait a minute. First, tell me what happened. Tell me everything, right from the beginning."

He told me the story of his bizarre evening. After Zack left the church, he and Eric decided to go light some fireworks, so they drove to a parking area not far from our house where recreational cyclists stowed their cars while they biked the scenic canyon road. There, they saw an empty commercial van parked in the darkness. They saw electronic equipment inside. The van was locked. They banged on the window and tried to open it. Dylan rationalized this by noting the van was deserted. When the window did not open, they broke it with a rock.

I asked Dylan if breaking the window was Eric's idea. He said, "No. It was both of us. We thought of it together."

They took the equipment and drove to a secluded spot close by. Minutes later, a deputy drove by and saw the damaged van. He found the two boys in Eric's car with the equipment a short distance down the road. As soon as the officer approached the car, Dylan confessed.

When I'd heard the whole story, I asked my question again. "You committed a crime against a person. How could you do something so morally wrong?" His answer shocked me. He said, "It was not against a *person*. It was against a company. That's why people have insurance." My jaw dropped. I cried out, "Dyl! Stealing is a crime against a person! Companies are made up of people!" I tried to appeal to his sense of reason. "If one of our renters decided to steal a light fixture from one of our apartments, would it be a crime against a rental company, or against us?"

Dylan relented, "Okay, okay. I get the point." But I didn't stop. I explained that the owner of the van would have to pay a deductible to the insurance company. "There's no such thing as a victimless crime, Dylan." I'd heard a story about a programmer who figured out a way to siphon tiny, nearly untraceable amounts of money from calculations that left an odd penny. "Before long, you'll know enough to do something similar," I told him. "Do you think that's ethical?" He said he knew it was not, and assured me he'd never do anything of the kind.

What he'd done was wrong, and I wanted him to know it. Appealing to his empathy, I asked him how he'd feel if someone stole from him. "Dylan, if you follow no other rules in your life, at least follow the Ten Commandments: thou shalt not kill, thou shalt not steal." I paused to consider which of the other commandments might have relevance, and then decided to stop haranguing him. "Those are rules to live by."

He said, "I know that."

We sat in silence for a little while. Then I said, "Dyl, you're scaring me. How can I be sure you'll never do such a thing again?" He said he didn't know, and seemed frightened to learn he could do something so bad on an impulse. He was obviously miserable. I felt no anger at that point, only compassion.

Before we stood, I told him he had broken our trust. We would be watching him more closely, and his activities would be restricted. He complained it wasn't fair for us to punish him on top of the Diversion program; weren't the legal consequences enough? But his actions had left us no choice. I also said I thought he should see a professional counselor. He said he absolutely did not want to do that. When I told him we would seek help if it was in his best interest, he said definitively, "I do *not* need counseling. I'll show you I don't."

I was grateful Dylan could get on with his life without going to jail. Years after his death, though, I visited a secure treatment program for juvenile offenders, the type of place Dylan would likely have been sent to, and learned that what I had feared so much would almost certainly have been better for Dylan than returning to school, especially if the culture at Columbine High School was as toxic for him as we believe it was.

The administrator told me, "We're into saving kids, not punishing them." He described the supports that would have been available to Dylan, such as professionals who specialized in dealing with mood disorders and PTSD, common in kids who have been bullied. The multidisciplinary team would almost certainly have diagnosed his depression, as well as any other brain health disorders he might have been living with. The staff worked closely with the offender's parents. There was even a computer training facility there.

We never know what lessons are in store for us, especially when our prayers are answered and events seem to turn out the way we want. At the time, we were grateful he'd qualified for Diversion. But I can't help wondering if sending Dylan to a juvenile detention facility would have saved his life, and the lives of everyone he took with him.

• • •

It took two months for the Diversion program to begin. In the meantime, Tom and I worked together to tighten the reins at home. We created a curfew schedule, limited Dylan's social activities, took away his computer keyboard, and restricted his driving privileges. We searched his room regularly, and told him he could not spend any free time with Eric. He was expected to spend time with us, and to be cooperative when he did. Work and his participation in plays at the school were constructive influences, and he would continue to be able to do those things.

Dylan was relieved when the rules were spelled out for him, and accepted our conditions willingly, but it was still a difficult time. He seemed withdrawn, and was quick to anger when we made any demands on him.

His relationship with the outside world didn't seem to be much better. Roughly a week after the theft, Dylan got a job at a grocery store. He disliked the job itself and hated wearing a flowered shirt as part of his uniform. His attitude was terrible, and his time there ended quickly. Next, he got a speeding ticket. Not long after, he ran a red light on his way home from renting a video, and got a ticket from the same officer who'd questioned him on the night of his arrest.

After the ticket, Tom and I warned him again that he needed to get his act together. Any more mistakes, and the consequences for his future could be positively disastrous. Felons can't vote or serve on a jury; he'd be disenfranchised. And who would want to hire him?

A month or so after the arrest, I called the Harrises to touch base. We all wanted what was best for our children, and I thought the two families should be in contact to coordinate the consequences we had meted out. Mrs. Harris and I talked about the advantages and disadvantages of keeping the two boys apart. She told me about Eric's angry outbursts, and said they planned to find professional help for him immediately. I told her we were trying to determine whether Dylan needed to see a therapist or not.

I felt strongly the boys should be separated, but Mrs. Harris did not want to remove the central friendship in her son's life at a time of crisis. I understood, but felt Dylan needed some distance. We agreed to keep them apart for a while, at least.

There were good times as well as bad. One night, Byron called after capriciously quitting another job. I was so discouraged with both of my sons, I did not know what to do. After Tom had gone to bed, Dylan sought me out. He listened carefully and quietly to my worries about Byron and made a few suggestions while supporting the way I'd handled the call. When I was done venting, he did his best to cheer me up. That night, I felt grateful he had not been sent to jail.

During that interim period, he and a friend started a fantasy baseball league. The activity seemed wholesome and I liked the boy he started it with. Eric did not participate. Dylan also did the sound for a production of *The Music Man*, which we attended at the end of February. There's nothing like a school play to make parents feel proud, and we certainly felt proud of Dylan that night.

Still, we were relieved when the Diversion program finally

started in March. During the intake process, Dylan was asked to select problems pertaining to him from a long list. Eric checked many of these, including *anger, suicidal thoughts,* and *homicidal thoughts,* but Dylan marked only two: *finances* and *jobs.*

The intake included an extensive assessment of our family. I stated that Dylan sometimes seemed "angry or sullen" and his behaviors were at times "disrespectful and intolerant of others." That certainly was my feeling about him that year, especially after the arrest. He never raised his voice, swore in our presence, or talked back, but I could hear disrespect in his voice sometimes when he talked about others. It was the worst thing, in my experience, that could be said about Dylan.

Later, these comments would be seen as incontrovertible evidence that we ignored warning signs and set the stage for violence by tolerating belligerence. At the time, though, I was simply eager for the counselors to know the worst about him, so the experts handling his case would be able to help him if he needed it.

When the counselors questioned Dylan, he admitted to using marijuana a couple of times. This surprised us, so Tom followed up with questions when we got home. Dylan didn't want to say where he'd gotten the drugs, but eventually confessed that the pot had belonged to his brother. Tom confronted Byron, and warned him that if he brought illegal drugs onto our property again, he'd turn Byron over to the police himself.

Juvenile records are usually sealed, but after the tragedy Dylan's Diversion reports were released. They stated that Tom and I had "kicked" our older son out of the house for using drugs. That brought me up short. The decision for him to leave home had been Byron's, made in consultation with a family counselor, and the move itself had been completely amicable. Plus, Byron was still very much in our lives after he moved out; we saw him for dinner at least once or twice a week. In the Diversion interview, Dylan said he loved his brother but that marijuana use was "a waste of time and money."

He claimed to have used alcohol "a couple of times," although his journals would reveal he was self-medicating heavily. After he died, I learned that his nickname, on the Internet and among some of his friends, was VoDKa, the capitalized D and K a play on his initials.

Dylan was upset to discover that Tom had confronted Byron about the pot, and Tom explained he'd do anything to keep his boys safe. After the tragedy, though, Tom blamed himself for Dylan's secret life and worried he'd unwittingly damaged their relationship by violating Dylan's trust. Had Dylan held back from telling us he was scared of Eric because he knew his father would talk to the Harrises? And of course Tom would have, if he'd had any inkling of the lethal dynamic between the two boys.

. . .

Years after the tragedy, I picked up a parenting magazine in a waiting room featuring an "ethical parenting" quiz. I got all ten questions "right" except for "Would you read your child's private journal?" The correct answer, according to the parenting magazine, was "no." I know it would have been my answer too, when Dylan was alive, but it would not be my answer now.

When we search our children's rooms or read their journals, we risk that they will feel betrayed. However, they may be hiding problems they cannot manage by themselves.

When Dylan was asked by the counselor to talk about his family relationship, he said it was "better than most kids'." He said Tom and I were "supportive, loving, dependable and trustworthy." In response to the question "What impact has this [arrest] had on your family?" Dylan answered, "A bad one. My parents were devastated as well as I." And to the question "What have been the most traumatic experiences in your life?" Dylan responded, "The night I committed this crime."

After interviewing Dylan and our family, the writer of the treatment status report concluded, "Based on history, it does not appear treatment is indicated." Despite this, when we finally met Dylan's Diversion counselor in March of 1998, it was the first thing I asked: Did she think Dylan needed therapy? When Dylan joined us, she asked him if he thought he needed a therapist, and he said no. I was a little disappointed she didn't give us more guidance—I already knew what Dylan thought. But Dylan kept assuring us he'd simply made a stupid mistake. "I'll prove to you I do not need to see anyone." We agreed to monitor the situation, and to change course if necessary.

Diversion took up a lot of his time that year. Dylan was provided with counseling, anger management training, and an ethics class. He was required to participate in community service activities as well as making restitution payments to his victim, and he was tested for drug use on a regular basis. We felt the gravity of the punishment would help Dylan to understand the seriousness of his offense.

Unfortunately, Dylan's and Eric's Diversion appointments were often scheduled together, and they saw each other at school. Though the boys did not talk about the arrest, their friends knew they were in serious trouble because their activities were so restricted. When Judy Brown heard Eric and Dylan were in trouble with the law, she assumed it was for the threats Eric had made against her son, Brooks.

Eric had a website, filled with hate speech and violent imagery. He made specific threats against Brooks, going so far as to include the Browns' telephone number and home address. I did not learn about Eric's website until the afternoon of the attack on Columbine High School. But Dylan had known about it—and, the day before he and Eric were scheduled for their Diversion intake interviews, he'd told Brooks. In the hallway at school, he'd slipped Brooks a piece of paper with the web address on it, warning him not to tell Eric how he'd found out.

This, to me, is striking—another one of Dylan's attempts to extricate himself from the relationship with Eric, or at least to call attention to the severity of Eric's disturbance. Everyone knew Brooks was close to his parents, particularly to his mother; Dylan had to assume Brooks would tell Judy about the site immediately. That is precisely what happened, and the Browns did go to the police. An investigator drew up an affidavit to search the Harris home, which was never shown to a judge. After Columbine, that paperwork disappeared.

Not knowing about Eric's website is a huge regret, and it emphasizes how important it is for parents to share information with one another, though the conversation might be uncomfortable. It's understandable Judy didn't come to me about the website: when the two boys were arrested, she believed the police had finally taken action. She had no idea Eric and Dylan had been arrested for a theft that had nothing to do with Eric's threatening behavior—just as I had no idea Eric had threatened Brooks or anyone at all until the afternoon of the tragedy, when Judy Brown was standing in my driveway and fifteen people were lying dead in the school, countless others injured and traumatized.

• • •

The limitations we placed on Dylan after his arrest felt restrictive to him, and he was short-tempered with us. Since there had been no indication on the Diversion screening of any psychological problems, we tolerated his irritability and tried to keep him engaged in family activities as much as we could. As always with Dylan, there were enough good times to keep me hopeful. For all the unpleasantness and disagreements in those months, there were many times when we got along and enjoyed each other's company.

When Dylan asked me what I wanted for my birthday at the end of March, I said I'd like some time alone with him. He took me out for breakfast. I tried to get him to talk about himself, but Dylan answered my questions as briefly as possible, then asked me about my job and my life. He was so adept at listening that I did not see how skillfully he turned the focus of the conversation away from himself. Before our pancakes were cold, I was babbling about my artwork, my job, and my dreams for the future without recognizing how deftly he had shielded his inner life.

By the close of Dylan's junior year, things seemed to be getting back to normal. Dylan spent afternoons and evenings at rehearsal for a school production of *Arsenic and Old Lace*. We began to talk about his life after graduation. He felt burned out and didn't want to go to college, but we encouraged him to think about it, and a few days later he agreed to come with us to the high school to look at college resources. Dylan was smart, but he hadn't been truly motivated by what he was studying since he'd left the gifted program. I felt sure he'd flourish at college, with more freedom to discover and pursue his passions.

On April 20, exactly one year before his death, he and Tom went to their first baseball game of the season. The following week, Tom and I went to see *Arsenic and Old Lace*. Dylan's contribution to the performance was flawless. Though I cannot say he appeared completely happy, he seemed more balanced, as if he was trying to get past the mistakes he had made.

That spring, we had the worst argument we ever had during his lifetime. It happened on Mother's Day, the last Mother's Day we had together, and it still hurts me to remember it.

I can't remember exactly what set me off. I was heartsick about the disastrous year I'd had with both my kids, angry about Dylan's continuing negativity and bad attitude, and quietly hurt he had forgotten Mother's Day. When I confronted him about his attitude, I had the feeling he was responding, not to me, but to some inner joke. It seemed disrespectful.

Fed up, I got in his face. I shoved him against the fridge, pinning him there with my hand. Then I waved my finger and gave him a real mom lecture. I didn't yell, but there was authority in my voice as I told him he had to stop being so crabby and selfish. "The world doesn't revolve around you, Dylan. It's time for you to think about the other people in this family. You need to start carrying your weight." Then I reminded him he had forgotten Mother's Day.

I dug my hand hard into his shoulder while I lectured. Until the day I die, I will never stop wishing that I had pulled him toward me instead of pushing him away.

Finally, in a soft voice that carried warning power, he said, "Stop pushing me, Mom. I'm getting angry, and I don't know how well I can control it." That was all it took; this wasn't my parenting style. Appalled that the conflict had progressed this far, I backed off. It was the worst confrontation we'd ever had, in seventeen years.

Later, we sat together at the kitchen table. We both felt awful. I apologized for losing my temper. Dylan apologized for forgetting Mother's Day, and volunteered to help me prepare dinner. That afternoon, he went out to buy me a card and an African violet planted in a tiny watering can. It was a perfect gift; I love miniatures, and we'd collected some together when he was little. We hugged. I thought it was okay, although I noted he'd only signed his name to the card, instead of saying "Love, Dylan."

Of course I wished we hadn't fought, particularly on Mother's Day, but I felt justified. Aren't you supposed to confront your kids when you feel like they're straying off the straight and narrow? I feel differently about that fight now. I know that hugging my son and telling him I loved him wouldn't have stopped him from hurting himself and others. Still, I wish I had taken his hand. *Sit down with me. Talk to me. Tell me what's going on.* Instead of telling him everything he was doing wrong, or what he had to be grateful for, I wish I'd listened, and validated his pain. If I had to do it over again, I'd tell him, *You've changed, and it's scaring me.*

But I wasn't scared. I should have been, but I was not.

. . .

I can now see there was a great deal to be concerned about in Dylan's junior year.

In the background, there was the worry of Tom's illness, financial uncertainty, and friction between Tom and Byron and me. All these factors increase the risk of depression in the vulnerable. Dylan's arrest and the bullying he was experiencing at school are both social factors associated with a higher risk of depression and suicidality. His increased irritability and an uncharacteristic lack of motivation were signs of depression, though these seemed well within the parameters of what a parent could expect from a teenage boy. He carefully hid his alcohol use—another risk factor—from us. Every time we felt truly concerned about him, he'd go out of his way to reassure us that everything was okay.

So how does a concerned parent parse out the difference between garden-variety adolescent behavior ("He's so lazy; he's got such a crappy attitude; she's such a drama queen") from real indicators of depression or other types of brain illness? The crucial question raised by a story like mine is how to tell when actions or words indicate something worrisome.

There is no fail-safe answer; in fact, these are some of the most troubling unresolved issues in the field of behavioral medicine. But Dr. Christine Moutier of the American Foundation for Suicide Prevention teaches medical students and physicians to pay attention to *changes*: in sleep patterns, expressions of anxiety, shifts in mood or usual patterns of behavior, or in a teen's "personality." Taken individually, these may indicate nothing more than a stressful week, but a constellation of changes may signal a more serious problem. Junior year, Dylan went from being the kid I didn't have to worry about to the kid I was worried about all the time. After sixteen years of no trouble at all, suddenly he was in conflict with the authorities at his school, with us, with other kids, and ultimately, with the law.

Dr. Mary Ellen O'Toole, a former FBI profiler and a forensic behavioral consultant, authored the FBI report "The School Shooter: A Threat Assessment Perspective," shortly after the tragedy. She warns against relying on a kid's self-reporting and advises parents to look at behaviors. If something seems inconsistent or inexplicable, get another pair of eyes on the problem, and don't allow yourself to be mollified.

Loving our kids makes us more susceptible to ignoring disturbing behaviors, or explaining them away. This is especially true when the kid in question is "a good kid," and when we have a good relationship. It's a fight to see these behaviors clearly, and to act when we notice something. But you'll never forgive yourself if you don't.

If you're worried, Dr. Moutier advises, seek expert help. If the child is okay, hearing it from a therapist will make you feel better; if there is a more serious problem, a therapist is more likely to recognize it, and can help.

Dylan did not want to get help. His journals show he was trying to manage his problems by himself. Given this aspect of his personality (and his innate stubbornness), I'm not convinced I would have been able to force him to see a therapist; even if I had gotten him to the office, he would have been perfectly capable of sitting there in sullen silence for an hour. I asked Dr. Langman, who specializes in adolescents, what he suggests to parents whose child won't cooperate; he told me he asks the *parents* to come in. Often a conversation with them is enough to determine whether further intervention, such as contacting a child's guidance counselor at school (or even law enforcement) is necessary.

Dylan promised he'd turn his life around, and then he did. According to Dr. O'Toole, that recovery might have been a sign in itself, one especially common among young women in abusive relationships. As soon as a parent moves to intervene—"I don't want you seeing Johnny anymore"—the girl returns to actively managing their impression of her.

There are, of course, no guarantees a child will be okay, even with professional help. Eric's parents *did* send him to a psychiatrist after the arrest, and he began taking medication—none of which stopped him from putting into motion the events of April 20, 1999.

These days, when I page through one of my old diaries and read an entry like "Dylan crabby when reminded to feed the cats," part of my brain howls: *How could you miss that?! Didn't you know depression often presents as irritability in adolescent boys?* I did not, and I am not alone. Somewhere out there in America right now, a suburban mom is pointing with exasperation at two hungry, hopeful cats threading around the ankles of a teenage boy who has forgotten to feed them. Chances are, that boy will grow up without event to lecture his own teenager over a pair of empty cat food bowls.

But for some percentage of families, this will not be the happy outcome. Some unlucky mix of a child's vulnerabilities and the circumstances that trigger them will combine to set off a much darker cascade.

CHAPTER 14

Pathway to Violence

Dylan's Senior Year

Robyn pinning a boutonniere on Dylan the afternoon
of their senior prom, three days before the shootings.
The Klebold Family

*It has always been my feeling that one of the great tragedies of Columbine
is the fact that yourselves and the Harrises shared nothing of your own
lessons from Columbine. That is, you've failed to respond to the questions
so many parents in the world have: What signs of hatred and despair did
you see? What warning signs did you miss? Were you a family that ever
spent much time at the dinner table together? What did your son talk
about? What would you have done differently in raising Dylan? . . .*

*The most nagging question to me involves what your son hid from
you. I've heard a number of people say that teens can be very good at
hiding items (e.g., bombs and guns) and secrets from their parents. I
don't disagree with that. But this was not just a case of hiding things.
Your son was so angry and distressed and hateful and so troubled that
he wanted to kill hundreds of his classmates. Hundreds! How in the*

world could you not have seen that your son was THAT hateful and
troubled? How did you become so disconnected that you did not see this
disposition of his? How could that happen?!?

I think you could do a great service if you were to speak publicly
about those lessons. Sure, it would be very difficult for you to do so.
Painful, yes. Might people say you were terrible, neglectful parents?
Sure. But obviously many say that already. To me what's most impor-
tant is that the pain you might encounter by being open and speaking
publicly could not possibly be worse than the pain you've already expe-
rienced in losing your son in such a tragic way, not to mention the guilt
associated with doing nothing as repentance.

—Excerpt from a September 2007 letter from Tom Mauser,
the father of Daniel Mauser, one of the boys killed on
April 20, 1999, at Columbine High School

I know that people want a window into the last days of Dylan's
life, and so I have opened my journals and Dylan's to build a
parallel timeline.

Threat assessment professionals talk about "a pathway to violence." Dr. Reid Meloy explained: "Targeted violence often begins
with a personal loss or humiliation. That incident becomes a decision point, where the person believes that the only way to resolve
this grievance is to carry out an act of violence. The first step is
researching and planning for the event. The next is preparation: the
accumulation of weapons, the selection of a target. The next is the
implementation of the attack."

Eric was on a pathway to violence, probably as early as April of
1997, when the boys first began to make little bombs. He believed
that Dylan was on that pathway too, but Dylan's journals tell a different story. He was pretty sure he was going to be dead long before
Eric had the chance to execute his plan. Dylan's personal pathway
was toward suicide, until January of 1999, when suddenly it was not.

It wasn't that Tom and I didn't know that something was
wrong with Dylan in his senior year. We simply—drastically and
lethally—underestimated the depth and severity of his pain and
everything he was capable of doing to make it stop.

• • •

Made Dylan spend a few minutes with us when we all sat in the den and ate dinner. It's so hard to connect with him—he just pushes us away. We've got to keep trying to have some kind of relationship. [8/20/98]

Dylan came home from school on his way to work & I fixed him a snack. He felt lousy, thinks he's getting a cold or worse. He picked out a yearbook picture before going to work. Tom got home late and I made a nice little dinner. Dylan came home and joined us before going out. [8/28/98]

During the summer between Dylan's junior and senior years, he acted like a typical teenage boy: sometimes funny, playful, and affectionate, other times withdrawn, cranky, and self-involved. I always had the feeling, though, that he was holding something back.

Dylan was still on a short leash at home. We searched his room to make sure he wasn't hiding drugs or anything stolen. He'd always been good with money, but he was short a lot that summer. Tom nagged him to get a job, but he didn't want to settle for fast food; he wanted to work with computers. He was making restitution payments to the victim of his crime, and while he picked up a little extra money by doing odd jobs for us and for our neighbors, we made up the difference when he fell behind on his car insurance.

At the Diversion orientation meeting, the parents had been asked not to contact the staff. *If you don't hear from us,* they told us, *it's going well.* Even though we found out later that he sometimes missed appointments or showed up late, we didn't hear a thing. When Dylan's original intake counselor left, a new one called to introduce himself, and that was it. Years later, I read the first counselor's case notes. She said Dylan was a "nice young man, kind of goofy, and a bizarre sense of humor, he makes me laugh."

I've talked to the friends Dylan spent time with that summer many times since then. I've asked point-blank if they saw signs of depression or rage, but Dylan's behavior seemed as normal to them as it did to us. Some of his sillier moments were caught on film. Devon's sixteenth birthday party had a luau theme, and she gave me a photo of Dylan in the lurid Hawaiian shirt and straw hat she'd lent him for the occasion. Underneath, she wrote: "He hated it, I could tell, but he put it on anyway." She goes on to describe how much he ate.

Nate slept over often. The two of them would stay up until nothing was on television but infomercials. They'd turn the volume down and make up dialogue to accompany the sales pitches, laughing so hard they'd give themselves stomachaches. Then the two of them would raid the kitchen. They ate Polish sausage, apple crisp, doughnuts, and ploughed through chips and salsa by the ton. Tom used to say we should buy stock in Oreos.

Despite this apparent normalcy, in the journal entry dated August 10, Dylan writes a passionate and secret final good-bye to the girl he secretly has a crush on—one suicide note in a journal filled with them.

Days before the start of Dylan's senior year, he was hired to do tech support at a computer store. He willingly accepted the store's dress code, a collared shirt and black pants, and worked eleven hours on his first day, arriving home tired and proud. Tom and I noted that Dylan's long day was likely the first of many if he chose a career in computers.

As the fall approached, incoming seniors at Columbine High School were asked to submit pictures for the yearbook. A local photographer shrewdly suggested Dylan ask a friend to the session to help him loosen up, so Zack tagged along, and I loved the shots the photographer took of Dylan looking relaxed and happy among the pink rocks in the valley not far from our home. One of those photos would later be featured on the cover of *Time* magazine, under the headline "The Monsters Next Door."

. . .

As Dylan began his senior year, life settled down for the whole family.

Tom and I were cautiously optimistic and proud when Byron finally landed a job he loved at a car dealership. His supervisors were mature, encouraging mentors, as eager to teach him about the business as he was to learn. He moved nearby to be closer to work, so we saw him more often, and Tom and I watched with growing pleasure as our older son seemed to grow up overnight. He even adopted a kitten, and I was touched to see what a loving and nervous new dad he was.

That job would prove to be a turning point in Byron's life, the place where he transitioned into manhood and became the hardworking, responsible, thriving adult he is today.

Tom and I purchased a second rental property downtown and rented the studio outbuilding on our property. The additional income alleviated our money worries, though we still didn't know how we'd manage Dylan's college expenses. Most important, Tom finally found a combination of medications to give him some relief from his chronic pain. He still had a few surgeries to go through, but he could do much more than he'd been able to.

I'd settled into my new job, too, and enjoyed the freedom granted by my four-day workweek. With more time to cook, I shamelessly used food as a lure to get the family together. I made beef stew and lasagna; the gloppy, layered Mexican casseroles both boys loved; Dylan's favorite pumpkin spice cake; and tapioca pudding by the vat. I put up triple batches: one to eat, one to freeze so I could get something on the table in a hurry, and the last so I'd have something extra to send home with Byron. Sunday dinner with the whole family happened almost every week. Byron and Dylan staged epic dish-towel-flicking fights in the kitchen; though they looked like grown men, they were really still boys.

I also had time to concentrate on my art. I'd always loved the technical challenge of translating a three-dimensional world into two dimensions, and over the years I'd taken the occasional class and sporadically attended figure drawing sessions on Saturday morning with my friends. But between raising my family, running a household, and work, months would go by sometimes without an afternoon free.

Certainly, I'd never before hit a creative groove the way I did that year. I could lose myself for hours in a drawing or a painting, thinking of nothing but how to more faithfully translate the colors and shapes I saw in nature onto the paper in front of me.

My journals from those days are filled with the issues preoccupying me: chalky whites, muddy colors, tricky shadows, composition, detail, and form. After Columbine, convinced my trivial preoccupations had blinded me to Dylan's distress and plans, it would be years until I could make art again.

• • •

11/5 Tom is having outpatient hand surgery tomorrow.

11/6 We were at the hospital til 5, then we began our slow trek home through traffic. We stopped for Chinese takeout and medication. We were glad that Dylan stayed home so we could actually eat dinner with him. His car is broken so he was stuck here until a friend picked him up at about 9 to go to a movie. I want so much to be closer to him, but he is absent so much of the time. This is such an important time. He really needs to be planning for his future but he just isn't moving ahead. At least he was pleasant tonight and ate with us.

11/9 Dylan was cute and pleasant today and actually talked about wanting to go to school in Arizona to escape the weather.

The previous year's problems appeared to be behind Dylan. He could be moody and irritable, but what teenager isn't? Sometimes we noted that he was tired, but the computer store job required a lot of hours, and he was taking calculus, advanced video production, English, and psychology, on top of an early morning bowling class.

Without any prompting from us, he kept his appointments with his Diversion counselor, participated in community service at a local park, and took routine drug tests. Although drugs had never been a problem with Dylan, we were relieved to have one less thing to worry about. He started earning back the privileges he'd lost after the arrest, and when his computer store job proved too difficult to maintain around his school and Diversion appointment schedules, he was rehired at Blackjack Pizza.

On September 11, 1998, Dylan turned seventeen. Our gift to him was a nod to his prodigious appetite—a small black refrigerator that he could take with him to college the following year. He loved it, and insisted on carrying it right up to his room, the cord dragging behind. As soon as Nate found out, he showed up with a companion gift: a supersized bucket of fried chicken, all for Dylan.

That month, he volunteered to do the sound for a Halloween production of *Frankenstein* at school, and rekindled his friendship with Brooks Brown. The two of them had drifted apart after the conflict between Eric and Brooks the previous year, but they fell back into an easy friendship while working on the play.

Dylan was proud of *Frankenstein*; he used a wide variety of unusual audio sources to develop the eerie soundtrack. The cast and crew recorded a surprise video to thank the drama teacher. In the video, Brooks, Zack, and Dylan clown around—saying they hope she'll buy them beer, or pay them to pass down their senior year production know-how to the next crop of students. Judy Brown threw the wrap party, and took a picture of Dyl laughing at the video along with everyone else.

Dylan promised he'd finish his college applications by Christmas. We had to nudge him a few times, but he did his usual thorough job, and Tom and I helped him to keep the paperwork straight. We asked him to consider some smaller schools, but he wasn't interested. He applied to two schools in Colorado and two in Arizona, and we all celebrated when he dropped the four college application packets into the mail.

Christmas was low-key and comfortable. As usual, Dylan led the way in finding and decorating our tree; he always wanted the biggest one we could fit on top of our car. It was an annual tradition for me to drag Tom and the boys to some festive event—a madrigal choir session, or a holiday event at the zoo. That last Christmas, it was dinner at a Moroccan restaurant, where we sat on cushions on the floor and ate without silverware, scooping the spiced dishes into our mouths with pieces of bread.

Dylan had asked Tom if he could borrow some money to buy Christmas gifts, and I was touched to find a hardbound writing journal from him under the tree Christmas morning. It was perfect— thoughtful without being extravagant. I had no idea I'd be pouring my sorrow onto its pages four months later.

Tom and I bought Dylan the long black leather coat he'd asked for. Tom thought it would look ridiculous on Dylan's lanky frame, and privately I agreed. But several boys at the school wore similar black coats, and he'd already bought a black cotton duster. He thought it was funny when a teacher or some other person in a position of authority saw him and Eric in the hallway and teased: "You look like you're in the Trench Coat Mafia." But I didn't know until after their death that there was a large, loose group of kids at the school who wore long black coats and called themselves that.

A great deal was made of Dylan's affiliation with the Trench Coat Mafia in the immediate wake of Columbine. It was one of the clues everyone hoped would elucidate what we'd missed—the key to unlock the mystery. Was the Trench Coat Mafia a gang of death-obsessed goths? Neo-Nazis? Satanists? A suicide cult? Like most such leads, the Trench Coat Mafia connection sputtered out without revealing anything—though not before a myth had been created. In fact, the Trench Coat Mafia was just a bunch of kids, some friends, some not, who favored a certain kind of coat to set themselves apart from the kids at Columbine High School who shopped at more conservative stores like Polo or Abercrombie & Fitch. Dylan and Eric hadn't even thought of themselves as members of the group, although they were friends with a boy, Chris, who was.

Regardless of how we thought the coat would look, it seemed harmless enough, and Dylan was thrilled when he unwrapped it on Christmas morning.

. . .

1/11/99 This long, hard day is over. Tom's surgery was today. We had to get up at 4:00 AM to be there by 6:00. After sitting and waiting for

13 hours, I just needed to get home. Good thing I did because Dylan hasn't exactly risen to a level of responsibility in my absence. He overslept and missed a class and was sleeping when I got home. Nothing taken care of that I needed him to do (like take care of the cats). What have I raised?

1/12 Tom is home from the hospital. . . . Dylan has been so reclusive. We've hardly seen him & attempts to engage him have been futile. He didn't even say hi to Tom or ask how he was. It was weird.

In January, about three months before the tragedy, Tom had surgery to replace a portion of his left shoulder joint. I came home from the hospital in the evening to find Dylan had not done what I had asked him to do. I no longer remember what the chore was— probably cutting up some broccoli for dinner, or picking up a quart of milk from the store. A recorded message informed me that he had missed a class. The cats had not been fed, and Dylan was asleep in his room. I was disappointed and irritated he had dropped the ball while I was looking after his father in the hospital, and I told him so.

I can't count the number of times I've shared this story with other suicide loss survivors. "I couldn't understand why she wasn't pulling her weight!" a mother I met recently told me, the tears streaming down her face. "I told her to stop being so selfish!" Four days after the argument, her daughter was dead. Sometimes a kid messing up at school or coming at you with a bad attitude about helping at home isn't a sign they need to be criticized and corrected, but a signal that they need help.

Dylan often appeared tired, and I worried aloud about his course load and Blackjack schedule. Tom and I were both concerned about how listless and withdrawn he was during the week of Tom's surgery, so we took him out for Chinese food as soon as Tom was up to it, a few days after the operation. The meal passed pleasantly, and we were placated.

In retrospect, I can see how often Dylan expertly allayed our concerns whenever we raised them. I don't know whether he was managing himself, or us—whether he was hoping whatever was wrong would get better, or that we wouldn't notice how bad it was. He'd always been the kid we could rely on to do the right thing, the kid who wanted to take care of everything himself. So when he said he was okay, we believed him.

His journals indicate a major sea change had taken place in his thinking. The entry on the twentieth of January reads: "im here, STILL alone, still in pain." He has not died by suicide, and he is angry. The syntactical irregularities noted by Dr. Langman come fast and furious, to the point that much of the entry is almost incomprehensible. "I love her, the journey, the endless journey, started it has to end. we need to be happy to exist timely. I see her in perfection, the halcyons. Love it, endless purity."

It is possible that he was drunk, but there is a sense of fantasy becoming reality for him. "The scenarios, images, pieces of happiness still come. They always will. I love her. she loves me. i know she is tired of suffering as I am. it is time. it is time." On the twenty-third of January, three days later, he secretly attended the Tanner Gun Show with Eric and Robyn, where they bought the shotguns they would use in the massacre and met Mark Manes, the young man who would sell him a TEC-9 semi-automatic pistol.

The irony is that I was never happier than I was in the winter of 1999. The weekend after Tom's surgery, Byron came over in the afternoon and the three men of the family worked on their respective cars, car parts scattered across the garage. Tom was not able to use his arms much, but he could give advice and oversee the work, and the three of them joked and helped each other.

I stayed inside where it was warm, working on a painting while a pot of homemade chili simmered on the stove. When the guys came inside, I watched a Denver Broncos game on television with them, just so I could bask in the pleasure of having my family together. Time was flying—Dylan would be off to college in the fall—and I didn't want to miss a single moment. After Byron headed home, Dylan and his dad drove off to rent a movie in Tom's cherished, carefully maintained classic car. On the way back, Tom let Dylan drive it for the first time, and Dylan came home puffed up with pride.

It had been an absolutely perfect day, a thought I recorded in my diary before bed. *I feel so lucky and thankful,* I wrote. *This day was golden.*

Of course, I have wondered many times about the ease of Dylan's deception. As it does for many people living with thoughts of suicide, making a plan may have made it easier for Dylan to function, and thus to mislead us into believing his life was turning around. It can be hard to differentiate between someone who is genuinely getting out of a cycle of depression, and someone who feels relief because they know they're going to die. (Dr. Dwayne Fuselier, who spent much of his career with the FBI in hostage negotiation, tells his students to pay attention when a crisis negotiation seems to be going well for the same reason—sudden cooperation may mean the hostage taker has made a decision to die.) But I still cannot reconcile the kid cracking up with me over Alec Guinness in *Kind Hearts and Coronets* with the boy I saw on the Basement Tapes, a boy who had already started making plans to slaughter innocent classmates.

The deception was universal. Two days after our chili dinner, Tom and I received an unexpected phone call from Dylan's Diversion counselor. Unless we had any objections, he was recommending early termination from the program for both Eric and Dylan. This was terrific news. Early termination from Diversion is rare, awarded to only 5 percent of participants. Both boys had done exceptionally well, the counselor told us, and he was convinced they were on solid ground. It was ten weeks before the massacre.

People tend to find this detail particularly upsetting, but it does not surprise me. If I didn't know what was in Dylan's mind—the child I bore and raised, who sat on my lap and emptied my dishwasher—then what on earth could a stranger have known? In his book *The Anatomy of Violence,* Dr. Adrian Raine cites a study in which children are left in a room and told not to peek at a toy when the experimenter leaves. Whether they do peek or not is caught on tape, as is their response—truthful or deceitful—when the experimenter returns and asks them if they did.

When the "did you peek?" interviews were shown to undergraduate students, they guessed correctly which kids were lying only 51 percent of the time, only a little better than sheer chance. Next, the researchers brought in customs officials, who, as Dr. Raine points out, have lots of experience sniffing out people traveling with contraband. These seasoned professionals correctly guessed which kids were lying only 49 percent of the time, which is *worse* than flipping a coin.

The researchers then brought in police officers to view the tapes. They guessed correctly 41 percent of the time—*significantly worse* than chance. You'd think it would be easier with the youngest children, but even four-year-olds could convincingly fool the pros. Somewhat gleefully, Dr. Raine sums up the study results: "Parents, you *think* you know what your kids get up to, but actually you don't even have a clue with your own toddler. That's how bad the story is. Sorry, mate, but you really are as hapless as I at figuring out who a psychopathic liar is."

It is a cold consolation to me. It does not surprise me that Dylan and Eric were able to deceive their teachers, a school counselor, Eric's psychiatrist, and the Diversion specialists. But, until April of 1999, I would have told you Dylan couldn't have fooled me.

• • •

The week after the call from Dylan's Diversion counselor, his college acceptance letters started to arrive. Dylan had been accepted to one school in Colorado, wait-listed at another, and accepted to two in Arizona. He seemed lukewarm about the Colorado school, but pleased to have some options in Arizona.

Life is falling into place for him, I thought as I arranged a dinner with the Harrises to celebrate the boys' termination from Diversion. Though we had made efforts all year to keep the two apart, our concerns about their relationship had receded. Certainly, Eric had shown us he was impulsive and emotional, but he was under the close supervision of his parents, and he'd started seeing a therapist.

The boys were about to graduate from high school, their mistakes behind them, and I was pleased for the families to be able to recognize their accomplishment. Life gives few enough opportunities to celebrate, and we had a great deal to be thankful for.

Some weeks earlier, I had asked Dylan about his friends' plans. He said Nate, Zack, and some of the others were off to college; Eric was hoping to join the Marines. Before our dinner with the Harrises, I asked Dylan for an update on Eric's plans. Joining the Marines had fallen through, he told me. Eric would be living at home, working, and attending community college instead.

During this conversation, Dylan had a faraway look, which made me worry he was having second thoughts about his own college plans. After an initial flurry of excitement over a warmer climate, he'd withdrawn, becoming even more pensive and quiet than usual, as if he had something on his mind.

"You're sure you want to go away?" I asked. Some of our friends' kids had started their college careers at community colleges closer to home, and I wanted to remind him there were other options. "I definitely want to go away," he said, sounding decisive. I nodded, believing I understood: he was nervous, naturally, but ready, too. I think now he was talking about his own death.

A couple of days later, we got written confirmation of the early Diversion termination. In his final report, dated February 3, Dylan's counselor wrote:

PROGNOSIS: Good

Dylan is a bright young man who has a great deal of potential. If he is able to tap his potential and become self-motivated he should do well in life.

RECOMMENDATIONS: Successful Termination

Dylan has earned the right for an early termination. He needs to strive to self motivate himself so he can remain on a positive path. He is intelligent enough to make any dream a reality but he needs to understand that hard work is part of it.

I finally allowed myself to exhale. Dylan was back on track. Maybe I *had* been overreacting by worrying so much about the theft. Boys did dumb stuff, as everyone said.

Dylan's journals tell a different story. By that point, things had decidedly taken a turn for the worst. Given the chance to travel back in time, I would ransack every nook and corner of my children's rooms, looking not just for drugs or goods we hadn't bought, but for any window onto their inner lives. There is nothing I wouldn't give to have read the pages of Dylan's journal while he was still alive, while we still had the chance to pull him back from the abyss that swallowed him and so many innocent others.

Later in February, Dylan and I had a conversation about his senior year coming to an end, and he mentioned a senior prank. Assuming the whole class was involved, I asked him for details. He smiled, and said he did not want to tell me.

He and Tom loved practical jokes, but the thought of a senior prank made me nervous. The Diversion counselor had been clear: even the smallest and most insignificant infraction, like toilet papering a house on Halloween, could jeopardize Dylan's future. If he made another mistake, he'd have a felony on his record.

"Don't even think about it," I warned him. He said, "Don't worry, Mom. I promise I won't get into trouble." Diversion was officially over, but Dylan had one last appointment with his counselor, so I called and asked him to please make sure Dylan understood the seriousness of the situation he was in. I didn't want him to take part in anything at school that might get him into more of a mess—no matter how silly, and not even if he did it with the entire senior class.

His Diversion counselor spoke to him about it at their last appointment, and made the rules clear. Dylan never mentioned the topic of a prank to us again.

. . .

Cheez. I'm stuffed. We just got back from dinner with Eric Harris and his parents. We went there to celebrate the end of Diversion for Eric and Dylan. Just hope they will stay out of trouble now for a year

so their records are expunged, whatever that means. My, I remember
what we were going through a year ago!

—Journal entry, February 1999

We met Eric's family on the second day of February at a local steak-house. It had been nearly a year since we'd seen them. The six of us sat in two adjacent booths, with the four parents in one booth, Eric and Dylan in the next.

When Eric's mom said they weren't sure what his plans were, I chirped that Dylan would be leaving for college in the fall. Secretly, I was relieved Dylan had a more concrete plan than Eric did. I will forever be humbled by the foolishness of my pride.

Mid-February, Dylan came downstairs dressed to go to work, though he wasn't scheduled. Eric's dog Sparky was seriously ill, so Dylan had picked up Eric's shift at Blackjack. I was fond of the little dog and felt sad for Eric; it's hard to lose a pet, especially an animal you've grown up with. As he left the house, I gave Dylan a hug and told him how proud I was that he was such a responsible employee and a good and loyal friend.

Later that week, the two of us looked at degree requirements for the schools he'd been accepted to, and we both revved up when we saw all the classes he could take. Tom grappled with financial aid forms while Dylan and I began to plan college visits.

One night at the end of February, I surprised Tom and Dylan by bringing home a couple of fruit pies and *Seven Samurai*, a classic Japanese film from the 1950s directed by Akira Kurosawa. Dylan had heard about *Seven Samurai* in a class at school, and was curious about it. I'd never seen it, although I knew the American Western remake from the sixties, *The Magnificent Seven*. Snowy and cold outside, it seemed like the perfect night to light a fire, pig out, and watch a movie, but I worried about my choice as soon as the film began: I wasn't sure Dylan was going to stick around for a long, black-and-white, subtitled movie about a sixteenth-century Japanese village.

I was wrong. Dylan was spellbound; we all were. Poor Byron dropped in for an unexpected visit in the middle, and even though we couldn't understand a word of the Japanese dialogue, we shushed him when he tried to talk. He sat down and tried to get into it with us, but he had the reaction I'd expected from Dylan. In a matter of minutes, he'd kissed me on the top of the head and let himself out. Rapt, we barely looked up long enough to say good-bye.

After the closing credits rolled, Tom, Dylan, and I stayed up late on the couch, talking about some of the more remarkable scenes. Because he'd made videos and done sound for plays, Dylan had deep appreciation for the technical challenges the movie presented. He was particularly knocked out by a complicated choreographed battle scene staged in a downpour, which I would come to learn had inspired directors like Martin Scorsese. I was thrilled he'd appreciated the subtle artistry of the film.

The first week of March, Dylan said he and some friends were going to the mountains to do an assignment for his video production class. Tom was scheduled for yet another surgery that week, to replace his right shoulder joint. I asked Dylan who was going on the trip, and who would be driving; I had not met two of the kids he mentioned. March is still winter in Colorado, and I reminded him to bring warm clothing, food, and water in case of a weather emergency. When I kissed him good-bye, I made him promise he wouldn't trespass. It was public land, he assured me; one of the boys knew the area well. He told me they were making an action film in a natural setting, using toy guns. In truth, they were filming the "Rampart Range" video, which I did not see or even know about until we were deposed, four years after the tragedy. In it, Dylan, Eric, and Mark Manes—the man who sold them one of the guns— shoot the weapons they have stockpiled.

On March 11, I took the day off so the three of us could visit the college in Colorado that Dylan had been accepted to. He was not overly enthused about the visit—he claimed to be intent on moving to a desert climate—but I was pleased to note he became more engaged when we took a tour of the computer lab. His academic performance in high school had always been a little mysterious to us; for someone who had shown so much early promise, he hadn't excelled. Watching him on that campus, I felt sure he was going to thrive at college.

That evening, Tom and I attended parent-teacher conferences at Dylan's high school. We'd received a midterm report the previous week showing that Dylan's grades had dropped precipitously in calculus and English. I was pretty sure it was "senioritis," a high school senior goofing off after being accepted to college, but wanted to touch base.

Dylan's calculus teacher told us Dylan sometimes fell asleep in class, and had not turned in some assignments. He'd taught Dylan before, and was disappointed Dylan wasn't more motivated. I was bothered to hear Dylan was slacking off, but not alarmed.

"Is he being disrespectful to you?" I asked.

The teacher replied with amusement, "Oh, no, not Dylan. Dylan's never disrespectful." I wondered aloud if being a year younger than his classmates explained his immature attitude, or if he was blowing off the subject because he planned to take it again at college. Then I worried I was making excuses for Dylan, and I shut up.

When I told the math teacher Dylan had been accepted at the University of Arizona, he seemed impressed and slightly surprised. When we mentioned the other Arizona university, he laughed and said, "Oh yes. That's where all the jocks go after they flunk out of UCLA." We later shared this comment with Dylan, who changed his mind about visiting the school. The upshot of our meeting was that Dylan wouldn't fail the course if he went to class and turned in the overdue assignments.

We sat down with Dylan's English teacher next. She'd taught both of my sons, and I felt a comfortable familiarity with her. I was relieved to hear Dylan had turned in some missing assignments after she'd sent out the midterm report, and his grade had moved from a D to a B. His teacher also praised Dylan's writing abilities. Tom and I were happily surprised. We'd always thought of Dylan as a math kid, and Byron as the son with the talent for language.

After this praise, the tone of the conversation shifted, and she told us Dylan had turned in a disturbing paper. (Tom remembers the word she used as *shocking,* because he wondered if it was a reference to sexual content.) We asked for details, but she only said the paper contained dark themes and some bad language. To illustrate the inappropriateness of Dylan's composition, she told us about a paper Eric had written, from the first-person perspective of a bullet being shot from a gun. Eric's story, she told us, could have been violent, but when it was read aloud the class was amused. Dylan's story, on the other hand, was dark. It had no humor in it at all.

Her comments on the paper, which I did not see until a year later, read as follows: "I'm offended by your use of profanity. In class we had discussed the approach of using *$!?** Also, I'd like to talk to you about your story before I give you a grade. You are an excellent writer/storyteller, but I have some problems with this one."

During our conference, Tom asked, "Is this something we should be concerned about?" Dylan's teacher said she thought it was under control. She'd asked Dylan to do a rewrite, and planned to show the original to Dylan's guidance counselor. Since I never wanted to leave a meeting without an action plan, I asked, "So, one of you will call us if you think this is a problem?" She confirmed they would.

She did show the paper to Dylan's counselor, who chided him about the language. I had the opportunity to meet with the counselor after the tragedy; he was understandably stricken by his failure to recognize an incipient threat. The professionals I have spoken with are divided on whether Dylan's paper (and possibly Eric's) would today qualify him for a screening in a public school system with a threat assessment protocol. It's entirely possible that both would have gone unremarked: teenage boys often write disturbingly about guns and violence. True threat assessment, though, is all about assembling disparate clues to arrive at a full picture, and it's likely that Dylan's arrest, his suspension in junior year, and the disturbing paper would together have added up to a red flag.

We did not perceive the paper to be a red flag, though, and the events of the rest of the night contributed to diminish the relative importance of it. Since no one else was waiting to talk to the English teacher, we continued to visit with her. I mentioned a presentation I'd seen about the differences between Generations X and Y children. We chatted about the district's language arts curriculum and one of the required reading books, *A Prayer for Owen Meany*.

We were all roughly the same age, and the three of us mused about what it had been like to be young during the Vietnam War. This prompted Dylan's teacher to share a story. She'd brought a folk record from the sixties, "Four Strong Winds," into class. The song featured the hardships faced by migrant farm workers, and it had always made her cry; but her students had laughed when she played it.

Tom and I leaned forward with concern. "Did Dylan laugh too?" She told us he had. I was bitterly disappointed; he often watched classic movies with us, and I would have expected better. Tom and I apologized for the insensitivity of our son and his classmates, and the three of us commiserated over the youth of today, like old-timers sitting on a park bench. We shook hands warmly when we parted.

It was Dylan's reaction to the song—not the paper—that Tom and I talked about on the way home. I hated that he'd laughed when his teacher shared a piece of art that moved her. Tom could never part with old books, science journals, or car parts, and his piles of junk ordinarily drove me nuts. That night, though, I appreciated his idiosyncrasies as he dug out the old record. We sat in the living room with a cup of tea, and I gave myself over to the song's melancholy refrain.

Tom saw an opportunity to teach Dylan a lesson, and to have a bit of fun, too. When he heard Dylan's car coming up the driveway, he queued up the record. When Dylan came in, we told him about the meetings with his teachers. Tom remembers that we talked about the paper during that discussion and asked him to get it for us; I don't remember asking for the paper until the following morning. As we talked, Tom hit Play. Eventually, Dylan recognized the song coming up in the background. Knowing he'd been set up, he started to laugh.

"Why are you playing that *horrible* song?!"

"Why is it horrible?" I asked him. He said he hated the "weird" sound of it. We told him what the song was about. "Just listen to it with an open mind," Tom requested. Without protest, Dylan listened to the rest of the song. When it was over, he admitted it wasn't that bad.

We told him how hurt his teacher had been, and talked about the importance of respecting the feelings of others. He admitted it had been wrong to laugh. Afterward, the three of us curled up on the couch to watch one of our favorite movies, Alfred Hitchcock's *Vertigo*. As we headed off to bed, Tom and I felt we had provided the best guidance we could. I will never know if Dylan was pretending to care, or if he did.

The next morning, I asked Dylan to show me the English paper. He said it was in his car and that he didn't have enough time to look for it. I said, "Well, I'd like to see it when you get home from school today. When will you be home?" He said, "I won't have time today because I have to work." I gave him a look that said, "Stop making excuses," and added with finality, "I want to see the paper. You can show it to me tonight when you get home." He said he would. But by the time evening came, Tom and I had both forgotten about it.

This lack of follow-through on my part was uncharacteristic, but indicative: I believed Dylan was a psychologically healthy human being. I never considered that the paper could be a reflection of deeply seated problems. I knew it contained some rough language and a dark theme, but had confidence that his teacher and the school counselor would handle the situation appropriately. If anything, I was interested in taking a look at Dylan's writing skills.

I finally saw Dylan's paper for the first time more than a year after his death; a copy of the story was among some of the items returned to us by the sheriff's department. The subject matter—a man dressed in black who kills the popular kids at a school—was indeed disquieting, but I cannot help but wonder if, as an artist myself, I would have seen it as a danger sign if I had read it before his death. Artistic expression, even when it's unpleasant, can be a healthy way of coping with feelings. I abhorred the violence so attractive to teenage boys—I could no more sit through an entire viewing of *Pulp Fiction* than lay an egg—but I never imagined Dylan would be capable of making that violence real.

. . .

That spring, whenever Dylan wasn't busy, and the world slowed down around him, I noticed how pensive and distracted he looked. A month or so before the shootings, I approached him one afternoon as he sat on the couch staring blankly into the middle distance.

"You're so quiet lately, honey. Are you sure you're okay?"

He stood up and said, "Yeah, I'm just tired and have a lot of homework to do. I'm going up to my room to get it done so I can get to bed a little early."

"All right," I said. "You want me to make you something to eat?" He was also very thin in those last months. He ate well at home, but I wondered if he was getting enough when he wasn't there, and would often offer to make him French toast or an omelet between meals.

He shook his head and headed upstairs. I returned to tidying the kitchen, trusting in the kid I'd raised, satisfied he knew he could tell me whatever was on his mind, and confident that he would do so in his own good time.

It's not that I didn't know that something was wrong, but I had no idea it was a life-and-death situation. I was just worried Dylan was unhappy.

There isn't a day since the tragedy that I haven't relived that interaction, that I don't see myself following him up the stairs. A faraway look—I have heard suicidologist Thomas Joiner refer to it as "the thousand-yard stare"—is a warning sign for imminent suicide, and one often missed. Hundreds of times I've imagined myself demanding, cajoling, wheedling, bribing Dylan: *Tell me what's going on with you. Tell me what it feels like. Tell me what you need. Tell me how I can help.* I've even imagined barricading myself in his room, refusing to leave until he tells me what he's thinking. Each one of these fantasies ends with me taking him into my arms, knowing exactly what to say and how to get him the help he needs.

. . .

For my fiftieth birthday, I arranged to meet a friend for a drink after work. I told Tom not to worry if I was late; I suspected my friend might be planning a get-together. Indeed, I found a dozen close friends and coworkers at the restaurant—plus Tom, who'd organized the party. The fact that he'd done such a kind thing warmed me.

As I settled in for a conversation with my friends, Tom leaned over and warned me not to fill up on snacks. "We're going out for dinner," he whispered.

Dylan and Byron were waiting for us at home, dressed up and ready to go. Byron presented me with a houseplant, and Dylan gave me a CD. Ruth and Don met us at the restaurant—yet another surprise. I was as happy that night as I can remember being, completely oblivious to the terrible disaster looming on the horizon.

Don took pictures as we were leaving the restaurant. Dylan had been quiet all evening, visibly self-conscious and uncomfortable as he always was in social situations, but polite—and, as usual, happy to have a good meal. In the pictures, which I saw for the first time only after his death, he looks annoyed.

Early the next morning, the three of us set off for Arizona. Although I'd slept barely a few hours, I was looking forward to spending time with Tom and Dylan. Tom relinquished the wheel to Dylan on the second day; we hoped to use the trip to help improve his highway skills. The first few hours were a trial. With his crooked glasses balanced on his nose, and his baseball cap turned backwards, Dylan tilted the seat back in a semi-reclining position and drove with only the index finger of his left hand touching the wheel. I sat in the backseat, clutching the door handle and praying silently until I finally asked him to slow down. Tom tried to keep both of us calm, though I noticed he did not need his usual reminder to fasten his seat belt.

Little by little, Dylan's driving improved and he ended up driving for several hours. Eventually I was able to fall asleep, and when I woke up, Dylan was driving like a pro. He seemed pleased when I complimented him, though he was probably just happy I'd stopped nagging. He listened to techno CDs through earphones until Tom asked if he'd play something for us. Tom preferred jazz and I usually chose classical, so we were both surprised by how much we liked what he played. All of us were excited to see Colorado's mountains give way to the desert vegetation. When Tom took the wheel, Dylan grabbed the camera so he could take pictures out of the car window, and said again how much he was looking forward to going to school in the desert.

Our tour was successful, and by the end Dylan had made up his mind: he wanted to go to the University of Arizona. We could skip the other school on our itinerary and head for home. We stopped for gas and asked Dylan to pose next to a saguaro more than three times his height. He looks remote and unkempt in the photo, developed after his death, standing with his arms uncomfortably out from his sides; to me, now, they look poised over invisible guns. At our hotel, Dylan watched a movie in his room while Tom and I made an early night of it.

The next morning, as we were all getting ready to join civilization at the continental breakfast, Dylan pulled his old baseball cap, one of his favorite possessions, over his long hair. We'd made the cap together: he'd carefully snipped the "B" (for Boston Red Sox) off another hat grown too shabby to wear, and I'd sewn the letter to the back of a new hat, so he could wear it backwards and still display the logo. It turned out remarkably well, and he never wanted to be without it.

Tom stepped in with his 1950s dress code standards and asked Dylan not to wear the hat to the hotel's breakfast buffet. Dylan argued that we were on vacation, and it couldn't possibly make a difference to anyone if he wore the hat. I shot Tom a "don't sweat the small stuff" look, but didn't want to sabotage his authority, so I gathered up a suitcase.

"I'll go down to the car and wait while you two work this out."

I'd forgotten the car key, though, so I leaned against the hood in the cold morning air, remembering how Tom would insist the boys tuck in their shirts and polish their shoes for church while the minister's own kids wore T-shirts and jeans. I was angry at him for harping on the hat. I guess I still am.

Eventually, Dylan came down to the car alone, his head bare. I wanted to say I agreed with him, and that it was okay with *me* if he wore the hat, but I did not. I only said, "I'm sorry the morning started out like this. I see you decided not to wear the hat." Dylan sounded tired but determined to brush it off. "It's not worth fighting about; it's just not a big deal."

I was frankly surprised. I'd expected a little more sputtering and complaining from a seventeen-year-old. "Wow, Dyl. I'm impressed," I said, mistaking his willingness to withdraw from the conflict for maturity. I praised him for controlling his anger but I wish now he had stomped and screamed, giving me a glimpse of the rage burning inside him. Now I wonder if he had stopped caring about anything at all.

There was one more odd incident on our way home, which at the time Tom and I chalked up to Dylan's desire to get back to his friends. The three of us stopped at a packed McDonald's in Pueblo for a quick bite. A large group of teenagers had taken over a couple of tables against the wall. We'd just unwrapped our sandwiches when Dylan leaned forward, hardly moving his lips, and said urgently, "We have to go. Those kids are laughing at me." I looked over. The teenagers were hooting and hollering and having a great time, and none of them was paying the slightest bit of attention to us.

"Relax, Dyl. Nobody's looking at you," I said. Besides, if a person didn't want to be noticed, why wear a floor-length leather coat? But Dylan grew more insistent, casting quick, paranoid glances over his shoulder at the oblivious kids. He was so uncomfortable that we bolted our burgers and hustled out of there; the teenagers didn't even look up at us as we left. The rest of the ride home was uneventful.

After our trip, Dylan jumped right back into his busy social life. Nate spent the night. One evening, after studying calculus with Robyn, Dylan asked if I would help pay for prom expenses. I was floored he was interested in going to the prom at all; so, I found out later, were his friends. He seemed amused himself.

The following night, March 30, I attended a pre-graduation

meeting for parents of seniors and ran into Judy Brown. Since our phone conversation about the snowball more than a year earlier, we'd seen each other only briefly, mostly after school productions, and so we were eager to catch up. Before long, our conversation veered off into our mutual interest in art—my figure drawing sessions, and some classes she'd taken. We looked at some drawings I had stashed in my car before saying good-bye. Neither one of us mentioned Eric.

. . .

One of the most painful questions people ask suicide loss survivors is whether or not we ever hugged our kids. The question hurts, not only for the obvious reasons (only thousands of times; what kind of mother doesn't hug her kid?) but, in my case, because of a specific incident—indeed, a specific hug—that took place in the last two weeks of Dylan's life.

One afternoon we passed each other in the hallway at the foot of the stairs. Spontaneously, I threw my arms around him.

"I love you so much," I told him. "You are such a wonderful person, and Dad and I are *so* proud of you." He rested his left hand gently on my back, barely touching me. With the jokingly haughty air we sometimes used to thank each other for elaborate and ridiculous compliments, he thanked me. But I didn't want him to make a joke of this, which I meant with all my heart, and so I took his thin jawbone in both of my hands and looked directly into his eyes.

"No kidding around, Dylan: I mean it. I love you so much. You *are* a wonderful person, and Dad and I are proud of you."

He looked down, embarrassed, and whispered his thanks.

For years, I replayed this scene in my mind. Afraid that it would become distorted through repetition, I wrote it down. I can see it like a movie now, two figures in the hallway, his hand on the small of my back, me reaching up to hold his face. The memory of that hug is one of the most painful I hold—and the knowledge that, to this day, I have no idea what on earth Dylan could possibly have been thinking.

. . .

On April 4, I decided to whip up a belated, last-minute dinner in honor of the combined Easter and Passover holidays, figuring I'd scrunch the two and make it a double celebration, as my family had often done when I was a child.

When I mentioned it to Dylan, he laughed in an irritated way, as if at some private joke, and told me he didn't want to attend. He gave in when I asked him to reconsider. I spent a happy day in the kitchen cooking, and a neighbor joined us for the meal. We never did get all the way through the service, but we had a good time.

The family celebrated Tom's birthday in early April by going out for fondue. Byron and Dylan took one car, and Tom and I rode in another, giving the boys some time to bond. It was the last time Byron was alone with his brother, and he would later tearfully recall how normal Dylan had acted.

At dinner, Byron did most of the talking. Dylan was so quiet, I fretted he wasn't getting enough attention—an old worry, familiar to many parents, that one child will feel less loved or validated than the other one. Dylan did get a few jokes in, one so funny I laughed about it all evening. Later, when I couldn't remember what the joke was (neither Tom nor Byron could remember, either), I was crushed that I hadn't paid more attention.

After dinner, the four of us gathered back at the house for home-made cake and gifts. I'd found Tom a small concrete bench, a place to rest his sore joints while tending to his favorite flowers, and my two sons effortlessly carried it into the garden from the trunk of my car. Byron gave him a CD, and Dylan gave him a box of little cigars. For many years, he smoked one on Dylan's birthday in remembrance.

Four days before the tragedy, I saw the Toulouse-Lautrec exhibit with a friend at the Denver Art Museum, while Tom and Dylan studied a map of the University of Arizona to find the dorm closest to the center of campus and tried to figure out which rooms were the largest. After they were through, Dylan picked up his tuxedo. He hung the bag from his closet door to keep the contents from wrinkling. We would see it, later, in the background of one of the Basement Tapes.

Tom and I both noticed Dylan was a little agitated that week. I was sure he was nervous about the prom. Robyn was flying back to Denver on Saturday afternoon after an out-of-state church function, and her flight time would cut it close. Dylan had to choose flowers and work out the logistics of dinner and transportation; the tasks were, to say the least, out of his area of expertise.

That Friday, Dylan asked if Eric could sleep over. We agreed. The guest room hadn't been cleaned since Nate had spent the night a couple of weeks earlier, and our sick cat Rocky had thrown up in there, so Tom and I wrestled a vacuum cleaner up the stairs and asked Dylan to clean the room and bathroom before his friend arrived.

Dylan was irritated we were making such a big deal about cleaning; he told us Eric didn't care if the room was clean or not. I overrode his protests. "Eric may not care, but we do. If you clean your room, Dad will do the bathroom and I'll do the guest room. It'll go fast if we all help." A few minutes later, Dylan left the house, saying he had a quick errand to run. I rolled my eyes, believing he was procrastinating; more likely, he was removing something he did not want us to see. After Dylan returned, we poked our heads into his room intermittently to check his progress. Neither one of us saw anything unusual.

I'd already gone to bed when Eric arrived about 10:00 p.m. He had brought a large duffel bag, so heavy he could hardly lift it, and he was dragging it over the threshold when Tom said hello. Dylan and his friends were always hauling computer parts and video equipment over to one another's houses, so Tom didn't think twice about the bag. He told the boys what snacks were available, said good night, and came to bed.

We slept without interruption, and when I came down to make breakfast, Eric had already gone. After all the fuss about cleaning the guest room, the bed had not been slept in at all.

• • •

We all focused on Dylan to get him ready for the prom. It was so cute.
A. came over and we took pictures. Robyn & he left at about 6, and he
has a big night ahead.

—Journal entry, April 1999

On Saturday, April 17, Tom and I remained on standby at home to help Dylan get ready for the prom.

Dylan woke much calmer than the day before; he seemed to be going out of his way to convince me he wasn't nervous. When I asked if he was concerned Robyn wouldn't make it from the airport in time, he shrugged and said, "It's no big deal. If we make it, we make it. If we don't, we don't. I'm not worried about it."

Late afternoon, his hair still wet from his shower, Dylan hauled his tuxedo into our bedroom, where we had a full-length mirror to work with. New to formal wear, he needed Tom's help to understand what all the tuxedo pieces were. Self-conscious in black socks, plaid boxer shorts, and a gleaming white shirt with a stiff, pleated front, he seemed to tower over his father, though there was only a two-inch difference between them.

He stood patiently while Tom awkwardly twisted tiny pieces of metal and plastic through the many buttonholes. The bow tie stumped Tom, and Dylan wrestled it away to try it himself; together, the two consummate problem-solvers figured it out. I sat on the bed to keep them company and told Dylan he looked like Lee Marvin getting outfitted in Western finery in *Cat Ballou*, one of our family's favorites. Both he and Tom laughed.

I had the camera, and Dylan tolerated a few shots before becoming self-conscious and annoyed as usual. I tried to catch one of his reflection in the mirror without him noticing, but he grabbed a towel and flicked it to block the shot. I developed the roll a few months after his death, using an assumed name so the press wouldn't get ahold of the pictures. In that photo, only a fragment of his face is visible behind the towel—a mischievous grin under tired eyes.

We'd spent that year begging Dylan to get a haircut, to no avail, but I convinced him to tie his hair back into a ponytail with one of my own elastics for the prom. He put his prescription glasses in his pocket and donned a pair of small-framed sunglasses. We thought he looked very handsome.

Alison, our renter, came over and offered to take a picture of the three of us. In the picture, Dylan is clowning around, hamming it up like a professional model, Zoolander-style. The sharp lines of his formal wear stand in stark contrast to the faded flannel shirts and worn blue jeans Tom and I are wearing. He kept his sunglasses on as he posed with us; he wore dark glasses often during the last weeks of his life. I believe now he was hiding behind them.

Tom had remembered to charge the batteries on our video camera, and he filmed Dylan briefly before Robyn arrived. The conversation between them is stilted; clearly, neither of them is comfortable on camera. But we have looked back on this pre-prom video many times, and shown it to others. It is absolutely stunning how normal Dylan seems.

He and Tom talk lazily about baseball; Dylan mimes his hero, Randy Johnson, pitching in an ill-fitting tuxedo. Tom makes some comment about growing up, and Dylan remarks he'll never have kids. Tom says he may change his mind, and Dylan says, "I know. I know. Someday I'll look back at this and say, 'What was I thinking?!!'" It is breathtakingly prophetic. When Tom persists in filming over Dylan's protests, Dylan pinches small handfuls of snow from a nearby bush, lobbing the miniature snowballs playfully at Tom until the camera stops running. The fondness between them is palpable. It breaks my heart.

Robyn arrived in good time, looking lovely in a deep blue-purple dress. Tom taped Dylan presenting her with her corsage, and smiling down at her as she struggled to pin a rose to his lapel. I made paparazzi jokes and asked them to move so I could get a picture without parked cars in the background. Since Dylan had assured us he and Robyn were just friends, I was a little surprised—and frankly tickled—to see him put his arm around her.

In the last few frames on the tape Tom shot, the two of them smile into the camera. Then, self-consciously but sweetly, they both begin to laugh.

. . .

When I heard Dylan's car arrive home from the prom after 4 a.m., I roused myself to talk with him. Though I was tired, I wanted to reach out.

We met at the foot of the stairs. He looked exhausted but happy, a kid who'd had a big night. As usual, he was reluctant to volunteer information, so I peppered him with questions about what he'd eaten and whom he'd hung out with. I was excited to find out he'd danced. He thanked me for paying for tickets and clothes, and I was pleasantly surprised by his effusiveness when he told me he'd had the best night of his life.

I had kissed him good night and turned to go back to bed when he stopped me. "I want to show you something." He pulled a metal flask from his pocket. Someone with a little skill and a lot of solder had fixed a large crack at the top with a messy patch.

"What is this?" I demanded. "Where did you get this thing?"

He said he'd found it. When I asked what it contained, Dylan said it held peppermint schnapps, and that he'd rather not say where he'd gotten the alcohol. I was about to launch into my well-worn concerns about drinking when Dylan held up a hand, silencing me. "I want you to know you can trust me and you can trust Robyn. I had filled this so we could drink it tonight. I want you to see only a little tiny bit is missing." He handed me the flask, and insisted I examine it closely, as if he were going to do a magic trick with it. "We had a little bit to drink at the beginning of the evening but no more after that. See? It's close to the top." I acknowledged the flask was nearly full.

"I just wanted you to know you can trust me," he said again. Still a little shaken, I thanked him for sharing the information with me before adding, "I *do* trust you." Then I headed off to bed, reassured. I'd never expected him to get through high school without experimenting with alcohol, after all. At least he'd told me about it.

I've given a lot of thought to that private moment between mother and son in the stillness of the night. In retrospect, I sometimes think that engaging me in that conversation about the flask was among the cruelest tricks Dylan ever played on me. Was he consciously manipulating me into trusting him, even as he was planning a massacre? Was he mocking me? If he was preparing to die within a few days, why was it necessary to establish my trust in him? Did he need reassurance, or was he trying to prevent me from searching his room?

I once shared these thoughts with a psychologist who then asked me, "How do you know he wasn't in earnest? Maybe he did want to earn your approval, and it had nothing to do with what was to follow." It's one of the many things I will never know.

. . .

Sunday after the prom, Dylan slept late, then left for Eric's in the afternoon. He looked terribly tired, which was only to be expected after the sleepover on Friday night and a late night at the prom. I made a large kettle of homemade vegetable soup with posole, but Byron had plans and Dylan didn't get home until later, so Tom and I ate alone. April 19 was a Monday, and Dylan let me know he wouldn't be home for dinner. He'd made plans to go to a steakhouse with Eric, the same restaurant where we had eaten with Eric's family two months earlier.

"What's the occasion?" I asked. (When Dylan ate with friends, they usually went for fast food.) He told me Eric had a couple of coupons. They didn't need a reason, as far as I was concerned. Three weeks from graduation, they were about to move on to the next phase of their lives and I applauded their impulse to celebrate. I told Dylan to have a good time.

He got home about 8:30, and I greeted him at the door. "How was it?" "Good," he said, as he removed his muddy shoes. Always trying to pull a little more information, I asked, "What did you have for dinner?" He looked up from his shoes, tilting his head to one side so he could give me a "Come on, Mom" look; they'd gone to a *steakhouse*. "Uh, steak?" he said. We both laughed.

Tom was reading in the living room, and I asked Dylan if he had time to sit down with us for a minute, but he said he had a lot of work to do, adding he'd probably have to be in his room all evening to get everything done. He seemed particularly evasive and eager to get upstairs; I assumed he had some last-minute, end-of-year homework to finish up. The phone rang a few times; I let Dylan get it. I do not remember kissing him, or going to his room to say good night. I am still trying to forgive myself for not remembering if I did or not.

The next morning, I got up in the dark to get ready for work. Before I had the chance to call him for bowling, Dylan bounded down the stairs past our bedroom. I opened the door, trying to catch him before he left. The house was dark.

I heard the front door open. "Dyl?" I called into the darkness.

"Bye," was all he said.

CHAPTER 15

Collateral Damage

I truly see no reason to continue living. I have a mammogram on Wednesday. I'm even fantasizing about having a fatal disease so I could say, "How long do I have to stick around before I can get out of here?" I make no contributions to life and derive no pleasure from it. Fantasize about saving a child from disaster and dying in the process, or offering my life to terrorists to save a planeload of people.

—Journal entry, January 2001

On Valentine's Day of 2001, almost two years after Dylan's participation in the massacre at Columbine High School, I was diagnosed with breast cancer.

In a sense, I wasn't surprised. You know those Halloween costumes made to look like the handle of an ax is protruding from your chest? That was what I felt like all the time. The heart is where you hold and nurture a child, and a virtual bomb had been set off in mine. My son was dead, and fourteen other people because of him. It made sense there would be some collateral damage.

Fear of death had been a constant companion of mine since childhood, and an intensified version of it set in quickly after my diagnosis, adding to already sky-high levels of anxiety. A few days afterward, Tom took me out to our favorite neighborhood Chinese restaurant. At the end of the meal, when I broke open my fortune cookie, there was nothing inside.

My oncologist approached me thoughtfully. Because they'd caught the cancer early, and because the tumor was small, she felt I might be able to do radiation treatment and avoid chemotherapy.

Due to persistent stomach problems related to grief and anxiety in the wake of the tragedy, I had already lost about twenty-five pounds—weight I could not afford to lose. Grief and guilt had dramatically depleted my physical and emotional reservoirs. The treatment path was my choice, but the truth sat unspoken between us. I was so run-down and haggard I did not look like someone who would survive a brutal round of chemotherapy. I elected not to do it.

There's a Susan G. Komen cancer outreach program in our community. After your diagnosis, a breast cancer survivor comes to your house to give you information and encouragement. (The American Foundation for Suicide Prevention has a similar visitation program for suicide loss survivors, called the Survivor Outreach Program. I'm on the board of our local chapter, currently working to bring that program to Colorado.) When I saw the breast cancer support group information my volunteer had brought, I could only shake my head. I needed a support group, *that* was true—but not for cancer.

Radiation causes exhaustion and physical discomfort, but I was already there. With the help of family and friends and a terrific medical team, I got through my treatment. After my final radiation session, the staff of the clinic presented me with a card they'd signed. It's likely this is a kindness they perform for every patient, but the gesture devastated me, and I fled to the safety of my car to cry.

I didn't know why I was crying. Maybe because it had felt so good to be taken care of. Or because the end of my treatment meant I'd have to go back, full-time, to grieving for Dylan and struggling to understand what he'd done.

It's funny I don't have more to say about surviving cancer; I certainly didn't feel detached or blasé about it when it was happening. It was treated, and I moved on with gratitude. But after I recovered, I realized I'd been wrong in the journal entry that begins this chapter: I did not want to die.

Tom would often say he wished Dylan had killed us too, or that we'd never been born at all. I prayed I'd pass away in my sleep, a quiet deliverance from the agony of waking up and realizing it hadn't all been a terrible nightmare. Sitting in traffic, I'd fantasize about being given the opportunity to trade my life for the people who had died at the school, or being presented with the chance to sacrifice myself to save a large group. Dying would be a relief, I thought, and dying to save others would give my miserable life purpose.

Surviving breast cancer helped me to see (as perhaps we all should) that my life was a gift. My work, going forward, would be to find a way to honor that gift.

CHAPTER 16

A New Awareness

It's widely acknowledged among those who grieve that the second year is often worse than the first. The first year, you're trying to adjust to the newness of the suffering, and to get through the days. It's during the second year that you realize you've lost sight of the shoreline. There's nothing but emptiness ahead and behind, a vast loneliness stretching out as far as you can see. This, you realize, is permanent. There will be no turning back.

My grief was amplified by the agony of knowing that so many families were going through something similar because of my son. The image of Dylan, so hate- and rage-filled on the tapes, battled with my own memories of the playful kid I'd loved so much. Some days, it felt like a war was taking place inside of me.

A few things helped. I couldn't yet make any art, but as I lay in bed I would sometimes imagine I was drawing. Specifically, I imagined I was drawing trees.

I have always loved trees. I'm inspired by their fortitude and character—their knots and scars and burls, the sites of so many injuries and so much life—and by their generosity, the way they uncomplainingly provide shade and oxygen and food and shelter and fuel. Trees are both deeply grounded and aspirational; they never stop reaching. They feel like friends, and the idea of drawing them became a safe and comforting place for me to park my mind. But I could not yet put pencil to paper.

Indeed, I would not achieve the integration I sought until I found two nutrients essential to so many survivors. First, I found community and then I found a way to contribute.

• • •

Met C. Her son D. killed himself at 12 after a bad day at school. It was
over a year and a half ago and she still cries all the time. I cried hard
all the way home and realized how much I want to be in a support
group. Will lock cats out tonight so I can sleep.

—Journal entry, July 1999

Less than three months after the shootings, my supervisor sent me
to a large regional conference for rehabilitation professionals. I de-
bated about whether to go; while I had come to feel a little more
comfortable with my coworkers, I wasn't sure I was ready to be out
in the wider world. Ultimately I asked the organizers to hold my
nametag behind the registration table until I asked them for it. By
then, such precautions had become a way of life.

When I went to claim my badge, one of the two women behind
the table looked up. "Sue Klebold?" she asked. I tensed, as I would
for years. But the lovely dark-haired woman reached across the
table for my hand. "I'm Celia. I want you to know many people
understand what you're going through right now." Her voice was
warm, but she did not smile. When she continued, I understood
why. "My twelve-year-old son died by suicide last year," she said.

I had received an enormous amount of sympathy, and many
letters of commiseration. Our friends and my colleagues had been
wonderful but I always felt the distance between their experiences
and my own. Celia's hand on mine, and those words—"many people understand what you're going through"—tethered me back to
the world, providing a deep and automatic consolation, the way
a distraught toddler's tears stop as soon as he's swept up into his
mother's arms. I asked Celia if she might have some time to sit and
talk, and she told me she'd be relieved from the registration desk in
half an hour.

The next thirty minutes were wasted. I cried in the bathroom for
half of it, and walked around in a daze for the rest. My need to talk
to another mother who had lost a child to suicide was even greater
than I had known. When Celia reached out, I grabbed hold of what
she was offering like I was grabbing for a rope, mid-fall.

We spent almost an hour in two plush chairs in the hotel lobby, holding hands and sharing. I was careful not to divulge specifics about Dylan that might put Celia in legal jeopardy. Meanwhile, her own story broke my heart. She'd lost her son so young! At least I had been able to see Dylan as a young man.

I knew I wasn't the only mother who'd had absolutely no idea how troubled her beloved child had been, but I'd had few opportunities to feel the kinship that comes from talking to someone who has also lost someone to suicide. It helped that Celia was so pretty and well put-together, so intelligent and articulate—the kind of woman I would have admired under any circumstances. Her sophisticated normality was a balm, as I had unwittingly bought into many of the ignorant myths about suicide.

As we tearfully hugged good-bye, I felt closer to her than I felt to anyone in the world. "I can't imagine what you're going through," people would say, shaking their heads—and they were right. I say that without judgment. Who could imagine going through something like this? I certainly could not have. Surrounded as I was by love and support, I felt completely adrift from normal experience—and indeed, from myself. It was, I came to realize, how Dylan must have felt at the end of his life.

There had been no relief for me on the horizon, no indication it would ever feel any different, until Celia put her hand on mine. With one gesture, she had connected me to a society of survivors who would welcome me without hatred or judgment. For the first time, I felt a gleam of hope that I might not have to spend the rest of my life spinning on my own solitary planet, grappling with feelings no one else could understand.

Somewhere out there, there was a tribe of people who would see me as a sister, a partner, a soul mate—who would allow me to join them in making a contribution.

· · ·

In the second year after Dylan's death, I finally found that community.

It had been painful to feel so profoundly alienated from the place where we had made our home. I had always chatted easily with the barista at Starbucks, and I knew the names of all the women at the supermarket checkout. After Columbine, I anxiously watched people's body language and facial micro-expressions to see whether they recognized me. Luckily, 99.9 percent of the people who did had something kind to say, but cringing like a frightened animal in the place where we'd made our home had shaken my sense of myself.

Much has been written about what happened in Littleton in the wake of the tragedy. As humans go into shock after an assault on their bodies, so do communities. As President Clinton said on the night of the massacre, "If it could happen in a place like Littleton . . ." This wasn't the drug-riddled inner city, or some supposedly godless corridor like New York or Los Angeles. People who lived in Littleton were upstanding citizens with nice suburban houses and happy, healthy, well-fed children. We expected our schools to be safe.

In the months after Columbine, everyone who lived in the area felt exposed and frightened. The whole place was a bundle of raw nerves, and people responded in all kinds of ways. Some tapped in to a vein of forgiveness and compassion. Others lashed out. Many who'd never had a voice before gained a sense of power and importance. Some were seduced by it; others genuinely felt they could do some good by speaking out.

Blame swirled. Too many guns were the problem, said one faction. There hadn't been *enough* guns, said another; every teacher should be armed. A lack of family values was to blame, shouted the Religious Right. Still others claimed that the Religious Right had co-opted the community's mourning. Amid all this, people were trying to mourn the dead and heal the injured, while scrambling to rebuild a sense of community, a sense of safety, a sense of self.

The natural response to tragedy is to look for meaning: How could this happen? Who is responsible? Tom and I were the chief suspects. "Those boys could only have learned hate like that in their homes," editorials thundered. The things people wrote and said were painful to us, but we were far from the only ones to find the climate divisive.

Like porcupines, people roll into a ball to protect their soft centers, projecting their spikes outward. This defensive mode is a natural response to being attacked, and there were a lot of spikes in Littleton in those days. The school, the media, the police—everyone involved seemed to be simultaneously fending off an attack while launching one of their own.

The sheriff's department was doing meticulous work, but the public was learning they had also failed to follow through on Judy and Randy Brown's repeated warnings about Eric. His website was quoted extensively in the search warrants served on the day of the massacre, proving someone in the department had known about it. One claim had even been pursued: when investigators had found evidence that Eric was building pipe bombs, they drew up a warrant to search the Harris house. But the warrant was never taken before a judge, the house was never searched, and the investigation report did not surface until long after the tragedy.

As the public lost confidence in the sheriff's department, people began to demand more information. The autopsy report of a minor is usually sealed, but the most important findings—that there had been no drugs in Dylan's system, for instance—had already been released. I did not see what anyone had to gain from knowing what was in his stomach when he died, or how much his organs weighed. Even with our lawyers' help, we lost that fight, and the autopsy results were picked over and published. I felt sick. Even in this, we had failed to protect Dylan.

The media swarm had receded somewhat, but there was still a Columbine-related headline on the front page of the local news almost every day. Some reporters were digging into the ongoing investigation, and trying to get a real understanding of the dynamics at the school. Others were less ethical. When Columbine crime scene photos of Eric and Dylan lying dead in pools of blood were sold to the *National Enquirer* and published, it seemed there was no line that couldn't be crossed. Later, though, I would learn that many journalists had also been traumatized by the time they spent in Littleton.

Meanwhile, Tom and I were sitting in the eerily silent eye of the storm. Even while our own inner circle continued to be an immense source of strength (and an insulation from the hostility of the outside world), the tension in our own relationship was rising. It would only get worse as the sense of solace and purpose I found in the company of other suicide loss survivors grew.

. . .

My friend Sharon was a survivor of suicide loss herself, and knew I needed to connect with other parents who had lost children to suicide. She also knew that my organizational skills make me a natural coordinator and administrator, the type of person you automatically ask to plan a meeting, or balance a budget, or type up minutes. So, in that second year after Columbine, Sharon put me to work. She invited me to join a small group of women who volunteered for the Suicide Prevention Coalition of Colorado.

Walking into the first meeting, I was scared sick. Would these people judge me? I didn't dare to hope they'd understand what Dylan had done, let alone what I had experienced. Ten minutes later, I was sitting around a kitchen table with five other mothers of children lost to suicide, tying raffia bows onto flowerpots containing forget-me-not seed packets. There was no discrimination in that room— nothing but love, and compassion, and an all-too-recognizable grief. (Three of the six women at the table—half—would also survive breast cancer, which strengthened my admittedly unscientific theory about what happens when a bomb goes off in your heart.) The tension I usually felt in the company of others melted away. The opportunity to grieve for Dylan as my son, no matter what he had done in the final moments of his life, was valuable beyond description.

I recently read an article in the *New York Times* by a therapist, Patrick O'Malley. He describes the respite one of his patients found at a support group for bereaved parents, despite her initial resistance. The group was "a place where no acting was required. It was a place where people understood that they didn't really want to achieve closure after all. To do so would be to lose a piece of a sacred bond." When I was with other survivors, Dylan was a boy who had died by suicide. Nobody was excusing what he had done, but they weren't discounting my grief, either, or my right to miss the son I had lost.

The next weekend, I attended a luncheon hosted by the Suicide Prevention Coalition of Colorado, the group Sharon chaired; our forget-me-nots were on the tables. For the first time, I was in a room filled with people who could relate to all my feelings, the ones that made me feel like I was hanging on to sanity by the merest thread.

I didn't need to tell the people in that room that I hadn't known what Dylan was thinking or planning. That place was all too familiar to them. "Bottom line: when someone lies to you, you feel like a fool," a woman said, and I startled myself with a ragged sob. (One thing about a suicide loss survivors' event? You're never the only person crying.) They understood the humiliation I felt at being duped, and the shame of knowing that I had not been able to help my child precisely when he had needed me most.

As I'd done with Celia, I scrutinized everyone I met for some indication of the underlying problem that had brought this nightmare upon them. Did this mother seem cold or checked-out? Did this dad seem abusive, or neglectful? Was there some identifying characteristic that would brand these people—and, by extension, myself—as deficient in some way? This was, of course, the way people scrutinized me.

But the people I met there were nice, smart, funny, kind—*normal*. Their stories poured out of them. They were elementary school teachers, social workers, truck drivers, dentists, pastors, stay-at-home moms. They had been active, attentive parents, sisters, husbands, wives, and children. They had deeply loved the person they lost. Like me, many of them had misread indicators of something drastically amiss.

Suicide is ugly. It's wreathed in disgrace. It screams to the world that a person's life ended in failure. Most people don't even want to hear about it. As a culture, we believe that people who die by suicide are weak, that they lack willpower, that they've taken "the coward's way out." We believe that they are selfish, and have acted aggressively. If they cared about their families/ spouses/work, they would have found a way to think themselves out of the spiral they were in. None of this is true, and yet the taint is pervasive and shared by the surviving families. Bewilderment, guilt, regret, and self-castigation are constant companions for a survivor of suicide loss.

One afternoon, I had lunch with an old friend—not a suicide loss survivor—who asked me, "Can you ever forgive Dylan for what he did?" I sat silent, dumbstruck, seeing how radically our lives had diverged. All I could think of was the scene in *Ordinary People* where Buck's wet hand slips out of Conrad's, and Buck drowns. I composed my thoughts so I could say what I felt without sounding defensive: "Forgive Dylan? My work is to forgive *myself*." Like Buck, Dylan had slipped out of my grip. I was the one who let *him* down, not the other way around.

If suicide is difficult to think and talk about, then murder-suicide is unthinkable. I hadn't simply failed to protect Dylan from himself, but everyone he killed, too.

In the years I've been involved with the suicide loss survivor community, I have seen that education and prevention can save lives. But participating in that first event—and in dozens of others since—solidified a realization that was simultaneously comforting and terrifying: *anyone could be here.*

Lots of people there hadn't known there was a problem, or— like me—had underestimated its gravity. Our first inkling that something was seriously wrong slammed into our lives in one catastrophic, irreversible moment. Even professionals didn't always know when they were dealing with a life-and-death situation. A psychologist spoke about losing her son. Respected, well-trained, she'd known all the right things to do; still, suicide hadn't even been on her radar. (We should never conclude from these stories that suicide comes without warning; simply that we don't always recognize behaviors that may be indicative of risk.)

Others were well aware of danger, but hadn't known how to help. Another woman's son had been hospitalized repeatedly for his bipolar disorder. After his doctor-recommended release, he continued to be treated. In fact, he saw both the family's pastor and his own psychiatrist on the day he shot his girlfriend and killed himself.

These stories made me realize the seriousness of the foe we were up against. By lunchtime at the first event I attended, three things had become starkly clear.

One: There is more to suicide prevention than loving someone and telling them so. As bottomless as my love had been, it had not been enough to save Dylan, or his victims, and here was an auditorium filled with people who could say the same.

Two: Many of us had believed there were no signs of trouble on the horizon when we hadn't recognized indicators of potential risk. In many cases, we hadn't even known there was cause to be on heightened alert.

Three: I learned that while there are effective interventions for depression and other risk factors for suicide, we cannot yet rely on their effectiveness. I'm hesitant to write that, out of fear that someone who needs help might be discouraged from seeking it. But many of the people I met that day had tried to help someone struggling with ongoing or intermittent illness. They'd persevered through weeks, months, years, or even decades of therapy, through rounds of meds and alternative treatments and hospitalizations. Some of them were success stories, but some were not. Many lived in fear for someone else, or waged a daily struggle with their own suicidal thoughts.

Whether the problem was finding a bed in a good facility (there is little consensus on whether hospitalization is the best treatment for suicidality at all; some recent studies indicate that it may not be), the inadequacy of staff training on brain illness issues in emergency rooms, or a hospital's failure to raise an alarm about risk levels post-release, I understood for the first time that there were challenges to securing targeted, appropriate treatment for a person in danger.

That first suicide prevention event was the dawning of a new awareness. The problem we were up against was multifaceted and tremendously complex. If something was going to change, there was a great deal to be done.

• • •

Suicide prevention summit. An emotional ride. Got hugged in eleva-
tor by people when I finally said who i was. There was lots of crying.
I felt at home.

—Journal entry, May 2002

To most people, it wouldn't have seemed like much: me sitting at the registration table at a conference held by the Suicide Prevention Coalition of Colorado, greeting people and finding their nametags for them, as Celia had greeted me two years before. The difference was that I was wearing a nametag of my own, with a colored sticker on it identifying me as someone who had lost a child to suicide. As I took my place at the table that morning, my heart hammered in my chest. Would I be caught off guard by someone from the press? Would an attendee realize who I was and spit in my face?

I greeted the conference participants and answered questions about the speakers and gave directions to the restroom, and nobody said anything, except occasionally to offer condolences for my loss.

After that watershed day, I became seriously involved in initiatives to prevent suicide and violence. I manned registration tables and folded programs. I joined thousands of others at community walks to raise money for suicide prevention. I shuttled presenters to restaurants from their hotels, packaged items for silent auctions, picked pamphlets up from the printer. I talked to people, I hugged them, and I listened.

Recent data from the Centers for Disease Control show that suicide is among the top ten causes of death in the United States, right up there with pernicious killers like diabetes, Alzheimer's, and kidney disease. But when it comes to funding for research, suicide prevention is at the bottom, perhaps because of the misguided and yet persistent belief that suicide happens by choice rather than illness. Funding for suicide prevention research comes largely from families who channel feelings of sorrow and helplessness into volunteering and fund-raising. Like all nonprofit efforts, suicide prevention organizations are often underfunded and understaffed, and I quickly discovered that someone with my administrative skills could make a difference. For the first time in a long time, I felt I had a contribution to make.

My motives weren't purely altruistic. Being part of a group, working shoulder to shoulder toward the same goal, was a gift I gave myself. Even if I couldn't officially attend a support group, I could link arms with other suicide loss survivors to make a good conference better. It was a privilege and a blessing to connect with a cause so deeply. I'd had many jobs and hobbies that I had cared about. I'd taught kids to read as a reading specialist, and I'd worked to provide adult students with disabilities the accommodations they needed to succeed in college. But my work in the suicide prevention community felt like a bona fide calling, a path out of the darkness, a way forward for a life that had careened off the rails.

Over the years of working with people with disabilities, I had observed that profound loss often brought with it a depth of gratitude for life, a sense of joy, and an ability to be in the present that people untouched by tragedy could not always access. I felt that among suicide loss survivors, too. We cried a lot, but we also laughed.

One told me, "You can't laugh and cry at the same time." Laughter, I found, helped me to recalibrate the gyroscope inside me that was swinging so wildly. I started to seek out *Seinfeld* reruns, *Whose Line Is It Anyway?*, movies to crack me up like the absurd spaghetti Western parody *They Call Me Trinity*. I read books by humorists like Erma Bombeck, Dave Barry, and Bill Bryson. I listened to musical satirists like Weird Al and P. D. Q. Bach, as well as comedy on the radio during my commutes. Comedy became a form of community, too, as the best of it comes from a place of tragedy. Some of the comedians I came to enjoy the most, like Maria Bamford and Rob Delaney, speak openly about their own brain health struggles.

Through other survivors of suicide loss, I learned to find compassion for those who judged me, too.

One day, I heard through the grapevine that a colleague had been overheard saying, "You can't tell me a mother wouldn't know her child was dealing with something like this." It hurt because the woman and I had been friendly. To find out she believed I had known about Dylan's plans—that I had stood by, idle, while he planned to hurt himself and murder others—put me right back in the rock tumbler I'd been living in since Dylan's death.

I couldn't stop perseverating about the comment, and mentioned it to a suicide loss survivor further along than I was. She nodded.

"I used to think, 'If this happened in your family, you wouldn't judge. May life give you the opportunity to learn what a foolish and cruel thing you've said.'" Hearing her say that shocked me a little; I'd never seen her be anything but unfailingly generous and kind.

She continued: "Of course, I wouldn't wish this on anyone. Anyway, they're only trying to convince themselves nothing like this could ever happen to them." We were in the parking lot by then, and she gestured to the box of suicide prevention pamphlets in the front seat of my car. "Ignorance is what we're out here to combat, right?" she said, shaking her head. "God knows, I didn't think it could happen to me, either."

Her comment helped me to realize why the suicide prevention community felt so much like a home. This is a grassroots movement made up of mothers and fathers and partners and daughters and sons. We donate our time because we believe our loved ones did not have to die, and we know firsthand that ignorance can be lethal. This lends a real sense of urgency to the work we do.

In the aftermath of Dylan's death, I entertained hundreds of fantasies about ways to atone for what Dylan had done. Finally, here it was. I didn't have to trade my life in a terrorist attack to save a school bus filled with children. I could write a paragraph for a website, populate a spreadsheet, go around a ballroom putting programs on plates, pick a speaker up from the airport. The suicide loss community taught me that showing up in small and simple ways could save lives too.

I read every book and article I could get my hands on. I worked conferences so I could hear the speakers. I struggled through academic papers I found online, even when the summary was the only part I could understand. I watched webinars, pored over educational resources, asked lecturers for their PowerPoint slides so I could make sure I hadn't missed anything. I asked as many questions as I could.

Eventually, the suicide loss community helped me to see that it was Dylan's behavior—not mine—that had been pathological. In the process, though, I began to develop an activist's passion. What had happened with Dylan was an outlier in terms of magnitude and scope and rarity. But it had also been part of a larger problem, one I hadn't even realized was there.

At any given conference, I meet people who have lost someone close to them. Some of them come from families riddled through the generations with suicide, violent behavior, addiction, or other brain illnesses. Others have no known biological history at all. Many will have lost more than one close family member; others have survived their own attempts, and share their stories so others might learn. Some help the bereaved, while others work every single day to keep their loved ones or their patients alive. All of us are united under the same banner: *It may be too late for the ones we have lost, but it may not be too late to save others.*

Even as I found solidarity in this community, I stood apart. Coming to understand Dylan's death as a suicide provided some degree of comfort for me, and I must admit part of me would have liked to stop there. But I was never foolish enough to delude myself that Dylan was the only one who had been lost on the day he took his own life.

Long after I came to accept Dylan's depression and desire to die by suicide, I was still grappling with the reality of his violence. The person I saw raging on the Basement Tapes had been completely unrecognizable, a stranger in my son's body. This person—raised in my home, the child I believed I had imbued with my values, whom I had taught to say *please* and *thank you* and to have a firm handshake—had killed other people, and planned even greater destruction.

Understanding his death as a suicide was an important first step. But it was only the beginning.

CHAPTER 17

Judgment

*I try to find something that gives me a sense of peace and I can't find
one thing. Not writing, drawing, nature. I feel on the edge of disaster
all the time. I'm still weeping over Dylan and hating myself for what
he did. The image of him on the video is plastered on my brain. I feel
as if his entire life and death are unresolved and I haven't grieved yet
or put any of this into perspective. Everything I think about to comfort
myself is a double-edged sword.*

—Journal entry, August 2003

Four years after Columbine, the date was set for our depositions. Finally, the nameless dread that had hung over us during four years of our grief had crystallized into an item on the calendar.

Our lawyers explained that a deposition was sworn out-of-court testimony that the plaintiffs could use to gather information for a lawsuit if the claims against us progressed to a trial by jury. Tom and I and the Harrises would each spend a day answering questions before a close-knit group of bereaved parents. We would sit, face to face, with the grieving parents of the children Dylan and Eric had murdered. I would see the sorrow in their eyes, and know my son was responsible for putting it there. The thought filled me with terror.

I had already resigned myself to financial disaster. The media had portrayed us as wealthy, in part because my grandfather had been a successful businessman. But he'd left his estate to a charitable foundation, and our home, which looked like a massive compound from the aerial shots that appeared on TV, had been a fixer-upper. So we'd lose our home and have to declare bankruptcy. What was that in comparison to what we'd already been through?

The depositions would be difficult, but once they were done—whatever the outcome—at least they'd be over.

• • •

Dream made me cry all the way to work. Dylan was a baby, about the size of a doll. I was trying to find a way to lay him down, but there was nowhere safe to put him. I was in a dormitory and found a room full of drawers like a morgue or mausoleum. All the women in the room had a place to put their babies. But I had neglected to put a name on a drawer for him, so there was no place to lay him down. He was tired and needed to rest but I had not managed to make a safe place for him to go.

—Journal entry, April 2003

We were already widely blamed, but the depositions would be the decisive appraisal of our competence as parents. Ultimately our fate would rest in the hands of people who hadn't known our son, and who hadn't interacted with us as a family. It didn't take an outside committee to make me feel I had failed Dylan. Each day I cataloged hundreds of things I wished I had done differently.

It seemed highly likely we would be held responsible. On the Basement Tapes, Dylan and Eric were blatantly homicidal and suicidal, whipping weapons around like toys. Tom and I had recognized Dylan's room in one segment, so the weapons had been in our home at least one night. The intensity of our son's rage on the tapes made the entire family seem culpable. What could possibly be said to prove his violent tendencies had been hidden? Although it was the truth, I couldn't see how anyone would believe it. I barely believed it myself.

I thought often in those days of a young woman I'd met while teaching in a program for at-risk young adults working to get GEDs. Over lunch, she'd told me a story from her childhood. A classmate kept stealing her lunch money. Tired of going hungry, she finally told her father, who threw her into an empty bathtub and beat her with his belt until she could not stand.

"Don't you ever come to me because you can't handle your own business," he told her. She went to school the next day with a rake handle, which she used to beat the girl who had been stealing from her. Nobody ever bothered her again.

"It was the biggest favor he ever did me," she said, openly amused by my shocked look and the sandwich I'd abandoned.

I had been appalled by the story; it haunted me for years. But as we headed toward the depositions, I thought a lot about what it meant to be a good parent. At the time, I'd judged her father to be abusive, but my student had told the story with love and respect. She believed her dad had parented her appropriately, and indeed he had prepared her for the rough environment in which they lived. Had I missed the point? Certainly I was in no position to judge. Perhaps all of us were doing the best we could with the experience, knowledge, and resources we had.

The only thing I knew for sure was that Dylan had participated in the massacre *in spite* of the way he had been raised, not because of it. What I didn't know was how I could possibly convey this to the families of the people he had killed. Even if I could, it would never alleviate the magnitude of their suffering. Nothing would.

. . .

Our original statement of apology had been published in the newspaper, as well as the one we released on the first anniversary of the massacre. But whenever anyone we knew said anything to the press, the quote was taken out of context. We were threatened, and often felt afraid. Unfortunately, our inaccessibility and failure to speak up in our own defense had led people to believe we were hiding secrets.

I'd written those difficult letters to each one of the victims' families. Then I had withdrawn to spare them the painful intrusion of hearing from me, even though I wanted nothing more in the world than a connection with them. I had spoken the names of their loved ones like a mantra every day, and yet the only points of contact between us came through our lawyers, or from reading about each other in the paper.

I wanted to bridge that distance. I knew from studying other violent incidents that it could significantly reduce trauma if the perpetrator's family could sit down with victims to apologize in person, to cry and hug and talk. As impossible as it was to envision, acknowledging each other's humanity seemed like the best course of action; as painful as that interaction would surely be, I craved it.

Eventually, I had to let that go. I was the last person who could ask for a meeting, and couldn't run the risk of re-traumatizing someone by imposing myself. Each family's recovery from loss is their own. I can only say here that if speaking with or meeting me would be helpful to any of the family members of Dylan and Eric's victims, I will always be available to them.

We have had some contact with a few of the victims' family members over the years, and I believe it *was* healing, for both parties. The father of a boy who died reached out to us about a year after the tragedy. We invited him to our home in December 2001. I was stunned by his generosity of spirit and found great relief in being able to apologize to him in person for Dylan's actions, and to express our sorrow for his terrible loss. We wept, shared photos, and talked about our children. When we parted, he said he didn't hold us responsible. They were the most blessed words I could have hoped to hear him say.

Around the same time, the mother of one of the murdered girls asked to meet. She was forthright and kind, and I liked her immediately. We both shed a lot of tears at that meeting, but I was able to apologize, and to ask questions about her daughter. I was touched she asked about Dylan and wanted to know who he was. A person of deep faith, this mother feels her daughter's death was predestined, and nothing could have been done to prevent it. I have told her I wish I could agree with her. But I felt a great relief to meet her, and believe she took comfort from it too.

I received a lovely note from the sister of a murdered girl, who wrote that she didn't think parents were responsible for the actions of their children. We also received a lovely, sad letter from Dave Sanders's granddaughter. She said she did not hate us or hold us responsible. I treasured both those letters and returned to them time and again for solace.

Four years after the depositions, eight years after the massacre, I would meet another father whose son was murdered at the school. But at the time we were deposed, I had met only two people who had lost children at the school, and thirty-six families were making claims against us. As the day approached, I had no idea what to expect or who would be there when we faced each other in the courtroom.

. . .

Still struggling with fear, anxiety and feelings of craziness. There is no safe place to park my overburdened mind. I feel frightened, beaten, and on the brink of crossing over a line to madness and not coming back. I'm constantly aware of myself thinking about my state of mind, and about death. I was OK until these damn panics started. I was making it OK. Now I'm afraid I'll never be OK again.

—Journal entry, July 2003

The pressure mounted as the date of the depositions approached. Over dinner one night, Tom and I had a long conversation about the afterlife.

I worried a great deal about Dylan, even after his death. I was terrified his spirit would not be allowed to rest in peace because of his crimes. It was hard enough to know Dylan had suffered in life; I could not bear the idea that he continued to suffer in death, too.

As we were getting into bed, I had a debilitating panic attack.

It was not the first panic attack I had ever experienced. I had been a nervous, fearful child, prone to late-night anxiety, but that night's attack was the worst I'd ever had. My thoughts spiraled out of control, and I trembled and cried as my mind pitched in terror.

Those panic attacks lasted through the time of the depositions, and beyond. They would strike without warning—at the hardware store, in a meeting at work, while I was driving in the car. Like a tsunami, a sudden, overpowering surge of blinding fear would rise up in front of me, then crash down. These floods of incapacitating terror were worse, by far, than the grief. Sometimes the attacks would run into each other, one after another, and I'd lose hours, even whole afternoons. I drank gallons of chamomile tea, tried every homeopathic remedy for anxiety I could find at the health food store. I was terrified I would not be able to get through my deposition, and tortured myself with imagining what would happen if I had an anxiety attack while on the stand.

Reading my journals from that period is revealing to me now. It is clear, on every single page, that I am hanging on by a thread.

• • •

I am not allowed to talk about what happened during the depositions, except to say it was terribly painful and (I believe) unsatisfying for everyone involved.

I can, however, share a regret. I wanted to apologize to the families in person at the depositions, but our lawyers didn't agree. "This isn't the time or place," I was told. I wish I had fought harder to say those words. I believe their absence was deeply felt by everyone in the room, and continues to be, to this day. Saying I am profoundly sorry is one of the reasons I wanted to write this book.

Neuroscientists like to say behavior is the result of a complex interaction between nature and nurture. At some time in the future, we will likely be able to point to the specific combination of neurotransmitters that lead a person to commit acts of unspeakable violence. I will personally rejoice on the day neurobiologists map the precise mechanism in the brain responsible for empathy and for conscience. Needless to say, we're not yet there. We do know, from researchers like Dr. Victoria Arango, that there are clear brain differences between people who die by suicide and people who do not. Dr. Kent Kiehl and others have demonstrated that there also appear to be some clear brain differences between people who commit homicide and people who do not.

I have spent a lot of time wondering whether Dylan had a biological predisposition toward violence—and if so, whether or not we were responsible. I did not consume alcohol while I was pregnant with Dylan. He was not abused in our home, physically, verbally, or emotionally, nor was he subjected to anyone else being abused. He was not raised in poverty, or exposed (to my knowledge) to toxins such as heavy metals, which have been connected to violent behavior. Neither of his parents abused alcohol or drugs. He was well nourished.

Even if Dylan *did* have a biological predisposition toward violence, biology isn't destiny. What forces had aggravated this tendency in him? The governor of Colorado cited parenting as a causal factor in his first public appearance after the shootings. But Tom and I knew exactly what had happened in our home all those years we parented Dylan, and we were equally sure the answer wasn't there.

This was what I wanted to say in the depositions—not because I had any thought of clearing our names, or setting the record straight, but because it was such a crucial opportunity to broaden our understanding of how tragedies like Columbine happen. Dylan did not learn violence in our home. He did not learn disconnection, or rage, or racism. He did not learn a callous indifference to human life. This I knew.

I wanted to say that Dylan had been loved. I loved him while I was holding his pudgy hand on our way to get frozen yogurt after kindergarten; while reading Dr. Seuss's exuberant *There's a Wocket in My Pocket!* to him for the thousandth time; while scrubbing the grass stains out of the knees of his pint-size Little League uniform so he could wear it to pitch the next day. I loved him while we were sharing a bowl of popcorn and watching *Flight of the Phoenix* together, a month before he died. I *still* loved him. I hated what he had done, but I still loved my son.

Morality, empathy, ethics—these weren't one-time lessons, but embedded in everything we did with our kids. I'd taught the boys what I myself believe—that we should treat others as we wish to be treated. Dylan was expected to help our neighbors with their yard work without the expectation of payment because that's what neighbors do, and to hold the door open for the person coming in behind him because that's what gentlemen do.

I'm a teacher by constitution. Everything I knew and cared about and valued, I poured into my kids. A trip to the grocery store wasn't merely a stopover to restock the fridge, but a way to show my boys how to select the freshest apple, an invitation to think about the hardworking farmers who had grown it, and to talk about the ways fruits and vegetables make a growing body healthy and strong. It was a chance for me to introduce the vocabulary words "carmine" and "vermilion." I showed Dylan how to be gentle putting the fruit into the basket; we let an elderly lady with one or two items slip ahead of us in line; we made eye contact and said a polite "thank you" to the cashier. Nervous about inattentive drivers, I would take his hand when we went to tuck our shopping cart back into its spot so it couldn't roll out and dent someone else's car.

My approach changed slightly as the boys grew, but the message never did. Driving home from Little League, I tried to counterbalance the sport's natural message of competition with one of empathy: the kids on the other team are just like you. Dylan came to work with me whenever the opportunity arose, and though I never saw the students I worked with as "teaching moments," he learned—better than most kids, and through exposure—that people were more than their cerebral palsy or their amputated limb. He saw, too, that even after terrible difficulty, people could create meaningful and productive lives.

Similarly, Tom had worked to help his boys become good men. Through sports, he helped them understand fair play, the importance of a heartfelt effort, and the pleasure of teamwork. Working with them on repairs, he taught them science and engineering and construction—as well as the satisfaction in solving a challenging problem, not to mention the thrift and gratification of fixing something broken instead of throwing it away. He prompted them to do their chores without complaining, and helped them to remember me on special occasions like Mother's Day.

We had not done everything right. The research I have done

has taught me better ways I might have interacted with Dylan. I wish I had listened more instead of lecturing; I wish I had sat in silence with him instead of filling the void with my own words and thoughts. I wish I had acknowledged his feelings instead of trying to talk him out of them, and that I'd never accepted his excuses to avoid conversation—*I'm tired, I have homework to do*—when something felt off. I wish I'd sat in the dark with him, and repeated my concerns when he dismissed them. I wish I'd dropped everything else to focus on him, probed and prodded more, and that I had been present enough to see what I did not.

Even with these regrets, there were no obvious indications he was planning something destructive. I have heard many terrible stories of good people struggling to parent seriously ill, violent kids. I have nothing but compassion for them, and feel we must rehabilitate a health care system that too often leaves them out in the cold. If you want to feel sick to your stomach, listen to a mom tell you about the day her volatile ten-year-old narrowly missed stabbing her with the kitchen shears, and how it felt to call the police on him because she was worried the lock on his younger sister's bedroom door wouldn't hold against his rage. Too often, parents of seriously disturbed kids are forced to get the criminal justice system involved—even though it is drastically ill-equipped to manage brain illness—simply because there is nowhere else to turn. Unless a family can afford a private clinic, the choice is often between denying the severity of the problem and calling the cops. The question of accountability is not theoretical for those mothers.

As huge as my empathy is for those mothers, my situation was very different. Dylan showed no clear and present danger, the way some children do. He was going to school, holding down a job in the evening, and applying to colleges. Days before the massacre he was eating dinner with us as usual, keeping the conversation light and carrying his dirty dishes to the sink.

He did hole up in his room, but he hadn't withdrawn from his peers. He did not have access to weapons in our home, nor did he display any unseemly fascination with them. He was occasionally truculent and irritable, as many teenagers are, but we never saw any hint of the rage he displayed on the Basement Tapes. He did not threaten us, get into physical altercations, or allude to plans to hurt others. Neither Tom nor I had ever—not once—felt afraid of him.

We thought we saw evidence our parenting was working. Dylan was a good and loyal friend, a loving son, and he appeared to be growing into a responsible adult. In his writing, there is ample proof that he had absorbed the teachings we had worked so hard to impart; his journals are filled with his struggles with conscience. And yet, at the end of his life, something overwrote the lessons we had taught him.

Not all influence comes from within the home, and this is especially true in the case of teenagers. "Nurture" refers to all the environmental factors a person encounters. Dylan *was* interested in gratuitously bloodthirsty movies like *Reservoir Dogs* and *Natural Born Killers*—but so was every boy we knew. We did not buy those movies, or take him to the theater to see them. We also did not forbid them in our home after he reached the age of seventeen, figuring he would get access to them if he wanted to; he was working, and had his own money. We did talk to him about our concerns.

He also played *Doom*, one of the earliest first-person-shooter games. I hadn't liked the game, but I'd mostly worried that Dylan's computer use would isolate him, which hadn't been the case at all. My primary complaint about video games was how dumb they were, a waste of time. As with everything, my take on video games was filtered through my primary belief in Dylan's goodness. It would never have crossed my mind that he was capable of making the leap from shooting people on-screen to shooting them in real life.

Looking back, that was a mistake. There is good research now to show that violent games like *Doom* decrease empathy and increase aggressive behavior. Detractors point out that millions play these games (an estimated ten million people have played *Doom*), and only a tiny fraction of those go on to commit violence. But Dr. Dewey Cornell, a forensic clinical psychologist—and author of more than two hundred papers on psychology and education, including studies of juvenile homicide, school safety, bullying, and threat assessment—gave me his take on entertainment violence.

"One cigarette won't give you lung cancer, and some people smoke their whole lives without getting lung cancer. That doesn't mean there's no correlation. Entertainment violence may not be sufficient cause for a rampage, but it is a toxic factor. A small number of the most vulnerable people will get lung cancer after smoking when other factors and predispositions come into play. The same thing can be said about violent entertainment and acts of violence: the most vulnerable are at special risk." But Tom and I did not perceive Dylan as vulnerable. Nor did anyone else.

Dylan's vulnerabilities were probably the same ones that had made him so susceptible to Eric, another toxic influence. I was blind to it because I never perceived Dylan to be a follower. He was agreeable by nature; a typical younger sibling, he'd go along with Byron's games when the boys were young, and Tom and I could generally get him to do what we needed him to do without pushback. But I had plenty of opportunity to observe Dylan with his friends, and those relationships were equally negotiated. I never felt Zack or Nate had the upper hand with him. If Nate had a hankering for pizza while Dylan was craving McDonald's, they worked it out.

I still resist the idea that Dylan was nothing more than a passive follower. Eric's charm and charisma were undeniable, and he was adroitly fooling adults, some of them mental health professionals, including a counselor and a psychiatrist. And yet I cannot easily explain how Dylan turned his back on seventeen years of empathy and conscience. Eric may have been the one who was single-mindedly focused on homicide, but Dylan went along. He did not say no. He did not tell us about the plan, or tell a teacher or one of his other friends. Instead he said yes, and entered into a plot so diabolical it defies description.

I will never know why Dylan latched on to the violence Eric suggested. His journals make clear that Dylan was profoundly insecure, and felt hopelessly inadequate. Eric probably made him feel validated and accepted and powerful in a way nobody else did—and then offered him the chance to show the world just how powerful the two of them really were.

Dr. Adam Lankford cites "a desire for fame, glory or attention as a motive" for mass shooters. Ralph Larkin calls it "killing for notoriety." Mark Juergensmeyer, who writes about religious terrorism, calls it "the public performance of violence" and argues that acts like these have symbolic, as well as strategic, goals. Sociologist Dr. Katherine Newman, author of *Rampage*, ties it directly to image rehabilitation when she says school shooters are "searching for a way to retire their public image as dweebs and misfits, exchanging it for something more alluring: the dangerous, violent antihero."

I was surprised not to be asked in the depositions the details of how we'd handled discipline, movies, video games, Dylan's friendships, drugs and alcohol, clothing, firecrackers. But an in-depth look at the root causes of the catastrophe was outside the purview of the proceedings. The depositions were not a place to talk about bullying, or gun safety, or school climate, or the immaturity of the adolescent brain. I had not yet begun to talk to experts myself. Even at that early stage, though, I was clear on one point: I did not—and do not—believe I made Dylan a killer.

If I had thought there was something seriously wrong with him, I would have moved mountains to fix it. If I had known about Eric's website or the guns, or about Dylan's depression, I would have parented differently. As it was, I parented the best way I knew to parent the child I knew—not the one he had become without my knowledge.

• • •

Unsurprisingly, the news reports after the depositions were highly inflammatory, as so much of the coverage had been. The sealed transcripts of the proceedings gave the impression we were hiding something—again.

I wanted to share the transcripts with the public. Why not? I was tired of fielding the implication I had something to hide when I spent my days hunting for answers. Perhaps naively, I still hoped releasing the transcripts might finally put to bed the idea there was a single reason the tragedy had happened. And, unlike the Basement Tapes, there was no danger of contagion from releasing them.

Unfortunately, it wasn't my decision. All four parents of the shooters had been deposed, and the attorneys never reached consensus on everyone's best interests. Eventually the judge decided to seal the depositions for twenty years.

I hadn't said everything I wanted to say when I was deposed, but I thought if the families could see and hear me, they'd understand that whatever the engine for Dylan's crimes had been, it had not started in our home. The papers the next morning showed me my folly. There it was again: conscientious parents would have known what their sons were planning; our failure to know meant we were responsible. Nothing would ever change how people perceived us.

I shredded the newspaper in my hands and pounded the bed with my fists until my wailing subsided. Hurt as I was, I also understood. I too had believed a good parent should know what her kids were thinking. If the situations had been reversed, if someone else's son had murdered Dylan while he was catching up on his homework in the school library, I would have blamed that family too.

. . .

I continued to experience high levels of stress, loss of sleep, and poor concentration after the depositions. Ten days afterward, we heard that the plaintiffs were ready to settle. The lawyers acted as if this was a great relief, but I didn't feel the least bit uplifted. No legal resolution would alleviate the dread that sat in the center of my chest, the hopeless feeling that I had reached the end of my ability to cope.

With medication and therapy, my panic attacks eventually subsided. We went back to our lives—continuing to learn to live without Dylan, and with the knowledge of what he had done.

CHAPTER 18

The Wrong Question

G rief has a life cycle.
Many people have told me they started to emerge from the fog after about seven years, and that was true for me as well. By 2006, I was starting to feel better. I did not miss Dylan any less, and an hour did not pass where I did not think with pain and sadness about his victims and their families. But I wasn't crying every day, or wandering through the world like a zombie. With the legal restrictions lifted, I began to wonder if I could help promote a better understanding of suicide by speaking out.

Through my work in suicide prevention, I'd met two other survivors of murder-suicide. It had helped us to talk to one another. Most suicide loss survivors struggle with grief, guilt, and humiliation, but when a family member commits murder in the last moments of his life, it changes him in your mind, and alters the way you grieve for him. You never stop asking if something you did caused him to behave as he did. The media attention can be traumatizing.

These other survivors of murder-suicide believed, as I did, that suicide had been a driving factor behind their loss, and yet the public persisted in seeing these acts exclusively as murders. We wanted to show that murder-suicide is a manifestation of suicide, and to help people to understand that suicide prevention is also murder-suicide prevention. So, when I found out the University of Colorado at Boulder was hosting a conference called "Violence Goes to College," I decided to organize a panel discussion on murder-suicide.

Tom had found my immersion in the suicide prevention and loss community depressing, and he felt even more strongly about my murder-suicide research. (He called our panel the Addams Family.) I think he thought I was refusing to move on, and I sometimes wondered if he was right. I amassed a library of books about the adolescent brain, about suicide, murder-suicide, and the biology of violence, seeking out inconvenient truths and uncomfortable realities.

Part of it, perhaps, was penance; another part, self-protection. If I sought out the very worst, then it could never catch me unawares. Underneath it all, though, there was simply a compulsion to understand: How could Dylan, raised in our home, have done this?

• • •

I wanted to claim Dylan as my son. I wanted to stand up and tell people that as much grief and regret as I felt for those he had hurt and killed, he was still loved. Unfortunately, I wasn't yet ready.

In the weeks leading up to my appearance on the panel, I went with a friend to see her daughter perform in a play at her college. It should have been a beautiful weekend, but being on campus with all those young people triggered something inside me. It was the first time I'd visited a college campus since I'd been to the University of Arizona with Dylan, and whenever I saw a tall, skinny boy enjoying college life, my heart would clutch.

Walking across the beautiful campus, I was jolted by a severe panic attack—my first since the spell I'd had during the depositions. I had another during the play we'd come to see, and another over dinner. Flipping through the channels in my hotel room while I was waiting for my friends to pick me up the next morning, I landed on *I'll Cry Tomorrow,* the 1955 biopic of singer Lillian Roth. During Susan Hayward's portrayal of Roth's alcohol-induced nervous breakdown, I had a panic attack so acute I thought it would kill me.

That weekend began a terrible period. It was as if my brain had an accelerator spring stuck in the floored position. In previous periods of panic, I had focused on death, but this time I thought about fear. I became afraid of being afraid.

Anything could trigger an attack. Driving past the coroner's office where they'd taken Dylan's body: *boom.* Watching an old movie where a cowboy throws dynamite into a barn: *boom.* Red flowers on a bush: *boom.* My digestive system has always been my Achilles' heel, and I became afraid to eat because of the constant intestinal upsets that came with the panic.

Because the attacks were triggered by anything that reminded me of Dylan's death, my therapist felt they were a manifestation of post-traumatic stress disorder. She was clear about my course of treatment: I needed to take the tranquilizers a doctor had prescribed. But I was afraid of becoming addicted to them, and so I'd only take half a pill, or a quarter—enough to dull the edge of my anxiety but not enough to give me a true sense of well-being or to allow my racing mind to rest. Underneath it all, I felt as if my suffering indicated an essential character flaw. *Cut it out,* I thought viciously to myself. *Get yourself together. You should be able to think your way out of this.*

My therapist believed I wasn't ready to appear on the panel. But I was compelled to follow through on my commitment, whatever the cost, and my compulsion to publicly represent "normalcy" made the pressure worse. I wanted to demonstrate that I wasn't controlled by my fear. In trying to prove it, I created a trap for myself.

As the day of the panel approached, my panic attacks became more frequent and intense. One evening on my drive home, the sensations were so acute that I was sure I'd cause an accident. I had never had a truly suicidal thought before, but now I looked over at the passenger seat and thought: *If there were a gun there, I would use it to make this stop.* I clutched at the steering wheel and thought clearly to myself: *This cannot go on.*

I got through the panel presentation—with some help. On my therapist's recommendation, a friend taped my answers so I could simply press Play if unable to speak. I ended up relying on the tape about half the time. It was a difficult day for everyone who appeared on the panel but a successful one nonetheless; the evaluations showed clearly that we'd made a real difference in the way people understood murder-suicide. One called it "a revelation." Another went so far as to apologize to us for the way she'd thought about our cases before.

I began taking the tranquilizers as they were prescribed, and with medication, therapy, and lots of long walks, the debilitating attacks eventually began to subside.

I now understand that anxiety is a brain disorder I will live with and manage for the rest of my life. Even when I am not in crisis, the possibility is always with me. Because of this vulnerability, I carefully monitor my response to stress, as people at high risk for stroke monitor their blood pressure. I meditate, do yoga and deep breathing exercises, and exercise daily. I see a therapist and take antidepressant medication if I need extra help. Over time, I have come to listen to my anxiety, and to recognize it as an indication of something amiss.

As the years passed, the distance between Tom and me continued to widen, leaving us with almost no common ground and no way to build a bridge back to each other. In 2014, after forty-three years of marriage, we decided to part ways—a decision I could only make after I realized that the thought of staying in the relationship made me feel more stress than the idea of leaving it. We ended our marriage to save our friendship, and I believe we will always care for each other. I am grateful for that.

As I emerged from the dark and terrifying period of those last panic attacks, I felt like Dorothy stepping cautiously into the Technicolor land of Oz. Once safe on the other side, I saw that my own crisis had served as an enlightenment of sorts. It had taught me some things I needed to know in order to better understand Dylan's life, and his death.

. . .

The World Health Organization defines mental health as "a state of well-being in which every individual realizes his or her own potential, can cope with the normal stresses of life, can work productively and fruitfully, and is able to make a contribution to her or his community."

My anxiety disorder showed me what it feels like to be trapped inside a malfunctioning mind. When our brains are impaired, we cannot manage our own thoughts. No matter what I did to try to think myself back to balance, I didn't have the tools to do it. I understood for the first time what it meant not to be in control of my brain.

Understanding this gave me a great deal of empathy for others who suffer. I'd been trying for years to understand how Dylan could have done what he did. Then my own mind ran out of control and I entered the world on the other side of the looking glass, a private, seething hell in which unwanted thoughts took control and called the shots.

The sad, scary truth is we never know when we (or someone we love) may experience a serious brain health crisis.

Once I was feeling better, I couldn't believe how distorted some of my thinking had been. For the first time, I understood how Dylan could have thought he was going in the right direction when it had been anything but.

I still can't fathom what Dylan and Eric did; I cannot understand how anyone on earth could do such a thing, let alone my own son. I find it easy, if painful, to empathize with someone who has died by suicide, but Dylan *killed*. It is not something I will ever get used to or get over.

Was he evil? I've spent a lot of time wrestling with that question. In the end, I don't think he was. Most people believe suicide is a choice, and violence is a choice; those things are under a person's control. Yet we know from talking to survivors of suicide attempts that their decision-making ability shifts in some way we don't well understand. In our conversation, psychologist and suicide researcher Dr. Matthew Nock at Harvard used a phrase I like very much: *dysfunction in decision making.* If suicide seems like the only way out of an existence so painful it has become intolerable, is that really an exercise of free will?

Of course, Dylan did not simply die by suicide. He committed murder; he killed people. We've all felt angry enough to fantasize about killing someone else. What allows the vast majority of us to feel appalled and frightened by the mere impulse, and another person to go through with it? If someone chooses to hurt others, what governs the ability to make that choice? If what we think of as evil is really the absence of conscience, then we have to ask, how is it a person ceases to connect with their conscience?

My own struggle showed me, in a way nothing else could, that when our thoughts are broken, we are at their mercy. In the last months of his life, Dylan turned his back on a lifetime of moral education, empathy, and his own conscience. Everything I have learned supports my belief that he was not in his right mind.

Brain illness is not a hall pass. Dylan is guilty of the crimes he committed. I believe he did know the difference between right and wrong at the end of his life, and that what he did was profoundly wrong. But we cannot dedicate ourselves to preventing violence if we do not take into account the role depression and brain dysfunction can play in the decision to commit it.

Of course, that is a risky thing to say. The idea that people with brain disorders are dangerous is among the most pervasive and destructive myths out there, and it is largely false. Most people with brain disorders and illnesses are not violent, but some percentage are. We must arrive at a way to discuss the intersection between brain health and violence in an open and nonjudgmental manner, and we cannot do that without first talking about stigma.

You can probably name several Olympic gold medalists and star quarterbacks who have blown out their knees, or major-league pitchers who've had Tommy John surgery. But most of us can't name a single celebrity who has struggled—successfully, anyway—with depression or another mood disorder. Even celebrities are afraid of losing their jobs or being seen as a danger to their children. Wealth, power, and the love of the public is no defense against that stigma.

My own experience with anxiety showed me the risk and shame involved in making my pain known to others. I believe I am a profoundly honest person—sometimes to a fault. And yet, when I was experiencing spikes of panic, I felt so ashamed of what I was going through, so humiliated by my inability to "get on top" of the problem, that I went to great lengths to conceal my experience. Afraid of being seen as weak or unstable, I had done my utmost to hide (or at least, disguise) my inner storms from colleagues and friends.

And I'd been able to do so with little difficulty, even though I believed my mind was trying to kill me. I'm sure my colleagues and casual acquaintances noticed all was not well. *Does Sue look thin/shaky/pale/distracted to you?* Except there was a perfectly good reason for me to seem under the weather. *No wonder she seems run-down—you know what she's been through.* Just as I had once said to Tom, *Dylan's course load must be too heavy; he looks tired,* and *Of course he'd rather play video games than hang out with his parents; he's a teenager!*

Once I'd emerged on the other side of my own health crisis, I could see how shrouding it had isolated me. But the experience also helped me relate to others who hide the enormous pain they're in. Most of these issues are treatable, as long as people get help. Yet many do not seek the treatment they need, and stigma is one reason why.

If you hurt your knee, you wouldn't wait until you couldn't walk before seeking help. You'd ice the joint, elevate it, skip your workouts—and then, if you didn't see any improvement after a couple of days, you'd make an appointment with an orthopedist. Unfortunately, most people don't turn to a mental health professional for help until they're in real crisis. Nobody expects to heal their knees themselves, using self-discipline and gumption. Because of stigma, though, we do expect to be able to think our way out of the pain in our minds.

As soon as my own anxiety disorder was under control and I began to emerge from the quicksand, it was suddenly as clear as day: a brain health crisis was a *health issue*, the same as a heart condition, or a torn ligament. As with those health issues, it can be treatable. But first it has to be caught and diagnosed. Every day, mammograms and breast exams help doctors catch and treat cancers they would have missed fifty years ago. I survived cancer myself because of these, and can only hope that someday we'll have screenings and interventions at least as effective for brain health.

Indeed, we must. Like many other diseases, brain illnesses can be dangerous if they are not recognized and treated. The person most likely to suffer from a destructive impulse is usually the one who has it. In some exceptional cases, people may behave violently toward others as well. That's not a given, or even a likelihood, but it does happen. Untreated illnesses can jeopardize the people who have them, and those around them.

When people who are struggling cannot get access to the life-saving treatment they need, it puts them at increased risk of doing harm to themselves or others. Self-medication with drugs and alcohol is common when people aren't getting proper treatment and support, and abusing those substances *is* a factor that dramatically increases the likelihood of violence among those with mental illness.

Whenever I interviewed an expert for this book, I asked them this question: How do we talk about the intersection of brain disorders or mental illness and violence, without contributing to the stigma? Dr. Kent Kiehl summed it up neatly: "The best way to eliminate the belief that people with mental health issues are violent is to help them so that they're not violent."

. . .

It's very hard to know who is going to commit an act of violence. Profiling doesn't work. But violence *can* be prevented. In fact, threat assessment professionals have a saying: *Prevention does not require prediction.* It does require, however, that we increase overall access to brain health interventions.

Dr. Reid Meloy, a pioneer in the field, uses this analogy: A cardiologist may not know which of her patients is going to have a heart attack, but if she treats known risk factors such as high cholesterol in all of them, cardiac events will go down. The rates will improve further if she attends closely to patients at increased risk— the smokers and the overweight—and they'll go down even more if she makes sure that patients who have already had heart attacks comply with heart-healthy programs and take their medications.

A similar tiered system is already working in some schools. At the tier-one level, everyone should have access to brain health screenings and first aid, to conflict resolution programs, and to suicide prevention education. Peer intervention programs teach kids to seek help from trained adults for friends they're worried about without fear of repercussion.

A second tier of attention is trained on kids going through a hard time—a student grieving a lost parent, one who has suffered teasing or bullying, or those in known high-risk populations. For instance, gay, lesbian, bisexual, and transgender kids are at disproportionate risk for bullying, so special efforts might be made to connect those kids to resources.

The third level of intervention comes into play when a child has emerged as a particular concern. Perhaps he or she has an ongoing emotional disorder, has talked about suicide, or—as Dylan did—has turned in a paper with violent or disturbing subject matter. The student is then referred to a team of specially trained teachers and other professionals who will interview him or her, look at the student's social media and other evidence, and speak to friends, parents, local law enforcement, counselors, and teachers.

The real beauty of these measures is not that they catch potential school shooters, but how effectively they help schools to identify teens struggling with all different kinds of issues: bullying, eating disorders, cutting, undiagnosed learning disorders, addiction, abuse at home, and partner violence—just to name a few. In rare cases, a team may discover that the student has made a concrete plan to hurt himself or others, at which point law enforcement may become involved. In the overwhelming majority of these cases, though, simply getting a kid help is enough.

"People who are involved in targeted violence are usually involved because of an underlying issue," Dr. Randazzo told me. "Often, that is a mental health issue. Usually, those mental health issues can be resolved if they are discovered and treated effectively. Better mental health resources can *without question* help to prevent violence."

If we are serious about preventing violence, we must also recognize the cost to society when we make firearms so easily accessible. Dylan did not do what he did because he was able to purchase guns, but there is tremendous danger in having these highly lethal tools readily available when someone is at their most vulnerable. These risks are demonstrated, and we must insert them into the equation when we are talking about how we can make our communities healthier and safer.

. . .

When tragedies like Columbine or Virginia Tech or Sandy Hook happen, the first question everyone asks is always "Why?" Perhaps this is the wrong question. I have come to believe the better question is "How?"

Trying to explain why something happens is how we can end up latching on to simple answers without actionable solutions. Only someone already in distress and with a vulnerability to suicide sees death as a logical solution to life's inevitable setbacks. It's dangerous to condition ourselves to view suicide as a natural response to disappointment, when it is really the result of illness.

The same thing, I believe, is true about what happened at Columbine. Dylan was vulnerable in many ways—unquestionably emotionally immature, depressed, possibly suffering from a more serious mood or personality disorder. Tom and I failed to recognize these conditions and to curtail the influences—violent entertainment, his friendship with Eric—that exacerbated them.

Asking "how" instead of "why" allows us to frame the descent into self-destructive behavior as the process that it is. How does someone progress along a path toward hurting oneself or others? How does the brain obscure access to its own tools of self-governance, self-preservation, and conscience? How can distorted thinking be identified and corrected earlier? How do we know the most effective treatments at various places along the continuum, and make sure they're available in any medical setting?

How long can we fail to recognize that brain health is *health*, and identify what can be done to maintain it?

These are the issues that urgently need our attention. Asking "why" only makes us feel hopeless. Asking "how" points the way forward, and shows us what we must do.

As I learned all too well, brain health isn't an "us versus them" situation. Every one of us has the capacity to suffer in this way, and most of us—at some time in our lives—will. We teach our kids the importance of good dental care, proper nutrition, and financial responsibility. How many of us teach our children to monitor their own brain health, or know how to do it ourselves?

I did not know, and the greatest regret of my life is that I did not teach Dylan.

Knowable Folds

A day does not pass that I do not feel a sense of overwhelming guilt—both for the myriad ways I failed Dylan and for the destruction he left in his wake.

Sixteen years later, I think every day about the people Dylan and Eric killed. I think about the last moments of their lives—about their terror, their pain. I think about the people who loved them: the parents of all the children, of course, but also Dave Sanders's wife, children, and grandchildren. I think about their siblings and cousins and classmates. I think of those who were injured, many left with permanent disabilities. I think about all the people whose lives touched those of the Columbine victims—the elementary school teachers and babysitters and neighbors for whom the world became a more frightening and incomprehensible place because of what Dylan did.

The loss of the people Dylan killed, ultimately, is unquantifiable. I think about the families they would have had, the Little League teams they would have coached, the music they would have made.

I wish I had known what Dylan was planning. I wish that I had stopped him. I wish I'd had the opportunity to trade my own life for those that were lost. But a thousand passionate wishes aside, I know I can't go back. I do try to conduct my life so it will honor those whose lives were shattered or taken by my son. The work I do is in their memory. I work, too, to hold on to the love I still have for Dylan, who will always remain my child despite the horrors he perpetrated.

I think often of watching Dylan do origami. Whereas most paper folders are meticulous about lining up the edges, fourth-grade Dylan tended to be more slapdash, and his figures were sometimes sloppy. But he'd only have to see a complicated pattern once to be able to duplicate it.

I loved to make a cup of tea and sit quietly beside him, watching his hands moving as quickly as hummingbirds, delighted to see Dylan turn a square of paper into a frog or a bear or a lobster. I'd always marvel at how something as straightforward as a piece of paper can be completely transformed with only a few creases, to become suddenly replete with new significance. Then I'd marvel at the finished form, the complex folds hidden and unknowable to me.

In many ways, that experience mirrored the one I would have after Columbine. I would have to turn what I thought I knew about myself, my son, and my family inside out and around, watching as a boy became a monster, and then a boy again.

Origami is not magic. Even the most complex pattern is knowable, something that can be mapped and understood. So it is, too, with brain illness and violence, and this mapping is the work we must now do. Depression and other types of brain disorders do not strip someone of a moral compass, and yet these are potentially life-threatening diseases that can impair judgment and distort a person's sense of reality. We must turn our attention to researching and raising awareness about these diseases—and to dispelling the myths that prevent us from helping those who most need it. We must do so, not only for the sake of the afflicted, but also for the innocents who will continue to register as their casualties if we do not.

One thing is certain: when we can do a better job of helping people *before* their lives are in crisis, the world will become safer for all of us.

ACKNOWLEDGMENTS

I would not have been able to complete this book without Laura Tucker. Hundreds of pages of writing and thousands of hours of heartache might have died with me had Laura not transformed them into a publishable manuscript. During the years we have worked together, Laura has been much more to me than a writer. She has been midwife, therapist, surgeon, researcher, architect, navigator, workforce, spirit guide, and friend. She was both mortar and mason, completely responsible for turning a pile of broken bricks into a solid structure. Until we teamed up, I was mired in problems that seemed unsolvable. How could I tell a story effectively when readers already knew the ending? How could I explain real-time experience when critical information about facts was learned later? How could I craft my voice when I started out as one person and ended up as someone else? Laura solved these and countless other problems. She has an uncanny ability to weave disparate incidents into threads of logic. She knew how to mine for detail and when to abandon it. I was continuously stunned by her sensitivity to nuance and her ability to hear what lay in the silence between words. Having the opportunity to work with Laura has enriched my life. I will always be grateful that she had the fortitude to undertake a book with such painful subject matter and "walk the walk" with me— even when it was difficult for both of us. I am, and will always be, in awe of her skills and deeply indebted to her.

My agent, Laurie Bernstein, from Side by Side Literary Productions, Inc., found me to ask if I might want to publish a book at a time when I was trying to find the right literary agent for the book I was writing. Her appearance on the scene was eerily prescient. After our first conversation, I knew that Laurie was the right person to safeguard my interests and help me realize my vision. To that end she assumed more roles than I can name. But I am especially grateful for her vision and guidance in helping develop a book proposal that made such a difference in all that would follow, and for steering me to Laura and to Crown Publishers. She's my champion and defender, and I thank her for her hard work and deft hand throughout the writing and publication process.

I thank Andrew Solomon for so many things. Before we met, I heard him speak at a mental health event in Denver and was so inspired by his message that I immediately purchased and read his book *The Noonday Demon: An Atlas of Depression*. When Andrew later asked if he could interview Tom and me for a book that would eventually become *Far From the Tree*, I didn't hesitate to accept the offer (and encourage Tom to participate). In the years that followed, I have appreciated every moment spent with Andrew, not only because he is witty, articulate, sensitive, and brilliant, but because he has encouraged and supported my desire to publish from the moment we met. He read not only excerpts but complete drafts of my manuscript at various stages in its development. His comments were invaluable. And ultimately, I am grateful for his willingness to join me at the finish line by contributing the Introduction to this book. I am very honored to know him and perpetually grateful for his generosity.

My appreciation for my partners at Crown Publishers could fill pages. I thank this extraordinary team for gently walking me along the path to publication. There is not space to list everyone by name, but I am sincerely grateful to everyone who contributed their excellence and support. Special thanks go to my editor, Roger Scholl, for his superb editorial eye, his great sensitivity, and his willingness to champion this book from day one. Thanks also to his wonderful assistant, Dannalie Diaz. Publisher Molly Stern's brilliance and heartfelt enthusiasm for the project and its mission have been breathtaking. My publicity team far exceeded any hopes I could have had for the experience of publishing. Working with Deputy Publisher David Drake, Director of Publicity Carisa Hays, and Associate Publisher Annsley Rosner has been a gift and a joy. I hope they know how grateful I am for their guidance and friendship. Thank you as well to Assistant Marketing Director Sara Pekdemir.

And many thanks to Crown Senior Production Editor Terry Deal, copy editor Lawrence Krauser, Director of Interior Design Elizabeth Rendfleisch, to Creative Director Chris Brand for designing the extraordinary cover for *A Mother's Reckoning,* and to Subrights Director Lance Fitzgerald, for expanding the book's reach around the world. And last but not least, my heartfelt thanks to Maya Mavjee, President of the Crown Publishing Group, for her faith in me and for helping me to get the message of the book out to the reading public.

Many thanks go to Dave Cullen for talking with me about his research on the Columbine tragedy, and for helping me recount specifics of the incident. He generously searched through piles of material to fact-check references when I needed his help with accuracy.

For pointing me in the right direction when I began my research, and for reading the finished manuscript to offer input and recommendations, I thank Dr. Christine Moutier, Chief Medical Officer, and Robert Gebbia, Chief Executive Officer, with the American Foundation of Suicide Prevention (AFSP). Their willingness to share their expertise on the topics of suicide and mental health was an invaluable contribution.

I thank many additional subject matter experts for their willingness to be interviewed, to share resources, and to connect me with others who could answer specific questions. Whether or not their research related directly to the Columbine tragedy, all of these individuals helped me understand the complexities of brain health and the challenges of trying to prevent violence toward self or others. By making themselves available, they provided answers to some of the mysteries I had been struggling to comprehend for years. Many thanks go to Dr. Victoria Arango, Dr. Brad Bushman, Dr. Dewey Cornell, Dr. Dwayne Fuselier, Dr. Sidra Goldman-Mellor, Dr. James Hawdon, Dr. Thomas Joiner, Dr. Kent Kiehl, Dr. Peter Langman, Dr. Adam Lankford, Dr. J. Reid Meloy, Dr. Terrie Moffit, Dr. Katherine Newman, Dr. Debra Niehoff, Dr. Matthew Nock, Dr. Frank Ochberg, Dr. Mary Ellen O'Toole, Dr. Adrian Raine, Dr. Marisa Randazzo, and Dr. Jeremy Richman. I am also grateful to Dr. Marguerite Moritz and Dr. Zeynep Tufekci for their input on the importance of appropriate media response to high-profile incidents of violence.

Many thanks go to my attorneys, Gary Lozow and Frank Patterson, not only for their ongoing care during the harrowing years after the tragedy, but also for allowing me to interview them for the book. Our conversations helped me recount some of the legal aspects of what we had endured together.

I am deeply grateful to Nate for being a dear friend to Dylan, and for continuing to be Dylan's friend and ours in the years since Dylan's death. He made it possible for me to vicariously enjoy many of the happy times they shared. For Nate's willingness to relive the past with me, and for his desire to do whatever he could to help with the book, I am truly thankful.

With humble gratitude, I thank many dear friends, neighbors, colleagues, and fellow survivors of suicide loss for their ongoing kindness and support. There are too many individuals and too many instances to cite, but in myriad ways, they gave me the sustenance to keep going when I didn't think I could.

I thank my brother and sister for shoring me up and watching over me like angels during a long and difficult journey. The constancy of their devotion is the wind beneath my wings.

Finally, and most important, I thank Byron and Tom for not opposing or hindering my efforts to publish, despite their discomfort with the idea. Though they both made it clear that they did not want to churn up difficult memories, sacrifice their privacy, or focus on a time in their lives they would rather forget, they honored my determination to do what I felt was necessary. For this I will always be grateful. I thank them both for their love, courage, and understanding.

Byron, your love and support are the greatest blessings in my life. Without them, I would not have had the strength to write this book. And Tom, I will always treasure our friendship, which has weathered so much and will always endure.

Chapter 7

84   Robyn, Dylan's prom date, had bought three guns for the boys My source for this, as well as for many of the other facts in this book, is the Jefferson County police report. These documents are available on a number of online sites, including http://www.columbine-online.com/etc/columbine-faq.htm, accessed May 2015.

Chapter 10

127   The massacre had been carefully planned I remember very little of what Kate and Randy told us that day and was not able to take notes, so I have reconstructed the events using the Jeffco report and others. I am profoundly grateful to Dave Cullen for his fastidious attention to detail and the help he gave me to ensure that this section is accurate. That said, any and all errors are my own.

137   Notes from a conversation Conversation with Dr. Zeynep Tufekci, February 12, 2015.

138   An investigation by ABC News published in 2014 P. Thomas, M. Levine, J. Cloherty, and J. Date, "Columbine Shootings' Grim Legacy: More Than 50 School Attacks, Plots" (October 7, 2014), www.abcnews.go.com/US/columbine-shootings-grim-legacy-50-school-attacks-plots/story?id=26007119, accessed May 2015. A months-long investigation by ABC News identified at least seventeen attacks and another thirty-six alleged plots or serious threats against schools since the assault on Columbine High School that can be tied to the 1999 massacre.

138   exposure to suicide or suicidal behavior can influence other vulnerable people A roundup of that research can be found at reportingonsuicide.org. I strongly recommend that all journalists reference these guidelines for covering suicide (reportingonsuicide.org/wp-content/themes/ros2015/assets/images/Recommendations-eng.pdf), which were developed in collaboration with the American Association of Suicidology, American Foundation for Suicide Prevention, Annenberg Public Policy Center, Associated Press Managing Editors, Canterbury Suicide Project–University of Otago, Christchurch, New Zealand, Columbia University Department of Psychiatry, ConnectSafely.org, Emotion Technology, International Association for Suicide Prevention Task Force on Media and Suicide, Medical University of Vienna, National Alliance on Mental Illness, National Institute of Mental Health, National Press Photographers Association, New York State Psychiatric Institute, Substance

Abuse and Mental Health Services Administration, Suicide Awareness Voices of Education, Suicide Prevention Resource Center, the Centers for Disease Control and Prevention (CDC), and UCLA School of Public Health, Community Health Sciences.

139 **mass shootings in the United States is inextricably linked** Zeynep Tufekci, "The Media Needs to Stop Inspiring Copycat Murders. Here's How," *The Atlantic*, December 19, 2012, www.theatlantic.com/national /archive/2012/12/the-media-needs-to-stop-inspiring-copycat-murders -heres-how/266439, accessed May 2015. Christopher H. Cantor, et al., "Media and Mass Homicides," *Archives of Suicide Research*, vol. 5, no. 4 (1999), doi: 10.1080/13811119908258339.

140 **Meg Moritz, a journalist and professor** Moritz directed the documentary *Covering Columbine*, which explores the effects of the media coverage of the tragedy on both the community and the journalists who covered it.

140 **Dr. Frank Ochberg is a psychiatrist** Conversation with Dr. Ochberg, February 2, 2015.

142 **In 2014, a conservative Canadian network** As reported by Public Radio International: www.pri.org/stories/2014-06-10/canadian-news-network -refuses-broadcast-mass-shooters-name, accessed May 2015.

Chapter 11

152 **According to Dr. Jeffrey Swanson, who has spent** Jeffrey Swanson, et al., "Violence and Psychiatric Disorder in the Community: Evidence from the Epidemiologic Catchment Area Surveys," *Psychiatric Services*, vol. 41, no. 7 (1990): 761–70, dx.doi.org/10.1176/ps.41.7.761.

152 **"most attackers showed some history of suicidal attempts"** Bryan Vossekuil, et al., "The Final Report and Findings of the Safe School Initiative: Implications for the Prevention of School Attacks in the United States," www2.ed.gov/admins/lead/safety/preventingattacksreport.pdf, p. 21, accessed May 2015.

153 **the result of a conversation I had with Dr. Jeremy Richman** I spoke with Dr. Richman March 13, 2015. For more information or to support the Avielle Foundation, dedicated to "preventing violence through research and community education," see www.aviellefoundation.org.

155 **I started into the stack of books that Sharon had brought me** Some of these were books that I now recommend to every survivor of suicide loss. They include: Kay Redfield Jamison, *Night Falls Fast* (New York: Vintage, 2000); Carla Fine, *No Time to Say Goodbye: Surviving the Suicide of a Loved One* (New York: Harmony, 1999); Iris Bolton and Curtis Mitchell, *My Son . . . My Son . . . : A Guide to Healing After Death, Loss, or Suicide* (Atlanta: Bolton Press, 1983).

156 **Someone in America dies by suicide every thirteen minutes** www.afsp .org/understanding-suicide/facts-and-figures, accessed May 2015.
    Indeed, the problem of suicide—and how many people we really lose to it every year—may be even worse than we believe. Many researchers believe that a large number of deaths categorized as accidents are, in fact, suicides.

Only a small percentage (18 percent to 37 percent) of people who die by suicide leave a note. (Valerie J. Callanan and Mark S. Davis, "A Comparison of Suicide Note Writers with Suicides Who Did Not Leave Notes," *Suicide and Life-Threatening Behavior*, vol. 39, no. 5 [October 2009]: 558–68, doi: 10.1521/suli.2009.39.5.558). In most police departments, there is not enough staff or money to do a thorough investigation of many suspicious deaths—even when there are no brake marks at the site of the crash, or when an experienced hiker makes a rookie mistake.

156   **suicide is the third leading cause of death** "Suicide Prevention," http://www.cdc.gov/violenceprevention/pub/youth_suicide.html, accessed May 2015.

156   **A 2013 study looked at almost 6,500 teens** M. K. Nock, J. Green, I. Hwang, et al., "Prevalence, Correlates, and Treatment of Lifetime Suicidal Behavior Among Adolescents: Results from the National Comorbidity Survey Replication Adolescent Supplement," *JAMA Psychiatry*, vol. 70, no. 3 (2013): 300–10, doi: 10.1001/2013.jamapsychiatry.55.

157   **the overwhelming majority—from 90 to 95 percent** "Understanding Suicide: Key Research Findings," www.afsp.org/understanding-suicide/-key-research-findings, accessed May 2015.

157   **biological (and possibly genetic) vulnerability** Conversation with Dr. Victoria Arango, March 12, 2015.

157   **a Venn diagram with three overlapping circles** Thomas Joiner, *Why People Die by Suicide* (Cambridge, MA: Harvard University Press, 2005).

160   **E-mail from Peter Langman, February 9, 2015** Correspondence with Dr. Peter Langman used with permission.

161   **This was one of the first things Dr. Peter Langman noticed** Dr. Langman's website, www.schoolshooters.info, contains many resources on the topic, including his annotated transcripts of some of Dylan's writing, schoolshooters.info/sites/default/files/klebold_journal_1.1_2.pdf.

161   **Dr. Langman told me he had originally intended to leave Dylan out** Conversation with Dr. Langman, January 21, 2015.

161   **may mean he suffered from a mild form of avoidant personality disorder** Peter Langman, PhD, *Why Kids Kill: Inside the Minds of School Shooters* (New York: St. Martin's Press, 2009), Kindle locations 259–60.

163   **nine out of the ten school shooters** Langman, Kindle locations 259–60.

163   **The breach between what we know and do is lethal** Kay Redfield Jamison, *Night Falls Fast: Understanding Suicide* (New York: Knopf, 1999).

163   **Even if a person does not discuss their intention** The CDC lists the following as risk factors for young people: a history of previous suicide attempts; a family history of suicide; a history of depression or other mental illness; alcohol or drug abuse; stressful life event or loss; easy access to lethal methods; exposure to the suicidal behavior of others; and incarceration. A complete list of warning signs that someone may be thinking about suicide is available at the American Foundation for Suicide Prevention's website: www.afsp.org/preventing-suicide/suicide-warning-signs,

accessed May 2015. The more warning signs observed, the greater the risk.

163   **Ed Coffey, a physician and vice president at the Henry Ford Health System** C. Edward Coffey, "Building a System of Perfect Depression Care in Behavioral Health," *The Joint Commission Journal on Quality and Patient Safety*, vol. 33, no. 4 (April 2007): 193–99.

Chapter 12

167   **Psychopathy is characterized** Those interested in psychopathy will be interested to read Robert Hare, *Without Conscience: The Disturbing World of the Psychopaths Among Us* (New York: Guilford Press, 1999, 2011).

167   **A 2001 study of adolescent school shooters** J. R. Meloy, A. G. Hempel, K. Mohandie, A. A. Shiva, and B. T. Gray, "Offender and Offense Characteristics of a Nonrandom Sample of Adolescent Mass Murderers," *Journal of the American Academy of Child and Adolescent Psychiatry*, vol. 40, no. 6 (2001): 719–28, forensis.org/PDF/published/2001_OffenderandOffe.pdf.

Dr. Meloy, a board-certified forensic psychologist and a clinical professor of psychiatry at the University of California, San Diego, has authored or coauthored more than two hundred papers and eleven books on psychopathy, criminality, mental disorder, and targeted violence. He is a consultant to the Behavioral Analysis Units, FBI, Quantico, Virginia. Dr. Meloy's website, forensis.org, provides a wealth of academic publications for those interested in violence prevention, threat assessment, motivations for terrorism and mass murder, and related subjects.

167–68   **these deadly dyads mean it's absolutely critical** Conversation with Dr. Reid Meloy, January 26, 2015.

170   **Criminal justice specialist Dr. Adam Lankford** Conversation with Dr. Lankford on February 5, 2015.

170   **rampage shooters, like suicide bombers** Adam Lankford, *The Myth of Martyrdom: What Really Drives Suicide Bombers, Rampage Shooters, and Other Self-Destructive Killers* (New York: St. Martin's Press, 2013).

170   **Almost half of them died by suicide as part of their attacks.** Forty-eight percent: 38 percent by their own hand, 10 percent "suicide by cop," according to Adam Lankford, "A Comparative Analysis of Suicide Terrorists and Rampage, Workplace, and School Shooters in the United States from 1990–2010," *Homicide Studies*, vol. 17, no. 3 (2013): 255–74, doi: 10.1177/1088767912462033.

170   **mass shooters almost always follow** Bryan Vossekuil, et al., "The Final Report and Findings of the Safe School Initiative: Implications for the Prevention of School Attacks in the United States," www2.ed.gov/admins/lead/safety/preventingattacksreport.pdf, p. 21, accessed May 2015.

170   **"suicide prevention is also murder-suicide prevention"** Thomas Joiner, *The Perversion of Virtue: Understanding Murder-Suicide* (New York: Oxford University Press, 2014), p. 11.

171   **planning with Eric for the rampage** Conversation with Thomas Joiner, December 3, 2014.

172   **"The difference is in what Eric thinks and how Dylan thinks"** Langman, Kindle locations 947–49.

172   **"They just don't care"** Conversation with Dr. Marisa Randazzo, February 19, 2015.

172   **Dylan wanted to die** Conversation with Dr. Dwayne Fuselier, January 29, 2015.

Chapter 13

174   **An estimated one in five children and adolescents** K. R. Merikangas, J. He, M. Burstein, et al., "Lifetime Prevalence of Mental Disorders in US Adolescents: Results from the National Comorbidity Study—Adolescent Supplement (NCS-A)," *Journal of the American Academy of Child and Adolescent Psychiatry*, vol. 49, no. 10 (2010): 980–89, doi: 10.1016/j.jaac.2010.05.017.

174   **Only 20 percent of those kids are identified** US Public Health Service, "Report of the Surgeon General's Conference on Children's Mental Health: A National Action Agenda," US Department of Health and Human Services, Washington, DC (2000).

     US Department of Health and Human Services, "Mental Health: A Report of the Surgeon General," US Department of Health and Human Services, Substance Abuse and Mental Health Services Administration, Center for Mental Health Services, National Institutes of Health, National Institute of Mental Health, Rockville, MD (1999).

174   **A disease like depression can also have much more serious** B. Maughan, S. Collishaw, and A. Stringaris, "Depression in Childhood and Adolescence," *Journal of the Canadian Academy of Child and Adolescent Psychiatry*, vol. 22, no. 1 (2013): 35–40.

174   **20 percent of teenagers experience a depressive episode** US Preventive Services Task Force, "Screening and Treatment for Major Depressive Disorder in Children and Adolescents," *Pediatrics*, vol. 123, no. 4 (April 2009): 1223–28.

174   **A recent CDC report** Centers for Disease Control and Prevention, "Youth Risk Behavior Surveillance—United States, 2011," *Morbidity and Mortality Weekly Report, Surveillance Summaries*, vol. 61, no. SS-4 (2012), www.cdc.gov/mmwr/pdf/ss/ss6104.pdf.

174   **teenagers (especially boys) tend to withdraw** National Institute of Mental Health Depression in Children and Adolescents (fact sheet), www.nimh.nih.gov/health/topics/depression/depression-in-children-and-adolescents.shtml, accessed May 2015.

178   **Losses and other events—whether anticipated or actual** www.suicidology.org/ncpys/warning-signs-risk-factors, accessed May 2015.

181   **unexplained somatic symptoms** Dr. John Campo and colleagues published a study of children with unexplained recurrent abdominal pain

in *Pediatrics* in 2001: 44.4 percent of the children they studied also met the criteria for major depressive disorder (MDD). They suggested that children who have recurrent abdominal pain might respond to life stress with physical symptoms. John V. Campo, et al., "Recurrent Abdominal Pain, Anxiety, and Depression in Primary Care," *Pediatrics*, vol. 113, no. 4 (2004): 817–24.

186   **the scratch read "Fags"** Dave Cullen, *Columbine* (New York: Grand Central Publishing, 2010), p. 200.

187   **Regina Huerter, director of Juvenile Diversion** The report was not made public, although Dave Cullen shared his copy with me. Huerter's testimony before the Columbine Review Commission was widely reported upon: extras.denverpost.com/news/col1202.htm, accessed May 2015.

187   **Ralph W. Larkin independently confirmed** Ralph W. Larkin, *Comprehending Columbine* (Philadelphia: Temple University Press, 2007).

188   **Of the forty-eight shooters** Peter Langman, *School Shooters: Understanding High School, College, and Adult Perpetrators* (Lanham, MD: Rowman & Littlefield, 2015).

190   **"Apparently such behavior was common enough"** Larkin, p. 90.

190   **Larkin reports that throwing trash from moving cars** Larkin, p. 91.

190   **A 2011 study by the Centers for Disease Control** Centers for Disease Control and Prevention, "Youth Risk Behavior Surveillance—United States, 2011," *Morbidity and Mortality Weekly Report, Surveillance Summaries*, vol. 61, no. SS-4 (2012), www.cdc.gov/mmwr/pdf/ss/ss6104.pdf.

190   **the number may be closer to 30 percent** National Center for Education Statistics and Bureau of Justice Statistics, "Indicators of School Crime and Safety" (2011), nces.ed.gov/pubsearch/pubsinfo.asp?pubid=2012002rev.

190–91   **four times the risk of developing antisocial personality disorder** W. E. Copeland, D. Wolke, A. Angold, and E. Costello, "Adult Psychiatric Outcomes of Bullying and Being Bullied by Peers in Childhood and Adolescence," *JAMA Psychiatry*, vol. 70, no. 4 (2013): 419–26, doi: 10.1001/jamapsychiatry.2013.504. This Duke University study found that, compared with kids who weren't bullied, those who were had four times the prevalence of agoraphobia, generalized anxiety, and panic disorder when they became adults. The bullies themselves had four times the risk of developing antisocial personality disorder.

191   **a strong association between bullying and depression and suicide** B. Klomek, F. Marrocco, M. Kleinman, I. S. Schonfeld, and M. S. Gould, "Bullying, Depression, and Suicidality in Adolescents," *Journal of the American Academy of Child and Adolescent Psychiatry*, vol. 46, no. 1 (2007): 40–9.

Y. S. Kim and B. Leventhal, "Bullying and Suicide," *International Journal of Adolescent Medicine and Health*, vol. 20, no. 2 (April–June 2008): 133–54.

191   **The connection between bullying and violence** T. R. Nansel, M. D. Overpeck, D. L. Haynie, W. J. Ruan, and P. C. Scheidt, "Relationships Between Bullying and Violence Among US Youth," *Archives of Pediatric*

and Adolescent Medicine, vol. 157, no. 4 (2003): 348–53, doi: 10.1001/archpedi.157.4.348.

191   **bully-victims are at the greatest psychological risk** T. E. Moffitt, A. Caspi, H. Harrington, and B. J. Milne, "Males on the Life-Course-Persistent and Adolescence-Limited Antisocial Pathways: Follow-Up at Age 26 Years," *Development and Psychopathology*, vol. 14 (2002): 179–207.

D. Pepler, D. Jiang, W. Craig, and J. Connolly, "Developing Trajectories of Bullying and Associated Factors," *Child Development*, vol. 79, no. 2 (2008): 325–38.

M. K. Holt, et al., "Bullying and Suicidal Ideation and Behaviors: A Meta-Analysis," *Journal of the American Academy of Pediatrics*, (January 2015), doi: 10.1542 peds.2014–1864.

W. E. Copeland, D. Wolke, A. Angold, and E. Costello, "Adult Psychiatric Outcomes of Bullying and Being Bullied by Peers in Childhood and Adolescence," *JAMA Psychiatry*, vol. 70, no. 4 (2013): 419–26, doi: 10.1001/jamapsychiatry.2013.504.

P. R. Smokowski and K. H. Kopasz, "Bullying in School: An Overview of Types, Effects, Family Characteristics, and Intervention Strategies, *Children and Schools*, vol. 27 (2005): 101–9.

192   **the individual has seen a physician within the year before their death** J. Pirkis and P. Burgess, "Suicide and Recency of Health Care Contacts: A Systematic Review," *The British Journal of Psychiatry: The Journal of Mental Science*, vol. 173, no. 6 (December 1998): 462–74.

192   **almost half of them** Ibid.

204   **Dylan's arrest** Recently arrested and incarcerated people are at higher risk for suicide. Thomas B. Cook, "Recent Criminal Offending and Suicide Attempts: A National Sample," *Social Psychiatry and Psychiatric Epidemiology*, vol. 48, no. 5 (May 2013): 767–74.

205   **Mary Ellen O'Toole, a former FBI profiler** Mary Ellen O'Toole, "The School Shooter: A Threat Assessment Perspective" (Quantico, VA: FBI Academy, 2000), www.fbi.gov/stats-services/publications/school-shooter, accessed May 2015.

205   **She warns against relying on a kid's self-reporting** Conversation with Mary Ellen O'Toole, February 23, 2015.

Chapter 14

217   **Dr. Adrian Raine cites a study in which children** Adrian Raine, *The Anatomy of Violence: The Biological Roots of Crime* (New York: Knopf, 2013), p. 171.

Chapter 16

247   **"a place where no acting was required"** Patrick O'Malley, "Getting Grief Right," *New York Times*, January 10, 2015, opinionator.blogs.nytimes.com/2015/01/10/getting-grief-right/?_r=0, accessed May 2015.

250   **Some of them were success stories, but some were not** There appears to be a high risk of suicide in the weeks immediately after discharge from a

psychiatric hospital. A. Owen-Smith, et al., "'When you're in the hospital, you're in a sort of bubble': Understanding the High Risk of Self-Harm and Suicide Following Psychiatric Discharge: A Qualitative Study," *Crisis: The Journal of Crisis Intervention and Suicide Prevention*, vol. 35, no. 3 (2014): 154–60, dx.doi.org/10.1027/0227-5910/a000246.

H. Bickley, et al., "Suicide Within Two Weeks of Discharge from Psychiatric Inpatient Care: A Case-Control Study," *Psychiatric Services*, vol. 64, no. 7 (July 1, 2013): 653–9, doi: 10.1176/appi.ps.201200026.

Chapter 17

260 **clear brain differences between people** K. Kiehl, et al., "Abnormal Brain Structure in Youth Who Commit Homicide," *NeuroImage: Clinical* vol. 4 (May 2014): 800–7.

261 **whether Dylan had a biological predisposition** In *The Anatomy of Violence* (New York: Knopf, 2013), Dr. Adrian Raine has identified these as the leading causes of a biological disposition toward violence. In our conversation on March 24, 2015, he went so far as to ask me about our family's fish consumption, as there is an impressive correlation between low omega-3 levels and violence. However, we ate fish at least once a week.

263 **Too often, parents of seriously disturbed kids** Liza Long's son is bipolar. Her provocative blog post "I Am Adam Lanza's Mother" went viral in 2012, and her subsequent book, *The Price of Silence: A Mom's Perspective on Mental Illness* (New York: Hudson Street Press, 2014), is a searing indictment of how our education, juvenile justice, and mental health systems deal with brain illness in children.

265 **"One cigarette won't give you lung cancer"** Conversation with Dr. Dewey Cornell, March 5, 2015.

266 **"the public performance of violence"** Mark Juergensmeyer, *Terror in the Mind of God: The Global Rise of Religious Violence*, third edition (Berkeley, CA: University of California Press, 2003).

266 **"searching for a way to retire their public image"** Conversation with Dr. Katherine Newman, March 16, 2015.

266 **the immaturity of the adolescent brain** Frances Jensen has written a fascinating book about adolescent brain immaturity and wiring: *The Teenage Brain: A Neuroscientist's Survival Guide to Raising Adolescents and Young Adults* (New York: HarperCollins, 2015).

Chapter 18

271 **"a state of well-being"** World Health Organization, "Mental Health: A State of Well-Being" (2014), www.who.int/features/factfiles/mental_health/en/.

RESOURCES

There are so many excellent resources out there that this list could easily be a thousand pages long. I've winnowed it down to the resources I recommend the most.

Suicide Prevention

If you or someone you love is in crisis (with or without thoughts of imminent suicide), call the National Suicide Prevention Lifeline for help.

National Suicide Prevention Lifeline
1–800–273-TALK (8255)
www.suicidepreventionlifeline.org

Your call will be automatically routed to a trained crisis worker who will listen and can tell you about mental health services in your area. The service is free and confidential, and the line is open 24/7. Everyone should keep this number handy.

The American Foundation for Suicide Prevention: www.afsp.org
Suicide Prevention Resource Center: www.sprc.org/Suicide

These two organizations provide amazing resources on a variety of topics, including how to recognize the warning signs of suicide and who's at risk, what you can do to help the bereaved survivors of suicide loss, how to talk to children about suicide deaths in the family, and much more. Invaluable for survivors, educators, activists, and people at risk, as well as anyone concerned about this issue.

With so many programs available for suicide prevention and mental health, how do you know which one to use? A good place to start is the Best Practices Registry (BPR) on the Suicide Prevention Resource Center (SPRC) website. Programs are listed only if they meet "best practice" standards.

www.sprc.org/bpr

Mental Health First Aid (for Youth and Adults)

Mental Health First Aid, a national organization, offers hands-on training to help people recognize the signs of addiction and mental health distress. I've taken the course three times and think everyone should. It's very powerful to know that for the price of one Saturday, you could save a life.

www.mentalhealthfirstaid.org/cs

Bullying

Bullying can be a problem with any age group; parents and schools can help.

www.stopbullying.gov

Peer Resources

Kids are more likely to talk to their friends than to an adult, so kids have to know what to do if a friend is struggling with suicidal thoughts. The "Save a Friend" tip sheet from the National Association of School Psychologists is a brief introduction to what every one of them should know. (Notice the importance of having access to a responsible adult or a crisis team member who has been trained to respond appropriately.)

Save a Friend: Tips for Teens to Prevent Suicide

www.nasponline.org/resources/crisis_safety/savefriend_general
.aspx

School Response to Suicide

In the aftermath of suicide, the safety of other students can depend on how a school handles the tragedy. This booklet (created by the American Foundation for Suicide Prevention and the Suicide Prevention Resource Center) provides a practical road map for a difficult time. Aside from the Lifeline, I recommend this resource more often than any other.

After a Suicide: A Toolkit for Schools
www.sprc.org/library_resources/items/after-suicide-toolkit-schools

Violence Prevention

The Centers for Disease Control's Division of Violence Prevention does important work. In particular, I would like to highlight the National Violent Death Reporting System, an invaluable tool in violence prevention.

www.cdc.gov/violenceprevention/nvdrs

This database offers comprehensive, anonymous reporting on violent deaths. Linking information about the "who, what, when, where, and how" from data on violent deaths helps us to understand why they happened. Over time, the database can show whether various efforts to prevent violence are working. Currently, only thirty-two states have the funding to participate.

Gun Safety

No matter where you stand on gun control and gun ownership, there is an undisputed relationship between access to firearms and increased suicide risk. The Means Matter program from the Harvard School of Public Health features informative and unique approaches to promoting gun safety for all. One of its initiatives, the New Hampshire Gun Shop Project, is a model for collaborative prevention without conflict.

www.hsph.harvard.edu/means-matter/means-matter

Media Guidelines

How the media reports on incidents involving suicide can affect public health and safety in the aftermath of tragedy. These are some guidelines:

www.afsp.org/news-events/for-the-media/reporting-on-suicide
www.sprc.org/sites/sprc.org/files/library/sreporting.pdf

I would like to see a similar protocol developed for reporting on murder-suicide. Everything we do to increase knowledge, inhibit myth-making, and minimize trauma makes our communities safer.

Threat Assessment

The Virginia Student Threat Assessment Guidelines provide schools with safe, structured, and efficient ways to respond to student threats of violence. This is a model for threat assessment that emphasizes early attention to problems such as bullying, teasing, and other forms of student conflict before they escalate into violent behavior. Now used in more than three thousand schools in eighteen states, this program trains multidisciplinary teams in a single day.

curry.virginia.edu/research/projects/threat-assessment

Threat assessment programs don't simply reduce student violence. They can help teachers and staff identify kids at risk of many kinds of harm, including suicide, partner violence, and child abuse.

INDEX